From Preachers to Suffragists

From Preachers to Suffragists

Woman's Rights and Religious Conviction
in the Lives of Three Nineteenth-Century
American Clergywomen

Beverly Zink-Sawyer

Westminster John Knox Press
LOUISVILLE • LONDON

Book design by Sharon Adamns
Cover design by Lisa Buckley
Cover photographs courtesy of the Schlesinger Library, Radcliffe Institute, Harvard University. (Left to right) Olympia Brown, Antoinette Brown Blackwell, and Anna Howard Shaw.

First edition
Published by Westminster John Knox Press
Louisville, Kentucky

This book is printed on acid-free paper that meets the American National Standards Institute Z39.48 standard. ♾

PRINTED IN THE UNITED STATES OF AMERICA

03 04 05 06 07 08 09 10 11 12 — 10 9 8 7 6 5 4 3 2 1

Library of Congress Cataloging-in-Publication Data is on file at the Library of Congress, Washington, D.C.

ISBN 0-664-22615-9

For Barbara

sister, colleague, best friend

Contents

Preface

I first "met" Antoinette Brown Blackwell, Olympia Brown, and Anna Howard Shaw, the three remarkable women who are the subjects of this book, a decade ago while I was in graduate school. In the process of refining a topic for my Ph.D. dissertation, I researched women preachers and clergywomen in nineteenth-century America. My hope was to study their sermons and, for the ordained women, their journeys to and experiences in ministry. On the way to what I believed would be an interesting dissertation, however, I encountered a few roadblocks. Most of the women who were preaching in the nineteenth century represented free church traditions in which extemporaneous preaching was the norm, leaving few sermons to study. And many of the materials of preaching women that *were* left behind have not been preserved or made available for public use. But most surprising of all was the discovery that several of the first women ordained by Protestant churches began their ministries as parish pastors but left those positions to work full time for woman suffrage. The dissertation took a different direction, but the common vocational paths of this group of early clergywomen remained in the back of my mind as a fascinating subject for a future project. The opportunity to pursue that project came with my first sabbatical leave a few years ago and has evolved into this book.

Writing a book, while most often a very solitary, even lonely enterprise, is really a group effort. Many individuals and communities have contributed to the realization of this book in a variety of ways. I am deeply grateful to my family of origin and my families of faith who affirmed and nurtured my call to ministry; my mentors on the faculty of the Graduate Department of Religion at Vanderbilt University for inspiring my curiosity; President Louis Weeks and the Board of Trustees of Union Theological Seminary and Presbyterian School of Christian Education for a sabbatical leave to pursue this project; the Association of Theological Schools for a Lilly Faculty Fellowship that enabled me to travel to libraries holding the papers of Brown Blackwell, Brown, and Shaw; the Schlesinger Library, Radcliffe Institute for Advanced Study, Harvard University, for use of its wonderful collection of American women's materials and to the even more wonderful people who tend that collection; my colleagues and students at Union-PSCE who have unfailingly expressed their support of and interest in my work; Stephanie Egnotovich of Westminster John Knox Press, a wise and gracious editor who believed in me and in this book long before I did; and my companions in life: my dear husband, Steve, who has patiently endured life over the past few years with three "other women" in addition to the one he married, and Charis, one of God's "creatures great and small," who warms my heart and occasionally my lap. Last but not least, I thank and celebrate the three brave and faithful women of this book who claimed their calls from God, enabling me and countless other women of faith to do the same. Thanks be to God.

Beverly Zink-Sawyer
Richmond, Virginia

"All men and women are created equal":

Religion and Rights for Women

The thirty-eighth annual woman suffrage convention met in the Lyric Theater in Baltimore, Maryland, February 7–13, 1906. Those who gathered for the annual meeting of the National American Woman Suffrage Association (NAWSA) added a unique tribute to their usual slate of political speeches and proposed legislation. They honored a special trio of woman's rights[1] pioneers who had led the movement valiantly since its inception in the mid-nineteenth century. Susan B. Anthony, Clara Barton, and Julia Ward Howe had distinguished themselves in particular ways among the plethora of gifted women who worked tirelessly for equal rights for American women and for the culmination of those rights in the elective franchise. Anthony had long been regarded as the "incomparable organizer"[2] of the movement. Barton's work went beyond her celebrated relief work and founding of the American Red Cross to include public advocacy for woman suffrage. Howe was beloved across the nation as the lyricist of the stirring "Battle Hymn of the Republic," which became the primary American anthem at the end of the nineteenth century. Her equally important and more extensive contribution to American society,

---

1. Throughout this work I maintain the historical usage of "woman's rights" and "woman suffrage."

2. Eleanor Flexner, one of the leading suffrage historians, characterized Anthony and other early leaders of the woman's rights movement this way: "If Lucretia Mott typified the moral force of the movement, if Lucy Stone was its most gifted orator and Mrs. Stanton its outstanding philosopher, Susan Anthony was its incomparable organizer, who gave it force and direction for half a century." See Flexner, *Century of Struggle* (New York: Atheneum, 1974), 84.

however, came through her oration and preaching on behalf of woman suffrage.

These "three great pioneers" of the woman's rights movement, as the recording secretary of the convention called them, were on the platform together for the first and only time.[3] All were in their eighties and nearing the end of their public activism if not their lives. Indeed, the 1906 convention would mark the last public appearance of Susan B. Anthony before her death a month later. The tribute to them at the Baltimore convention, then, represented a sincere expression of gratitude for those who had fought the battle for woman's rights for half a century as well as a generational "passing of the torch" from those who had established and led the movement to those who would see the movement through to a successful conclusion.

At the same annual convention, another trio of women appeared on the platform together. While they were less celebrated at that particular gathering than the three great pioneers, their collective efforts toward the equality of women equaled—perhaps even surpassed in some ways—those of their older suffrage sisters. Not only did they share a lifelong commitment to woman's rights, they *lived* that commitment by shattering what was perhaps the most ideologically rigid barrier to the professional equality of women: the ecclesiastical barrier. Antoinette Brown Blackwell, Olympia Brown, and Anna Howard Shaw were among the first women ordained to the ministry by American Protestant churches, Brown Blackwell being the acknowledged pioneer, the first woman known to be ordained by any church in the modern era.[4] Although they had been together at previous gatherings of suffragists and would be together at

3. Ida Husted Harper, ed., *History of Woman Suffrage*, vol. V, *1900–1920* (New York: National American Woman Suffrage Association, 1922), 151. The *History of Woman Suffrage* was published in six volumes. Volumes I-III were edited by Elizabeth Cady Stanton, Susan B. Anthony, and Matilda Joslyn Gage, with the first two volumes published in Rochester, New York, in 1881 and the third in 1886. Volume IV, edited by Anthony and Harper, was published in Rochester in 1902. Volumes V and VI were edited by Harper and published in New York in 1922. The citations hereafter will refer to *History of Woman Suffrage* with the appropriate volume and page numbers.

4. Karen Jo Torjesen has documented the presence of women in official ecclesiastical roles such as bishop and elder in the early centuries of the church. The evidence suggests that women performed liturgical functions equal to those performed by men in certain times and places. Since that time, however, there is no indication that women were ordained as most Christian communities understand that term or granted full ecclesiastical and clerical rights until 1853. See Torjesen, *When Women Were Priests: Women's Leadership in the Early Church and the Scandal of Their Subordination in the Rise of Christianity* (San Francisco: HarperSanFrancisco, 1993).

subsequent gatherings,[5] their simultaneous appearance on the platform of the 1906 convention of the NAWSA was unique and symbolic. These three ecclesiastical mavericks shared in the leadership of the convention's Sunday afternoon worship service, reported as follows in the narrative of the convention:

> The Rev. Antoinette Brown Blackwell made the opening prayer; the Rev. Anna Howard Shaw read the Scripture lesson and gave the day's text: "Be strong and very courageous; be not afraid, neither be thou dismayed, for the Lord thy God is with thee withersoever thou goest." The Battle Hymn of the Republic was beautifully read by the Rev. Olympia Brown and sung by Miss Etta Maddox, the audience joining in the chorus.[6]

Few if any convention delegates that Sunday afternoon would have recognized the poignancy and symbolism of a liturgical event led by Brown Blackwell, Shaw, and Brown in succession. Their presence and participation in the worship service, however, bore witness both to their ecclesiastical achievements and to their common commitment to a vision of political equality for women, a vision inspired by their religious convictions. The smooth and natural way in which they segued between their roles as clergywomen and political activists is symbolic of their understanding of the sacred and secular worlds in which they lived and worked, worlds that were, for them, continuous and whole and equally imbued with God's presence and goodness.

This is the story of those three women whose lives were shaped by their unyielding belief in the political *and* ecclesiastical equality of women. At times their lives intersected, such as at their 1906 NAWSA convention appearance, in interesting and seemingly predestined ways. At other times their lives had little in common beyond their itinerant preaching and their public speaking on behalf of woman suffrage as they followed different domestic and professional paths. They were always linked, however, by a common vocational path that led them from service as preachers to work

---

5. For instance, Brown Blackwell, Brown, and Shaw all took part in the NAWSA convention of 1902, with Brown Blackwell and Brown delivering addresses and Shaw presiding as vice president, and in the 1908 NAWSA convention, with Brown Blackwell and Brown both praying and speaking and Shaw presiding as president. See *History of Woman Suffrage*, V:23–54 and V:213–42.

6. *History of Woman Suffrage*, V:179.

as suffragists. Brown Blackwell (ordained by the Congregational Church in 1853), Brown (ordained by the Universalist Church in 1863), and Shaw (ordained by the Methodist Protestant Church in 1880) all entered parish ministry following their ordinations. Given the small number of women who were ordained during the nineteenth century, their ecclesiastical status alone places them within an elite group.

What makes these three women a subset of that elite group and thus worth studying, however, is the fact that they all left parish ministry to work full time for woman suffrage. Their vocational move from preachers to suffragists raises provocative questions about the experiences of the earliest ordained women in America as well as questions about frequently overlooked theological and ecclesiastical dimensions of the woman suffrage movement and its ideological and rhetorical foundations as women of faith rose to leadership positions in the organizations that fought for woman's rights.

Religious Roots of the Struggle for Woman's Rights

When Brown Blackwell, Brown, and Shaw joined other clergywomen and suffrage leaders for the Sunday afternoon service held during the NAWSA convention of 1906, few suffragists would have found the inclusion of an explicitly religious ritual in the context of a political gathering to be incongruous. From its inception, the woman's rights movement had significant theological and ecclesiastical dimensions, not unlike the antislavery movement, the earlier nineteenth-century social movement from which it grew and whose organizational and rhetorical style the woman's movement mimicked. Both movements had deep roots in theological values and ecclesiastical structures, and both movements used those values and structures in promoting their causes. The first woman's rights gathering in America, the Seneca Falls Convention held in Seneca Falls, New York, in July 1848, was spearheaded by a group of Quaker abolitionists, most notably Lucretia and James Mott, who regarded human equality as a divinely granted right and who had gained prominence in the antislavery movement. They were joined by others of various denominational backgrounds who acted out of a common theological belief in the equality of all human beings—regardless of race or gender—in the sight of God. When Lucretia Mott, Elizabeth Cady Stanton, and the others who issued the call for the Seneca Falls Convention sought a place for the gathering, they logically turned to the church, particularly those churches that had already demonstrated their support for human freedoms through their abolitionist activity. Thus, the first convention to discuss woman's rights was held at the Wesleyan Chapel in Seneca Falls.[7] Subsequent gatherings of women found shelter in churches when other meeting places turned them away.

More important than the physical welcome given to the incipient woman's movement by churches were the religious assumptions that formed the foundation of the movement. The rhetoric of the movement for woman's rights, from its earliest public statements, was replete with theological language and ecclesiastical concerns. In addition to their debates over political, legal, economic, and educational equality for women, leaders of the movement recognized the importance that religious beliefs and language had in shaping attitudes toward women and debated those as well. As historian Donna A. Behnke notes,

> If women were to reverse centuries of social and political suppression and conditioning, they would have to confront the ideological bases supportive of their subordination. The women were quick to see that theology, enforced throughout the centuries of church history, had provided the main argument for woman's subjection by insisting that woman was man's divinely ordered subordinate and convicted introducer of sin into God's perfect world. Thus, theological and ecclesiological questions were readily debated, and conventions continually acknowledged the priority and importance of religious prejudice. Succinctly worded resolutions were drawn up and passed, setting forth the injustices thought to proceed directly from male-dominated biblical and theological scholarship.[8]

The Declaration of Sentiments concerning woman's rights that was adopted at the Seneca Falls Convention in 1848 illustrates Behnke's

---

7. The *History of Woman Suffrage* notes that when the conventioneers arrived at the Wesleyan church, "lo! The door was locked. However, an embryo Professor of Yale College was lifted through an open window to unbar the door; that done, the church was quickly filled" (*History of Woman Suffrage*, I:69). Whether the church leaders simply forgot to unlock the door or had a change of heart remains a mystery. In any case, it is not surprising that the Wesleyans would be radical enough to welcome the woman's rights activists since they were in the forefront of other social and political movements of the mid-nineteenth century, such as abolition and temperance. And it was a Wesleyan minister, Luther Lee, who agreed to preach the sermon at the ordination of Antoinette Brown Blackwell in 1853.

8. Donna A. Behnke, *Religious Issues in Nineteenth Century Feminism* (Troy, N.Y.: Whitson Publishing, 1982), 2.

assertion. It opened with reference to certain "laws of nature and of nature's God" and declared that "all men and women are created equal" and "are endowed by their Creator with certain inalienable rights." It went on to chastise man for allowing woman "in Church, as well as State, but a subordinate position, claiming Apostolic authority for her exclusion from the ministry, and, with some exceptions, from any public participation in the affairs of the Church." Man had "usurped the prerogative of Jehovah himself, claiming it as his right to assign for [woman] a sphere of action, when that belongs to her conscience and to her God." The Declaration ended by vowing to fight woman's "social and religious degradation" and, to that end, endeavored "to enlist the pulpit and the press in our behalf."[9]

A set of resolutions attached to the Declaration was even more pointed in its theological assumptions and identification of necessary religious reforms. The resolutions reiterated the Declaration's assertion of woman's equality with man as intended by the Creator but also targeted specific areas of ecclesiastical constraint upon women, including the limitations imposed by "a perverted application of the Scriptures" and the prohibitions against women's promotion of "every righteous cause by every righteous means," including public speaking and teaching "in any assemblies proper to be held." The final resolution unanimously passed at Seneca Falls vowed to overthrow "the monopoly of the pulpit" and to secure to woman "an equal participation with men in the various trades, professions, and commerce."[10]

The Denunciation of "Women's Agitation"

Despite the obvious religious convictions of the early leaders of the woman's rights movement and their inclusion of theological arguments in support of their demands, the tide of "women's agitation," as it became known in the mid-nineteenth century, met more vehement opposition from the ecclesiastical world than from the secular world. "Religion formed the cornerstone of the case against feminine equality," observed historian William L. O'Neill.[11] No sooner had it begun than the movement faced, according to suffrage historian Aileen Kraditor,

9. *History of Woman Suffrage*, I:70–71.
10. Ibid., 72, 73.
11. William L. O'Neill, *Everyone Was Brave: The Rise and Fall of Feminism in America* (Chicago: Quadrangle Books, 1969), 11, 13.

a problem identical to one that faced its parent, the abolitionist movement. In the middle of the nineteenth century, most Americans accepted the "plenary inspiration" of the Bible, believing that the Scriptures were literally the word of God, infallible not only in matters of moral and religious truth but also in regard to statements of scientific, historical, and geographical fact.[12]

The public silence of women was among the infallible matters most nineteenth-century Americans believed to be decreed in the Bible. That silence and its assumed ratification in Scripture began to be challenged by some brave women in the 1830s. The catalyst for the first public debate over woman's rights in America was a clerical response to the 1837 New England speaking tour of Quaker abolitionists Angelina and Sarah Grimké. The Grimké sisters provoked outrage by speaking on behalf of the American Anti-Slavery Society, their behavior prompting the General Association of Massachusetts (Orthodox) Clergymen to issue a "Pastoral Letter" to all Congregational churches denouncing the Grimkés and all public speaking and teaching by women.[13]

The literal interpretation of Scripture and the unwillingness to challenge traditional gender roles shaped the response of most mid-nineteenth-century clergymen to any intimations of expanded rights for women. The Massachusetts clergymen who denounced the Grimkés supported the belief expressed in a sermon by their Presbyterian colleague Jonathan F. Stearns that while religion "seems almost to have been entrusted by its author to [woman's] particular custody," women themselves were not to step beyond the thresholds of their homes. A woman played an essential role in forming religious character within members of her family, but "shrinking from public exposure, [she] should be content to 'let her own works praise her.'"[14] Stearns and most of his mid-nineteenth-century colleagues subscribed to the gender ideology associated with what historian Barbara Welter has termed the "cult of True Womanhood" that prevailed throughout the century. "Woman, in the cult of True Womanhood presented by the women's magazines, gift annuals and religious literature of

12. Aileen S. Kraditor, *The Ideas of the Woman Suffrage Movement, 1890–1920* (Garden City, N.Y.: Doubleday, 1965), 75.

13. A report about and excerpts from the "Pastoral Letter" may be found in *History of Woman Suffrage*, I:81–82.

14. Jonathan F. Stearns, *"Female Influence, and the True Christian Mode of Its Exercise." A discourse delivered in the First Presbyterian Church in Newburyport, July 30, 1837* (Newburyport, Mass.: J. G. Tilton, 1837), 11.

the nineteenth century, was the hostage in the home," Welter asserts. "If anyone, male or female, dared to tamper with the complex of virtues which made up True Womanhood, he was damned immediately as an enemy of God, of civilization and of the Republic."[15]

Because of its emphasis on piety and its association with divinely ordained social and gender roles, the ideology of True Womanhood found its greatest allies in the church and in Christian doctrine. As a result, most gender battles of the nineteenth century (and, indeed, up to the present day), regardless of their particular contexts, were fought against a backdrop of biblical, ecclesiastical, and theological issues. "Political arguments for 'woman's rights and wrongs' required a praxis which explicitly addressed women's place before God," states Nancy Gale Isenberg.

> Indeed, crucial philosophical assumptions about "Woman" remained grounded in religious terms throughout the nineteenth century. Popular prescriptions for "Woman's sphere" relied upon fundamental theological and biblical references. If women were to challenge the social order, they required a dissenting stand toward the epistemology of traditional religion.[16]

A woman's behavior in both church and society was continually judged against biblical injunctions and theological rationales that were routinely and authoritatively quoted by religious and political leaders who viewed any female behavior that fell outside these norms as inappropriate and even dangerous to the religious and social order. It is not surprising, therefore, that as the woman's rights movement gained momentum through the nineteenth century, it generated increasing resistance from church leaders and religious organizations as feminist ideology clashed with cultural norms that were undergirded by theological and biblical assumptions of the prevailing mid-nineteenth-century American Protestantism.

Early in the movement, calls for particular rights for women prompted sermons on women's appropriate sphere of activities by individual clergymen and church leaders, such as the 1837 sermon by Jonathan Stearns.

---

15. Barbara Welter, *Dimity Convictions: The American Woman in the Nineteenth Century* (Athens: Ohio University Press, 1976), 21.

16. Nancy Gale Isenberg, " 'Co-Equality of the Sexes': The Feminist Discourse of the Antebellum Women's Rights Movement in America" (Ph.D. diss., University of Wisconsin, Madison, 1990) 183.

Later in the nineteenth century, however, as the woman's movement became highly organized, well financed, and focused on the specific goal of the ballot, the opposition to woman's rights grew commensurately in strength. State antisuffrage organizations had been prevalent prior to the turn of the twentieth century, especially in the South, but the imminent prospect of the passage of an amendment permitting woman suffrage shortly after 1900 prompted the founding in 1911 of a National Association Opposed to Woman Suffrage from what had previously been unrelated state societies.[17] This antisuffrage movement was supported in large part by Protestant churches. Some Protestant denominations went so far as to make official pronouncements that if not blatantly opposed to woman suffrage at least clearly delineated appropriate female activities. In 1897, for instance, the Synod of Virginia of the Presbyterian Church in the United States commissioned a study to consider the question of the "woman's sphere" in light of "the movement, now current, bearing upon woman in the home and church." While the report of the study committee did not explicitly mention suffrage, it stated that "the same principle of subordination" found in Scripture concerning "woman's place, duties and rights in the home and in the church" applied also to "her place and rights in the state."[18]

By the close of the nineteenth century, the movement had become associated with the anticlericalism of Elizabeth Cady Stanton and other leaders who challenged traditional Christian doctrines and questioned (or even rejected) biblical authority, finding their vision of gender equality increasingly at odds with traditional beliefs.[19] Their religious dissent

17. Several recent works address the organization and influence of the antisuffrage movement as it grew at the end of the nineteenth century. See especially Jane Jerome Camhi, *Women against Women: American Anti-Suffragism, 1880–1920* (Brooklyn: Carlson Publishing, 1994) and Elna C. Green, *Southern Strategies: Southern Women and the Woman Suffrage Question* (Chapel Hill: University of North Carolina Press, 1997).

18. *The Sphere and Rights of Woman in the Church* (Richmond: Presbyterian Committee of Publication, 1899), 3, 15. Historian Wayne Flynt has identified the Presbyterian Church in the United States as one of the denominations most adamantly opposed to woman's rights. See Flynt, "Feeding the Hungry and Ministering to the Brokenhearted: The Presbyterian Church in the United States and the Social Gospel, 1900–1920," in *Religion in the South*, ed. Charles Reagan Wilson (Jackson: University Press of Mississippi, 1985), 119–20.

19. Throughout the nineteenth century, Stanton had distanced herself increasingly from traditional Protestant doctrine and practices. In the 1890s, she organized a group of women to serve as a Revising Committee to create a commentary on biblical texts about or involving women. The first volume of the *Woman's Bible* was published in 1895 and met vehement opposition from both church and political leaders.

"implied not only disagreement with church dogma, but the rejection of church practices and creeds which upheld male-defined authority."[20] As a result of this clear opposition to the church's beliefs and practices, something of a backlash arose against the tremendous gains women had made through the nineteenth century, making the closing decades of the woman suffrage movement as riddled with theological controversy and literalistic biblical interpretation as the opening decades half a century before. That backlash was demonstrated in a poll that revealed that "by 1890, the number of people who believed that the Bible sanctioned woman suffrage was far smaller than the number of people who, in 1830, thought it condemned slavery."[21]

Because of the intricate and inextricable relationship between the rights and roles of women and the gender and social norms of the nineteenth century that were rooted in biblical and theological interpretation, it is not difficult to document opposition to woman's rights that came from church leaders and denominational groups. Voices from all corners of the church, including clergymen, theologians, biblical scholars, and even lay men and women, condemned the advocates of woman's rights who were perceived as determined to destroy the moral and religious foundations of the nation. As Donna Behnke notes,

> Indeed, some of the richest theological minds in America expended time and energies developing defensive exegeses against these female insurgents.
>
> Whether women denounced religion and the church to embrace atheism or whether they sought to meet religious opposition on the appropriate battlefield of biblical and historical scholarship their opposition was awesome. Amateur and professional alike reared their heads to quote biblical passage after biblical passage condemning women to social and ecclesiastical serfdom. Anathemas were hurled from pulpits and echoed in the halls of the nation's legislatures.

20. Isenberg, "'Co-Equality of the Sexes,'" 182.

21. Kraditor, *Ideas of the Woman Suffrage Movement*, 75–76. Interestingly enough, the Massachusetts Woman Suffrage Association surveyed Massachusetts clergymen in 1901 and found that the overwhelming majority of the ministers surveyed were in favor of full or limited woman suffrage. (See *Woman's Journal*, January 25, 1902.) But the following year the NAWSA leaders realized the struggle they still faced in winning church women to the cause of suffrage and set up a Committee on Church Work to seek "ways and means of interesting conservative church women" as well as ministers and religious groups. (See NAWSA, *Proceedings*, 1902, 61.)

Figureheads among America's theologians and politicians wrote erudite treatises chiding female demands.[22]

As a result of such widespread and official opposition, woman's rights advocates had no choice but to confront the religious arguments used against them. Of necessity, they became skilled exegetes and theologians, learning how to justify their beliefs using the same tools—Scripture and theology—that were used against them. "Throughout the nineteenth century," according to Behnke, "feminists showed an intense interest in the theological and ecclesiastical barriers which were reared before them; and, spurred by religious insights of their own, they developed an impressive theological rationale for their movement."[23]

Ecclesiastical Support for Woman's Rights

Despite the essentially religious nature of the arguments both for and against woman's rights that characterized much of the gender debate of the nineteenth century, the religious dimension of the woman's rights/woman suffrage movement has often been ignored or discounted by scholars. In a 1990 essay, historian Evelyn A. Kirkley relates a conversation she had with a colleague when she began researching the role of religion in the woman suffrage movement in the southern United States. " 'There really aren't any sources,' " her colleague warned. " 'That will be a short paper.' "[24] Because of the polarizing nature of the issues surrounding woman's rights, the public debate can easily appear distorted in historical retrospect. That is, the debate can be viewed simplistically as between woman's rights advocates who addressed religious issues from a secular mode of vilification and religious leaders who opposed any expansion of rights for women, especially the right to vote. As a result, the historiography of the woman's rights movement regards the religious dimension of the movement as ranging from having an insignificant influence on the movement to being an impediment to its success. This has resulted in considerable disagreement among historians of woman suffrage concerning the role of religion in that political movement for social change.

---

22. Behnke, *Religious Issues in Nineteenth Century Feminism*, 5.
23. Ibid., 1–2.
24. Evelyn A. Kirkley, " 'This work is God's cause': Religion in the Southern Woman Suffrage Movement, 1880–1920," *Church History* 59 (December 1990): 507.

Indeed, most suffrage historians have either been concerned with other aspects of the movement or have ignored, for various reasons, its religious dimensions. "A great deal has already been written about the sociological, economic, and political aspects of the nineteenth century woman's rights movement," Behnke observes. "So much, in fact, that it has dwarfed an equally important aspect of the movement—its concern for religious and theological issues."[25] In her study of the spirituality of abolitionist women, Anna M. Speicher suggests that contemporary historians have difficulty "transcending the secularism of our own age in order to interpret accurately the religiosity of a previous one."[26] Thus, the religious values and assumptions that inspired reformers and, consequently, shaped reforms are often misunderstood or ignored.

Another reason for the discounting of the religious dimensions of the suffrage movement is offered by Nancy Gale Isenberg. Isenberg studied the primary nineteenth- and twentieth-century accounts of the woman's rights movement and notes what she believes to be the misreading and selective editing of early narrative accounts of the movement by modern scholars, leading to a distorted interpretation of the origins of the movement. Among the elements ignored in several modern interpretations is the fundamental role of religious and theological ideology in shaping and inspiring woman's rights activists. "Like their historical accounts," Isenberg maintains, "nineteenth-century feminists readily employed religious rhetoric and biblical figures of speech to make their political claims. The source of their radicalism, rather than limited to only secular or rational traditions, encompassed religious language and assumptions."[27]

Because of the attention given to other influences on the movement and the mixed, at best, relationship between woman's rights and religious convictions, the prominent role of religious leaders and religious ideology in *supporting* expanded rights for women is often neglected or ignored by interpreters of the woman's rights movement. But as Evelyn Kirkley notes, religion had a significant impact on the movement in three ways:

> First, religion was used in both pro- and anti-suffrage arguments, if not as the primary argument, at least as an element. Second, it played

25. Behnke, *Religious Issues in Nineteenth Century Feminism*, 1.

26. Anna M. Speicher, *The Religious World of Antislavery Women: Spirituality in the Lives of Five Abolitionist Lecturers* (Syracuse, N.Y.: Syracuse University Press, 2000), 7.

27. Isenberg, " 'Co-Equality of the Sexes,' " 39.

an important role in the motivations of individual suffragists. Third, and most important, suffragists made the vote a religious crusade, imbuing it with respectability and righteousness.[28]

I have already noted the significant role that religious ideology played in the Seneca Falls Convention. An understanding of the inextricable relationship between human equality (in this case, the equality of men and women) and divine intention shaped the beliefs, and thus the rhetoric, of the Seneca Falls organizers. By claiming their cause was consistent with their interpretation of God's laws and intentions for humanity, they set the theological bar, as it were, quite high from the beginning of the woman's movement. And naming the church with its often "perverted" applications of Scripture as complicit in the degradation of women moved from theoretical arguments about religion to concrete examples of the church's efforts to thwart the progress of women. It was also evident from the beginning of the movement that religion played an important role in the motivations of individual suffragists. The preachers, pastors, and other openly religious women and men who gathered at Seneca Falls and at the annual woman's rights conventions that followed wore their religious affiliations openly. Many woman's rights activists and suffragists who joined the movement as it expanded made it clear that they acted out of a sense of divine call or religious obligation to reform American society much as their forerunners in the abolitionist movement had done. Social reform—in this case, woman's rights—became for them what Robert H. Abzug refers to as a "radical religious calling,"[29] their response to a divine impulse to reconfigure the world according to a vision of justice and equality. As a result of their religious motivation, suffragists demonstrated Kirkley's third means of religion's influence on the women's movement: they made the securing of rights for women—especially the vote—a religious crusade.

Kirkley's three dimensions of religion's influence on the woman's rights movement are revealed early in the movement by several mid-nineteenth-century male preachers and counter the traditional interpretation of the church's negative response to female activism. Following the formal organization of the movement, several clergymen who had already established their political positions as abolitionists became early and ardent supporters

28. Kirkley, " 'This work is God's cause,' " 508.
29. Robert H. Abzug, *Cosmos Crumbling: American Reform and the Religious Imagination* (New York: Oxford University Press, 1994), viii.

of woman's rights. They participated in conventions, contributed to publications, and even promoted the idea of female social and political equality from their pulpits. They advocated the cause of women through their words and actions, opening their churches for meetings, speaking and preaching on women's issues, and offering theological and social justification for female equality.

Two of these pastors, Samuel J. May and William H. Channing, represented a group of Unitarian clergymen who were prominent spokesmen at early woman's rights conventions. In 1846 May "preached a sermon at Syracuse, New York, upon 'The Rights and Conditions of Women,' in which he sustained their right to take part in political life." The sermon was printed as a pamphlet and widely circulated among religious leaders and reformers. In 1853, Channing authored and arranged for the circulation of a petition that was presented to the Legislature of the State of New York representing "advocates of woman's just and equal rights" and requesting the redress of "woman's legal and civil disabilities," including their entitlement "to Freedom, Representation, and Suffrage." Earlier that year, during a particularly contentious convention held in New York City, he defended the public speech of Antoinette Brown Blackwell shortly after her ordination by the Congregational Church. Theodore Parker, another Unitarian minister, delivered a sermon that same year on "The Public Function of Woman." "A woman has the same human nature that a man has," Parker declared, "the same human rights, to life, liberty, and the pursuit of happiness; the same human duties; and they are as inalienable in a woman as in a man." Then, from his philosophical understanding of woman's equality he extrapolated a defense of woman's political involvement: "By nature, woman has the same political rights that man has—to vote, to hold office, to make and administer laws."[30]

May, Channing, and Parker were joined by a number of other liberal clergymen who became public advocates for woman's rights and whose names and words appear frequently in the historical record of the movement. At the New England convention of 1859, the Reverends James Freeman Clarke and John T. Sargent distinguished themselves by their remarks. Clarke spoke in favor of giving women "every chance to fit themselves for new spheres of duty. If a woman wants to study medicine, let her study it; if she wants to study divinity, let her study it; . . . If she finds faculties within her, let them have a chance to expand." Sargent

---

30. *History of Woman Suffrage*, I:40, 588, 277, 278.

spoke to the gathering, he noted, "under the pressure of an obligation to testify in behalf of an interest truly Christian, and one of the greatest that can engage the reason or the conscience of a community." He addressed the particular hardships of impoverished women who suffered most greatly, he said, due to the denial of woman's rights. Another clergyman, T. W. Higginson, served as an officer of the Seventh National Woman's Rights Convention in 1856 and addressed the convention following a debate concerning the question of whether the claims of women were founded on nature or revelation. Higginson, the convention recorder noted, concluded that he was among "those who simply believed that God made man and woman, and knew what He was about when He made them—giving them rights founded on the eternal laws of nature."[31]

The most notable male preacher to join the movement for woman's rights was Henry Ward Beecher. Few Americans in the second half of the nineteenth century would have failed to recognize his name. As pastor of the large and influential Plymouth Congregational Church in Brooklyn for forty years, as a political orator, and as an interpreter of the social and theological upheavals that characterized Victorian America, Beecher gained national renown. Never one to fear mingling politics with religion, Beecher preached, wrote, and worked against slavery and in support of the Union, and, as for many a suffragist, his abolitionist activity led naturally to his support for woman's rights. He became an ardent supporter of the movement and its coalescence around the issue of the ballot, appearing frequently on suffrage platforms and preaching sermons in defense of the equality of women and of their full participation in the church, and was eventually elected president of the newly formed American Woman Suffrage Association (AWSA) in 1869. Beecher believed that woman's qualities of "refinement, tenderness, and moral purity" were God's gift and that her vote "would carry into human affairs a power almost like the right hand of the Almighty."[32] In 1870, he concluded his presidential address to the second annual convention of the AWSA with these words:

> I, for one, need not assert that I am from my whole heart and conviction thoroughly of the opinion that the nature of woman, the purity and sweetness of the family, the integrity and strength of the

31. Ibid., 265, 270–71, 647.
32. Henry Ward Beecher, "Woman Suffrage Man's Right" in Halford R. Ryan, *Henry Ward Beecher: Peripatetic Preacher* (New York: Greenwood Press, 1990), 104, 105.

State, will all be advantaged when woman shall be, like man, a participator in public affairs.[33]

While the support of male clergy such as Henry Ward Beecher, Theodore Parker, and James Freeman Clarke was critical for the establishment of the early woman's rights movement, the ultimate credibility of any pursuit of woman's equality depended on the success of female reformers in claiming public space for themselves. Karlyn Kohrs Campbell notes the significance of early woman's rights activists who

> were constrained to be particularly creative because they faced barriers unknown to men. They were a group virtually unique in rhetorical history because a central element of woman's oppression was the denial of her right to speak. Quite simply, in nineteenth-century America, femininity and rhetorical action were seen as mutually exclusive. No "true woman" could be a public persuader.[34]

Women Reformers Find Their Voices

By the time of the Seneca Falls Convention in 1848, several iconoclastic women had already defied the "true woman" designation by invading the sacred male spaces of platform and even pulpit. Several women had followed in the dangerous footsteps of the Grimké sisters and had earned reputations—positive ones for the quality of their presentations and negative ones for their audacity in transgressing gender roles—for their speeches before "promiscuous," that is, mixed-gender, audiences. Most of them found themselves participating in the public arena as a result of their abolitionist convictions. In the process, many abolitionists recognized the incongruity of advocating freedom and political rights for African Americans while American women of all races remained constrained by oppressive political, economic, and ecclesiastical laws. Many antislavery women were rudely awakened to their own plight when they tried to address public antislavery gatherings and were jeered, mobbed, and even expelled from their own antislavery societies.[35] Thus, "in advocating liberty for the

33. *History of Woman Suffrage*, II:768.

34. Karlyn Kohrs Campbell, ed., *Man Cannot Speak for Her*, vol. 1, *A Critical Study of Early Feminist Rhetoric* (New York: Greenwood Press, 1989), 9–10.

35. The American Anti-Slavery Society divided in 1840 over the question of women's participation. Women were welcomed as full members of the American National Anti-Slavery

black race," the narrative of the woman's rights movement declared, several reformist women "were early compelled to defend the right of free speech for themselves. They had the double battle to fight against the tyranny of sex and color at the same time," with many of their most vociferous opponents coming from the ranks of the clergy and their fellow abolitionists in the United States and abroad.[36] It was no coincidence, then, that the antislavery and woman's rights movements had a number of participants in common, including Abby Kelley Foster, Angelina and Sarah Grimké, and Lucretia Mott, whose rhetorical skills were honed on the antislavery platform. Donna Behnke notes the critical juxtaposition of the two movements and the importance of the abolitionist movement in giving rise to woman's rights activists:

> While the early decades of the century provided few women articulate enough to present bold, well-reasoned arguments intent upon reversing theological prejudices adverse to women, the Abolitionist Movement and other reform movements which gripped the century would bring strong-willed, well-educated women into the public arena.[37]

If the antislavery movement provided women reformers with an incipient opportunity to engage in public rhetoric as they promoted a cause, the woman's rights movement provided an opportunity for the blossoming of their rhetorical skills as they claimed public space to promote their own equality. Women speaking on behalf of woman's rights became a doubly subversive activity, a twofold act of defiance against cultural norms, as these women defied propriety both through their words on behalf of female equality and through their actions as women speaking in public settings to mixed audiences. Women publicly promoting the freedom of others—men and women who were enslaved, women trapped in prostitution, children abused by the labor system—was one thing, for even though they were transgressing social norms, their transgressions were mitigated by their selfless intentions. Women publicly promoting their *own* freedom was something else, however—something deemed

---

Society while the American and Foreign Anti-Slavery Society split off and disallowed the full participation of women.

36. *History of Woman Suffrage*, I:53.
37. Behnke, *Religious Issues in Nineteenth Century Feminism*, 2.

unacceptable and even selfish. Thus, the platform became both the vehicle for the promotion of a political message concerning woman's equality and a symbol of that message itself by the very embodiment of the speaker's words in the form of a woman speaking publicly.

To add yet another complicating layer to the subversive activities of some mid-nineteenth-century women, some women became engaged in *religious* rhetorical activity, praying and testifying in public religious gatherings and even preaching. The "monopoly of the pulpit," as the Seneca Falls leaders had termed it, was weightier than other professional barriers women encountered because it struck at the heart of a social structure based on prescribed gender roles believed to be established by divine decree. Although women who entered male professions such as education, law, and medicine throughout the nineteenth century met fierce opposition, they were at least spared the recitation of biblical injunctions commanding women's silence in church. Thus, in the nineteenth century as in the twenty-first, it was not unusual to find both men and women who readily accepted professional women in any field other than ministry.

In an auspicious alignment of historical events, the first organized calls for woman's rights occurred just as women were beginning to gain access to sacred ecclesiastical space. The rise of both new theologies that emphasized individual experience over ecclesiastical dogma and new church traditions that embraced practices once considered anathema, along with changing gender and social assumptions during the first half of the nineteenth century, fostered acceptance of women preachers, evangelists, and even pastors. It was not surprising, then, that the religious leaders recruited for the cause of woman's rights included a small but well-known group of women, such as Quaker preacher Lucretia Mott and intinerant evangelist Sojourner Truth, who by the 1850s had invaded the male bastion of the pulpit. Their titles and status varied and often did not conform to the professional categories of the major Protestant denominations, for most of these women were from sectarian groups that had no ordained offices or from denominations that had an array of recognized leadership positions. Most women preachers were, for example, recorded ministers of the Society of Friends, licensed (or nonlicensed) lay preachers of the Methodist Episcopal and African Methodist Episcopal Churches, or recognized preachers in the Holiness, Baptist, and other free traditions.

What did not vary, however, was the recognition and respect they were accorded by the budding woman's rights movement. Leaders of the movement regarded these renegade women as a badge of honor in the crusade against gender barriers. From the earliest woman's rights conventions, women preachers were asked to open and close the meetings with prayer. They were often invited to give sermons—both from the convention platform and from local church pulpits—during convention gatherings. They even organized Sunday services when necessary en route to conventions, such as the service held on the train in June 1905 as suffragists traveled to their first Pacific Coast meeting in Portland, Oregon.[38] The women who bore the hard-earned title "Reverend" were always addressed by that title in the minutes of woman's rights meetings. As ecclesiastical doors opened for women, milestone events, such as the first women ordained or licensed by particular denominations, as well as the difficulties and setbacks religious women faced received mention in the journals that chronicled the woman's movement. The *Woman's Journal*, the most widely circulated journal of the suffrage movement, which was published from 1870 until 1919, reported ordinations, calls, and other ecclesiastical decisions concerning women under its regular columns titled "News and Notes," "Concerning Women," and "Women in the Churches." Attempts of women to obtain full ordination in the Methodist Episcopal Church were reported in the January 23, 1875, and May 22, 1880, issues. The latter issue reported the decision against Anna Howard Shaw and Anna Oliver, who had sought ordination first by the New England Conference and then by the General Conference of the Methodist Episcopal Church in May 1880. The January 25, 1902, issue reported the ordination of Martha Curry in the Wesleyan Church as well as the evangelistic services led by evangelists Mary Frost and Fannie Simpson from Long Island. Occasionally an article appeared under the title "Woman in the Synagogue." The February 21, 1874, issue reported the *Jewish Messenger* as gloating that " 'as yet, the Woman's Rights movement has not reached the synagogue,' " with no Jewish woman desiring " 'to preach to her brethren. . . . Even the important matter of voting at synagogue meetings is a subject of no concern to our ladies.' " The response to these statements from the *Christian Register* as reprinted in the *Woman's Journal* advised the *Jewish Messenger* " 'to beware of premature exultation. When human nature has had its perfect work among the daughters of Israel some of the kinswomen of Miriam and Deborah may entirely eclipse the Universalist and Presbyterian prophetesses.' "

38. See *History of Woman Suffrage*, V:118.

Three Pioneers of the Pulpit

In this book I present the story of three women who represent those who transcended the ecclesiastical and cultural boundaries that circumscribed women's ambitions in the nineteenth century in order to work for—and demonstrate—the equality of women in all sectors of society. Their lives and work embodied many of the religious and social changes that defined nineteenth-century America. Beyond their common vocational path from preachers to suffragists, the lives of Antoinette Brown Blackwell, Olympia Brown, and Anna Howard Shaw reveal many similarities in philosophy and experience that enabled them to surmount the numerous obstacles placed before women of their era. Most notably, all three women were influenced more significantly by their relationships, their life experiences, and their inner senses of vocation than by the dictates of their times. Interestingly, all three were raised in frontier or rural communities where their activities and aspirations were perhaps less constrained than they might have been in more established communities. In addition, they all were raised in families that, to varying degrees, valued education, even education for women. And all three testified in their autobiographical materials to the importance of mentors and influential people—both men and women—whose paths through life crossed their own and who inspired these women to pursue long-held dreams and convictions.

What perhaps most obviously unites the lives of Brown Blackwell, Brown, and Shaw, however, is their religious conviction and their commitment to the church in some ecclesiastical form while they pursued, through rhetorical and organizational leadership of the suffrage movement, women's equality. These three women are convincing examples of the three ways in which religion played a role in the suffrage movement, as suggested by Evelyn Kirkley. All three women relied heavily on religious arguments to support the enfranchisement of women. They were challenged early in their lives—usually as college or seminary students—to defend, on biblical and theological grounds, their own clerical ambitions as well as their belief in female equality. They all acknowledged the spiritual motivation for their involvement in the suffrage movement. As they wrestled with the move from parish ministry to suffrage leadership, they made it quite clear through their public and private writings that they regarded their expanded "ministries" as simply different expressions of the lifelong and costly calls to ministry they had pursued and obtained. And it is abundantly evident from their sermons, speeches, and other writings that women's equality as represented in the vote was, for them, a religious crusade. Rarely did they speak of woman suffrage, even in decidedly secular settings such as before Senate committees and at congressional hearings, in purely secular terms. Instead, they always equated women's enfranchisement with a divine quest for justice.

Since the advent of an academic discipline of women's studies in the last quarter of the twentieth century, several fine inquiries into the relationship between women and religion in the nineteenth century have been published. One such work argues that women helped shape liberal Protestant religion in nineteenth-century America through their alliance with liberal clergymen, creating what has been termed a "feminized" version of traditional Christian doctrine.[39] Another work addresses the spiritual motivation for the work of several women abolitionists in the nineteenth century, all of whom rejected traditional ecclesiastical expressions of American Protestantism and instead shaped their own style of spirituality.[40] Other works have uncovered the vast numbers and influence of women preachers in nineteenth-century America.[41] Yet another work examines the many women who neither stayed within the institutions of traditional Protestantism nor abandoned their faith but instead founded new religious groups that in turn evolved into traditions outside the mainstream.[42]

My work in this book echoes elements of all those works, particularly as I seek to locate religious women in their rightful place among those who shaped both church and culture in the United States in the nineteenth century. It is different, however, in that I identify religious women who claimed ordained, public leadership positions in traditional ecclesiastical communities and, on moving from those communities to work in the political realm, did not eschew their religious identities and convictions but claimed them as the basis for their new work. Brown Blackwell, Brown, and Shaw represent an alternative to previously identified ways in which women interacted with religion in the nineteenth century. They neither directly shaped liberal Protestantism nor abandoned the church and orthodoxy. Instead, they confronted both American Protestantism

---

39. See Ann Douglas, *The Feminization of American Culture* (New York: Avon Books, 1977).

40. See Speicher, *Religious World of Antislavery Women.*

41. See Catherine A. Brekus, *Strangers and Pilgrims: Female Preaching in America, 1740–1845* (Chapel Hill: University of North Carolina Press, 1998) and Bettye Collier-Thomas, *Daughters of Thunder: Black Women Preachers and Their Sermons, 1850–1979* (San Francisco: Jossey-Bass Publishers, 1998).

42. See Catherine Wessinger, ed., *Women's Leadership in Marginal Religions* (Urbana: University of Illinois Press, 1993).

and the American political system with the sin of exclusion and constructed theological rationales that justified their work. They pursued paths that were different from—even antithetical to—those of their white, female, middle-class counterparts of the nineteenth century, demonstrating an inexplicable and very personal sense of divine claim on their lives.

To seek to determine how and why they pursued calls to ministry is to deny the very nature of those calls as mysterious and ineffable. Nevertheless, the experiences that shaped how those calls were nurtured and fulfilled is instructive for others, especially women who continue to discern such compelling calls in their own lives and who are still too often thwarted in their attempts to answer them. Brown Blackwell, Brown, and Shaw, who have not been studied together before in any sustained way,[43] testify to the compatibility of a commitment to both woman's rights and religious convictions. What historian Mary D. Pellauer said of Anna Howard Shaw applies to all three women: "In Shaw's work can be seen a case study in the terms by which the woman suffrage movement became respectable, in attaching itself to mainline Christianity."[44] These women demonstrate how these two belief systems—belief in the equality of women and belief in traditional Christian doctrine—that were often portrayed as conflicting could be held together and employed for social change.

The formative experiences of Brown Blackwell, Brown, and Shaw are critical to any interpretation of their work and thought. For that reason, chapter 1 presents biographical sketches of the three women. The people and circumstances they encountered, especially as young women, shaped the direction of their lives in obvious ways. At the same time, it becomes evident through their biographies that the convictions and determination inherent in each of these three women were equally responsible for their accomplishments. They were influenced by their historical circumstances but rarely constrained by them; otherwise they would not have pursued such a radical break with tradition in seeking

43. Carl J. and Dorothy Schneider present biographical sketches of Brown Blackwell, Brown, and Shaw and make reference to them as a group in their chapter on the first women ordained ("Ordination for the Few [1853–1900]"), but they offer no sustained study of their common experiences and work. See Carl J. and Dorothy Schneider, *In Their Own Right: The History of American Clergywomen* (New York: Crossroad Publishing, 1997), 60–70, 92.

44. Mary D. Pellauer, *Toward a Tradition of Feminist Theology: The Religious Social Thought of Elizabeth Cady Stanton, Susan B. Anthony, and Anna Howard Shaw* (Brooklyn, N.Y.: Carlson Publishing, 1991), 256.

ecclesiastical ordination. Their lives bear witness to an interesting inter-
play of internal fortitude and external forces that resulted in creative and
passionate legacies.

Chapter 2 presents a history of the opening of ordination to women in
the United States. By the time Antoinette Brown Blackwell obtained her
theological training at Oberlin College, women were already embracing
new public roles in American religion and shaping the direction of several
American Protestant traditions through their leadership and participation. After tracing the origin of and debates concerning the ordination
question, I recount the events leading to the ordinations of Brown
Blackwell, Brown, and Shaw. A woman's ordination to the ministry of
Word and sacrament, that is, full clerical ordination, was unprecedented
in the United States—or anywhere in Christendom, as best as scholars can
discern—before Brown Blackwell's ordination by a congregation of the
Congregational Church in 1853. Her ordination was followed ten years
later by Olympia Brown's ordination by the Northern Universalist Association, the first ordination of a woman in the United States by action of
a denominational body beyond the local church, and in 1880 by Anna
Howard Shaw's by action of the Methodist Protestant Church. These
three ordinations were radical and monumental breaks with ecclesiastical
tradition. The events and factors precipitating them in American religious
history are worthy of exploration. How did their calls to ordained ministry first manifest themselves? How did they articulate and pursue those
calls amidst ecclesiastical, educational, familial, and other prohibitions
against them? How did they justify, especially biblically and theologically,
the significant requests they made for ordination?

It is also important for interpreting the work of these three women to
understand their experiences in ordained pastoral ministry and their
moves from pastoral ministry to work for woman suffrage. This is the subject of chapter 3. Brown Blackwell, Brown, and Shaw all served churches
immediately following their ordinations, although for quite different
lengths of time. Their experiences in pastoral contexts not only provide
insight into the evolution of their future work and the manifestation of
their theological convictions but are instructive for the many women
entering pastoral ministry today who face similar circumstances, questions, and challenges.

After various periods of time and personal struggles, however, all three
women left full-time parish ministry to devote their efforts to the movement for woman suffrage. They broke down the most significant ecclesiastical barrier against women, but they recognized "the need for women's

rights before women could serve the church to their full capacity."[45] Their vocational shift raises several interesting questions. Why did they move from parish ministry to suffrage work? How did they see work for suffrage as an extension and fulfillment of their calls? How did their experiences as women in ministry influence their later vocational paths? This study argues that neither Brown Blackwell nor Brown nor Shaw "left" ministry for work as a suffragist as most historians state it.[46] Instead, I contend that all three women regarded their work for women's equality as an *extension of* their ministries. They could be numbered among the "anomalous men and women" described by Robert Abzug who "did not abandon the realm of the sacred in championing 'social' causes. Rather, they made religious sense of society, economy, race, politics, gender, and physiology."[47] The wider social and political worlds of America became their "parishes," and their ultimate goal became the spiritual transformation of American society rather than the spiritual transformation of individual hearts. They pursued a vision of the kingdom of God on earth that transcended the walls of individual churches and permeated every structure of American society and political life.

That vision of the kingdom of God on earth is evident in their rhetoric delivered from pulpits and platforms. Their theological understandings shaped their worldviews, their experiences in ministry, their move from preachers to suffragists, and especially their argumentation in support of women's equality. Thus, a study of the theological argumentation for woman suffrage offered by Brown Blackwell, Brown, and Shaw is the subject of chapter 4. By means of a decidedly religious rhetoric, all three women facilely bridged the divide between sacred and secular space. Their speech on the suffrage platform was replete with biblical references, theological language, and spiritual meaning. At the same time, they readily employed the pulpit in the quest for women's equality, never hesitating to promote woman suffrage as the text or occasion gave rise to issues of gender and justice. Their "religious imaginations"[48] inspired them to pursue political ends—in this case, women's enfranchisement and equal-

45. Schneider and Schneider, *In Their Own Right*, 69.
46. While Carl J. and Dorothy Schneider suggest that Brown Blackwell, Brown, and Shaw all probably left parish ministry in response to "a recognition of the need for women's rights before women could serve the church to their full capacity," they also state that "any New Woman could see that their experiences in the church had led Antoinette Brown Blackwell, Olympia Brown, and Anna Howard Shaw, and many members of the Iowa Sisterhood [an association of Unitarian clergywomen] to opt out of the clergy into other careers." See ibid., 92.
47. Abzug, *Cosmos Crumbling*, 4.
48. Ibid., viii.

ity—through theological means. As a result of their support for suffrage within the framework of familiar biblical and theological concepts, Brown Blackwell, Brown, and Shaw tempered fears of the radical nature of woman's rights, making it more acceptable among a broader constituency of American society at a crucial time in the suffrage movement.

In the concluding fifth chapter, I review the closing years of their lives and seek to assess the contributions of these three remarkable preachers-turned-suffragists to both church and society in the United States. Their most obvious and lasting legacy was their crucial role in opening the doors of the church to ordination for women. As pastors, they did their jobs well and came to be loved by communities of faith. Their influence came to be felt by much larger "parishes," however, as they became leaders of the suffrage movement. Through their inspiring rhetoric, Brown Blackwell, Brown, and Shaw came to be loved—and respected—by the American public. They demonstrate the faith and courage that comes from following an inner, God-inspired sense of vocation rather than acquiescing to the demands of others or the constraints of church and society. They maintained belief in biblical authority but interpreted Scripture in ways different from those who opposed them. They never really gave up ministry nor faith in the viability of the church even as they moved beyond congregations and specific denominations. They lived long, full, productive lives, with Brown Blackwell and Brown living to cast their votes in 1920, the first national election open to women voters.

The lives and work of Antoinette Brown Blackwell, Olympia Brown, and Anna Howard Shaw provide valuable insight into two little-studied subjects: the experiences of the earliest ordained American clergywomen and the religious dimensions of the movement for woman's rights in the United States. In assessing the contributions of women's theological scholarship in the nineteenth century, Donna Behnke states:

> Although the [nineteenth] century did not bring total victory for feminist theology (indeed, such is not the case even today), it did succeed in outlining the crucial issues and shaping those theological and biblical foundational arguments which remain valid and vital today.[49]

The questions and issues that shape the debate over women's ordination and participation in ecclesiastical communities today at the beginning of

---

49. Behnke, *Religious Issues in Nineteenth Century Feminism*, 6.

the twenty-first century are little changed from those that arose from the experiences of Brown Blackwell, Brown, and Shaw. Thus, their justifications of their calls to ministry, their ecclesiastical experiences, and the insights they gained from lives lived faithfully are invaluable for shedding much-needed light on the gender debates that continue to vex the church.

This work also addresses the timely issue of the relationship between church and state. These three women represent a significant number of other woman's rights supporters who not only found equality for women compatible with their theological and biblical beliefs but in fact were compelled to support woman's rights because of those beliefs. As America continues to struggle with the fragile and often inscrutable relationship between church and state even in the twenty-first century, and as churches continue to debate or struggle with the presence of women in all ecclesiastical roles, these three women exemplify a far more perfect way in their assumption of the compatibility of woman's rights and religious conviction. While they employed both sacred and secular means to promote their political and religious beliefs, they were never coercive in their zeal and never used religious language in a shallow, manipulative way. They were sincere in their religious and political beliefs and in their assumption that the two could not just peaceably coexist but were indeed two essential parts of one whole. As a result, their work provides a model for the kind of constructive public discourse and advocacy for reform that can arise from deeply held convictions, even religious convictions.

Chapter One

"Strangers in a strange land":

The Formation of Radical Religious Callings

Early in the fall of 1850, Antoinette Brown Blackwell's best friend and Oberlin classmate Lucy Stone invited her to attend the First National Woman's Rights Convention to be held in Worcester, Massachusetts.[1] Brown Blackwell initially declined the invitation (although she later relented and attended), citing her disagreement with the radical philosophy of the Garrisonian abolitionists, many of whom made up the core of the leadership of the incipient woman's rights movement. In a letter to Lucy Stone she expressed her ambivalence concerning the budding woman's rights movement:

> I might go there and speak against them in many things for I do not believe exactly with your party even on the subject of woman's rights and I would not be bought to silence. . . . I should still like to attend the convention but do not know that it will be best. I should be a stranger in a strange land and it would be hard for the people to understand me.[2]

1. The 1848 Seneca Falls Convention was the first called, national gathering of woman's rights advocates, but what was intended to be, and indeed became, the first *annual* national woman's rights convention was this one held in Worcester, Massachusetts, October 23–24, 1850.

2. Antoinette Brown Blackwell to Lucy Stone, August 13, 1850, Blackwell Family Papers (A-77), Schlesinger Library, Radcliffe Institute for Advanced Study, Harvard University, Fol. 26. Subsequent citations to this collection will read "BFP, SL" with the appropriate folder number(s).

Brown Blackwell's self-image of "a stranger in a strange land" serves as an appropriate metaphor not only for her own life but for those of Olympia Brown and Anna Howard Shaw as well. All three women found themselves driven, compelled, yes, *called*, as theological language would describe it, to ministry, but the call would lead inevitably to serious conflicts with cultural, familial, and ecclesiastical traditions. As Brown Blackwell, Brown, and Shaw sought the educational qualifications and ecclesiastical recognition necessary to fulfill their sense of divine call, they repeatedly found themselves to be strangers in strange lands: students in hostile classrooms, daughters in families appalled and embarrassed by their vocational choices, women fighting exclusively male denominational boards and church leaders. Nor did their feelings of alienation end once they moved beyond their parish positions. Although they gained respect and admiration for their work for suffrage, many of their secular colleagues regarded their religious commitments with a degree of skepticism.

While their particular battles varied in terms of their denominational contexts and life situations, all encountered alienation and obstacles on the way to ecclesiastical acceptance. Their grace and tenacity in claiming an ecclesiastical place for their gifts is both remarkable and exemplary for women who continue to feel like strangers in the often-strange world of the church even in the twenty-first century. Their lives bear witness to that grace and tenacity and to their conviction that the call of God will triumph over all earthly powers.

"A preacher for the people": Antoinette Brown Blackwell (1825–1921)

Of the three women portrayed in this book, perhaps Brown Blackwell felt the sense of being a "stranger in a strange land" most deeply and continuously throughout her life. Her call to ministry in a time and place that prohibited women's ordination, her liberal theological ideas in an increasingly conservative religious landscape, her moderate views on gender issues amidst radical feminist voices, and even her amateur intellectual forays into the worlds of philosophy and science in an age of increasing academic specialization all bear witness to this brilliant stranger finding herself and her abundant gifts in many strange lands. The struggles Brown Blackwell faced in pursuing her calls and interests, however, did not hamper her indomitable spirit nor diminish her commitment to her goals. In the course of her ninety-six years, she made herself at home enough in those strange lands to break down many nineteenth-century barriers that had circumscribed women's activities. She was one of the first women to complete the theological course of study at Oberlin College and the first woman to be ordained by a recognized Protestant denomination in the United States. She was among the first female orators of the social movements—temperance, abolition, woman's rights—that dominated the nineteenth century and also was among the first women elected to membership in the American Association for the Advancement of Science. Perhaps the crowning achievement of her life, however, was the simple act in November 1920 of casting a ballot in a voting booth as one of the first women to vote in a national election after the ratification of the Nineteenth Amendment.

This remarkable life began rather unremarkably in Henrietta, New York, in May 1825. Born into a devout Congregational family, Brown Blackwell felt compelled to request membership in her family's church at the unusually young age of nine. "I was as deeply and truly religious at that time," she later commented, "though but nine years of age, as I have ever been at any age."[3] As a child of the "burned-over district" of upstate New York, the region of phenomenal religious fervor and innovation during the second quarter of the nineteenth century, it was not surprising that Brown Blackwell developed a keen theological awareness at an early age. The evangelistic tours and ideas of Charles Grandison Finney were popular in the area of New York where the Brown family's farm was located. She recalled:

> Professor Finney who taught in the Theological School was a noted revivalist & sometimes held meetings in Rochester. It was he who converted my father & sister in the early days. My father always wanted to be a minister but felt that he must wait till he received a call from Heaven, joined the Church under Professor Finney.[4]

3. This reference (and many references in this and ensuing chapters) is from an unpublished manuscript of memoirs told by Brown Blackwell in 1909 to Mrs. Claude U. (Sarah) Gilson, a young suffragist, titled "Antoinette Brown Blackwell, The First Woman Minister," which is part of the BFP, SL, Fols. 3–14. There are two versions of the manuscript in the Schlesinger Library collection. The first version (from which the references in this book are taken) is identical to the second version in terms of its text but includes additional essays, articles, and the like by and about Brown Blackwell. This particular quotation is found on page 70. Citations to this manuscript hereafter will read "Gilson ms." followed by the appropriate page number(s).

4. Antoinette Brown Blackwell, "Childhood," 4, ms., n.d., BFP, SL, Fol. 1.

Brown Blackwell's oldest sister "originally induced the other members of the family to attend, and they all became warm admirers of Prof. Finney and his methods."[5] From that time on, religion played an even more central role in the Brown household. The family never, however, accepted the harsh Calvinist orthodoxy prevalent at the time that emphasized a transcendent, vengeful God and a helpless, sinful humanity. Instead,

> [the Brown family] belonged to the more liberal type of orthodox Congregationalists. The terrors of future punishment were not largely dwelt upon either in church or at home. To me from a child the whole matter of endless punishment seemed so terrible that I put it out of mind as far as possible, falling back upon the comfortable assurance that God was always just as well as merciful and that no wrong could or would be done.[6]

Even as a child, Brown Blackwell recognized her ambivalence about the doctrines propounded by Finney and his evangelist colleagues: "I was greatly impressed by his graphic doctrine of eternal punishment. . . . I seemed to believe it but even at that day had no real faith in it."[7]

Just as the Brown household encouraged Antoinette's less-than-orthodox theological beliefs, it also abetted her inclination toward less-than-orthodox occupational choices for a young woman of the mid-nineteenth century. She was allowed to engage in farm work usually reserved for boys, encouraged in her obvious giftedness for writing, and provided with an excellent secondary education that enabled her in 1846 to fulfill her "one great desire"[8] of acceptance at Oberlin Collegiate Institute in Ohio. Her unorthodox vocational choice had evolved through her young life:

> From earliest childhood I intended and expected to have a definate [sic] life work. In the very early days I intended to continue somewhat along the lines of the accepted Woman's Sphere. I supposed St. Paul must be right in what he said about women. As soon as I came to real thought on the subject I realized that he talked for his own times not for ours.[9]

---

5. Gilson ms., 70.
6. Ibid., 71.
7. Brown Blackwell, "Childhood," 4.
8. Ibid., 17.
9. Antoinette Brown Blackwell, "Life Work," 1, ms., n.d., BFP, SL, Fol. 1.

Her family and even her community embraced and encouraged her child-hood interest in pursuing a religious vocation even as they steered her toward work as a missionary or minister's wife, vocations that were more acceptable for women than ordained ministry:

> My mother finding how determined I was begged me at least to carry on my work in some foreign mission. My father gave me to understand that his assistance would cease with my college education at Oberlin and my brother, then a minister, would not assist me to do what he considered an impossible work. My teacher, a former minister, remonstrated and also urged work in a foreign mission.[10]

After a few years spent convincing her family that a higher education would help her in whatever she chose to do, Brown Blackwell's "persistent desire to be sent to Oberlin was gratified by [her] family. It was the only college in the country which would, at that time, admit women to a regular collegiate course and it was then in its thirteenth year." And so shortly before she turned twenty-one in the spring of 1846, she recalled, "I started for Oberlin and my college life."[11] When she arrived at Oberlin, however, she discovered that the gender equality on which the school's reputation had been built was often eclipsed by traditional understandings of women and their roles. The course of study that Brown Blackwell, her friend Lucy Stone, and other women were permitted to pursue was limited to certain literary and classical disciplines meant to prepare women to serve in the traditional female roles of wives and mothers and moral leaders of American society. Brown Blackwell voiced her discontent with these expectations and joined with Stone and others to organize the Ladies Literary Society in order to, among other things, gain experience in public speaking and debate, activities otherwise forbidden to the Oberlin women. She did what was necessary to complete the program leading to a literary diploma, graduating in the summer of 1847, but during her time at Oberlin she also took every opportunity to gain teaching and speaking experience, her heart still set on a career in ministry.

Undaunted by Oberlin's official stance on women's participation in any profession other than teaching, Brown Blackwell returned to Oberlin in the fall of 1847 to study theology. In a poignant, honest reflection, however, she admitted that "no where and by no person was there one word

10. Ibid., 2.
11. Ibid.

of encouragement for me in my intention to become a minister."[12] In fact, her presence provoked continual reaffirmation by the school's faculty and administrators of traditional roles for women. Charles G. Finney, then professor of theology and spiritual leader of the community, and James Fairchild, professor of mathematics and natural philosophy, were particularly vocal in their defense of the limitations placed upon the activities of women. Their repeated refusals to allow Brown Blackwell to speak publicly or pursue training for ordination is ironic in that both Finney and Fairchild were leading proponents of Oberlin's coeducational policy. They were not unlike many men (and women) of their era, however, in that they advocated an expanded domestic and moral role for women while continuing to place limitations on their spheres of public activity.

Even her best friend and confidante, Lucy Stone, expressed opposition to Brown Blackwell's pursuit of ministry, not because of any transgression of cultural norms (indeed, Brown Blackwell's ministry "will be a good to the sex," Stone believed) but because Stone had nothing but contempt for the "outgrown creed" of religious belief that had erected a "*wall* of bible, brimstone, church, and corruption, which has hitherto hemmed *women* into *nothingness*."[13] "How well I remember walking with her at sunset," Brown Blackwell recalled, "and hearing her say, 'You never can do it'— and my answer was, 'I am going to do it.'"[14] But unlike Stone, as Brown Blackwell's biographer Elizabeth Cazden notes, "Antoinette Brown made a concerted effort to integrate orthodox Christianity with reform politics and especially with woman's rights."[15] That effort enabled Brown Blackwell to break down many ecclesiastical and social barriers for women, but it came at the cost of knowing she was regarded by many in both church and society as a stranger in strange lands.

Despite opposition from all sides, Brown Blackwell continued to sit in on classes in the Theological Department, and Oberlin eventually acknowledged her with the ambiguous designation of "resident graduate pursuing the theological course."[16] What appeared to be a reasonable

12. Brown Blackwell, "Childhood," 4.

13. Lucy Stone to Antoinette Brown, August 1849, in Carol Lasser and Marlene Deahl Merrill, eds., *Friends and Sisters: Letters between Lucy Stone and Antoinette Brown Blackwell, 1846–93* (Urbana: University of Illinois Press, 1987), 54.

14. Gilson ms., 59.

15. Elizabeth Cazden, *Antoinette Brown Blackwell: A Biography* (Old Westbury, N.Y.: Feminist Press, 1983), 42.

16. This is the designation given to Brown Blackwell in the *Oberlin Catalogue of the Officers and Students* for the three years she was in the theology program. At the time, Brown Blackwell

compromise was not, however, since she was still prohibited from speaking publicly in an academic venue. This obstacle proved to be insurmountable since her course of study required the practice of preaching and other public recitations. She recalled one such awkward occasion when the new theological students were asked to state their reasons for pursuing ministry:

> The students who were asked to speak were called upon alphabetically. My name came early in the list and Professor Finney asked after a few speakers, "Who comes next?" Someone answered, "Antoinette Brown" . . . Professor Finney looked rather surprised and said, "Oh the women, we don't ask them to speak now." This was near the close of the meeting and I went home feeling really hurt, but when Professor Finney was informed that I was to become a regular student of theology, he said, "Oh, of course then, she must tell us why she wishes to become a minister."[17]

Finney eventually did allow Brown Blackwell full participation in his classes and made her position "both easy and satisfactory"[18] as she continued her theological study. Other professors, however, especially John Morgan and James Fairchild, were more adamant in their opposition. In one class her assignments included an essay on the New Testament passages commanding women's silence in church. This mean-spirited act turned out to benefit Brown Blackwell by challenging her to become a skilled biblical exegete. Her first presentation on the national woman's rights platform in 1850 was a revision of that very essay,[19] and from that time onward she was regarded as the foremost biblical interpreter of the movement.

---

said to one of the professors who opposed her presence in the program, " 'I expect some day to wake up & find my name on the regular class list' & I did. . . . It was not until nearly 40 years later that Oberlin gave me the degree of A.M., and later the degree of D.D. [1908]. So times change" (Brown Blackwell, "Childhood," 5, 7).

17. Gilson ms., 110.

18. Ibid.

19. The minutes of the First National Woman's Rights Convention held in Worcester, Massachusetts, October 23–24, 1850, state, "Antoinette L. Brown, a graduate of Oberlin College, and a student in Theology, made a logical argument on woman's position in the Bible, claiming her complete equality with man, the simultaneous creation of the sexes, and their moral responsibilities as individual and imperative." See Elizabeth Cady Stanton, Susan B. Anthony, and Matilda Joslyn Gage, eds., *History of Woman Suffrage*, vol I (6 vols.; Rochester, N.Y.: National American Woman Suffrage Association, 1881–1922), 224.

In the summer of 1850, at the conclusion of her work in theology, Brown Blackwell left Oberlin without official academic or ecclesiastical sanction. She returned to her home and family, where she was discouraged once again from pursuing her call to ministry:

> It was not until I reached home after graduating in 1850 that my family began to feel the imminent need of discouraging me in my plan to become a public speaker. They brought up all the objections that appealed to them urging the certainty of failure and the hard strain and suffering it must be for me to combat public opinion in this unusual way.

Even a trusted clergy friend, the Reverend Freeman, who had been her teacher in the secondary academy, warned her that she would become "a hopelessly handicapped woman minister in a civilized community," and an elderly relative warned that should she pursue such a radical profession, she "should be classed with Fanny Eisler the toe-dancer, in the estimation of the public."[20]

While she considered how she might fulfill her lifelong call to become what she referred to as "a man-acknowledged minister,"[21] Brown Blackwell developed her skills as a speaker and preacher. Her friend Lucy Stone, already deeply involved in the leadership of the woman's rights movement, invited her to address the First National Woman's Rights Convention held in Worcester, Massachusetts, in October 1850, arguing that the movement needed all the women it could gather who were trained in public speaking. It was at that convention that Brown Blackwell presented her Oberlin essay refuting biblical injunctions prohibiting woman's public speaking. Her eloquent and thoughtful presentation was well received, and as a result, she "was drawn into the loose-knit network of women and men throughout the Northeast who were working actively for a variety of social reforms."[22] For the next three years, she earned her living on the lyceum circuit, traveling across the northern United States from Ohio to New England to lecture on woman's rights, abolition, temperance, and other mid-nineteenth-century social reforms.

20. Gilson ms., 132.

21. Antoinette Brown to Lucy Stone, August 4, 1852, Blackwell Family Papers, Manuscript Division, Library of Congress, Washington, D.C. Subsequent references to this collection will read "BFP, LC."

22. Cazden, *Antoinette Brown Blackwell*, 57.

Because of her theological training and her acquaintance with liberal clergymen such as Samuel J. May and William Ellery Channing, who were among her fellow reformers, Brown Blackwell found many opportunities to preach. Woman's rights speakers were often invited to preach in churches of the cities that hosted their conventions (which were usually held over weekends), so Brown Blackwell's theological training and speaking ability provided her with numerous such invitations and quickly gained her a reputation as an outstanding preacher. She continued to encounter opposition to her preaching, however, including an experience she noted in this anecdote from her early itinerant preaching career:

> In one place they invited me to speak in the Church but said that no woman should stand in the pulpit and I was asked to stand on the floor just in front of the pulpit. One woman disapproved of my doing that. It was not Biblical. She felt called upon to reason with me and show me that I was wrong. To defend her own position she took her stand just outside the door of the Church and addressed me from across the doorsill upholding her position that it was not lawful for a woman to speak in the Church. She even followed me to another Church taking the same position.[23]

As a result of her preaching and speaking tours, two offers for permanent ministries came Brown Blackwell's way during the autumn of 1852. The first offer came from a group of abolitionist and reform leaders in New York City, where she had spoken several times:

> A number of gentlemen including Horace Greeley, Charles H. [sic] Dana, later of the [New York] Sun, consulted together, and wrote me offering $1000 salary with board and washing additional, they procuring a suitable hall, if I would become a minister there for one year.

Brown Blackwell "thought the matter over very seriously but decided that I was too inexperienced at that time to take a position of so much responsibility."[24] The New York venue would have showcased her rhetorical skills, but it would not have afforded her the pastoral ministry she desired. Her "congregation" there would not have been an identifiable group of

23. Brown Blackwell, "Life Work," 11.
24. Gilson ms., 155.

committed believers whose lives she shared throughout the week but rather a gathering of individuals, perhaps different each week, who had come primarily to hear her preach. She longed for ordination and ministry with an established congregation.

One of her speaking tours at about the same time took her to South Butler, New York, a town midway between Rochester and Syracuse, where members of a "struggling Congregational Church in that little town" heard her speak. They were searching for a minister and, whether progressive or desperate, invited Brown Blackwell to fill the position.[25] The South Butler church could only offer her an annual salary of $300, but she accepted the invitation anyway several months later and settled into the community in the spring of 1853.

The ordination question remained, but it was answered affirmatively that summer when the board of the church voted to ordain her in recognition of her good work.[26] The community gathered on September 15, 1853, in spite of protests from various quarters of church and society, to breach the "great wall of custom," as Brown Blackwell had once called the church's resistance to women ministers, and to welcome her into the male-only bastion of the ordained clergy. In her memoirs, she remembered the clergymen and lay leaders who were brave enough to participate:

> The ordination sermon was preached by the Reverend Luther Lee, a celebrated minister of the Protestant Methodists then located in Syracuse. . . . Prayer was offered by Elder McCoon, Baptist minister at South Butler. Rev. Mr. Hicks of Walworth gave the charge to the pastor, an address was given by Gerrit Smith who was then himself preaching in Peterboro, New York, and was still orthodox although he soon afterwards became more or less heterodox. . . . Another minister in Central New York, Rev. Mr. Fox, also officiated. Some friends came from a distance to assist at the rather unique ceremony. . . .
>
> We made the ordination service a little more formal and more lengthy than is usual. It seemed to me a very solemn thing when our

25. An African American minister had served the church some years earlier, confirming the congregation's progressive leanings, but the meager salary they were offering confirmed their desperation, as well. See Gilson ms., 155, 158.

26. Congregational church polity empowers local congregations to call and ordain ministers of their own choosing. The lack of any required denominational or hierarchical sanction for the ordination certainly made Brown Blackwell's ordination more feasible.

three deacons and these clergymen all stood around me each placing a hand upon my head or shoulder and gravely admitting me into the ranks of the ministry.

The whole hearted and cordial words of Gerrit Smith he spoke not only for the cause of womanhood, fully endorsing the equality of the sexes, but his charge to the church was fine and timely and his remarks to the minister were sympathetic, encouraging and strengthening.[27]

Brown Blackwell's great triumph in acceding to the ranks of the ordained ministry, however, had been somewhat tempered by her mistreatment just days earlier at the World's Temperance Convention held in New York City early in September. She was easily seated as a delegate to the convention from a local temperance association, but when she rose to the platform to speak, the acceptance of her credentials changed. She was shouted down and crowded off the platform on two occasions by those opposed to women's public speaking, and her attempts to speak prompted the crowd, made up primarily of clergymen, to pass a resolution prohibiting women's speech on the temperance platform. Brown Blackwell remained calm and resolute throughout the chaos. She later presented an extensive narrative of the incident to the Fourth National Woman's Rights Convention held in Cleveland in October 1853, recalling:

> There were angry men confronting me, and I caught the flashing of defiant eyes; but above me, and within me, and all around me, there was a spirit stronger than they all. At that moment not the combined powers of earth and hell could have tempted me to do otherwise than to stand firm.[28]

A report of the incident in the *National Anti-Slavery Standard* based on an article in the *New York Tribune* appears in Brown Blackwell's memoirs:

> A correspondent of the Tribune states that Rev. Antoinette L. Brown, since her return home, has received from this city by mail, a letter of appreciation on account of her sermon at Metropolitan Hall, and of sympathy in view of her trying position in the Temperance Convention. The letter made her the almoner to the poor of her parish of a

27. Gilson ms., 155–156.
28. *History of Woman Suffrage*, I:159.

hundred dollar note. This may be set down as one of the fruits of vulgar abuse heaped upon Miss Brown by the "Satanic Press."[29]

The report recounted Brown Blackwell's recent ordination by the South Butler congregation and made this astute and ironic observation:

> Miss Brown's theology being orthodox, her Presbyterian and Congregational maligners hardly know how to deal with the fact of her induction into the pastoral office. They will probably wish that her creed was that of a Unitarian or Universalist, for then they could set it all down as the fruit of "infidelity."[30]

The incident at the temperance convention demonstrated the divisiveness of women's public activity, whether in sacred or secular contexts. The treatment she received from fellow temperance workers was surely embarrassing and painful for Brown Blackwell, but the event gained her national recognition as a strong and committed reformer and a convincing orator, for immediately after she was "gagged," as one report put it, on that particular temperance platform, she walked down the street to the Broadway Tabernacle, where a woman's rights meeting was in progress. Upon learning of Brown Blackwell's treatment at the temperance gathering, the woman's rights advocates demanded that she report on her experience, which she did in the form of an extensive narrative that appears in the *History of Woman Suffrage*.[31] Both the incident itself and the sympathy she received in response to it provided her with notoriety that resulted in numerous invitations to lecture and preach.

Despite her newfound and hard-won recognition, Brown Blackwell returned to South Butler after the convention for her ordination and settled into the routine life of a parish pastor. Her ministry among the people of South Butler fulfilled her deepest desire to serve the church in a pastoral context.

At the same time, her commitment to expanded rights for women and her success as a reform orator kept Brown Blackwell traveling on the lecture circuit. Two weeks after her ordination, she traveled to Cleveland to address the Fourth National Convention. The minutes noted these words

29. From the *National Anti-Slavery Standard* (New York), September 24, 1853, as recorded in the Gilson ms., 352.

30. Ibid., 353.

31. See *History of Woman Suffrage*, I:152–60.

of convention president Frances D. Gage as she opened the meeting: "Before proceeding farther, it is proper that prayer should be offered. The Rev. Antoinette L. Brown will address the throne of grace." The secretary then recorded a brief statement in defense of Brown Blackwell's public prayer:

> She came forward and made a brief, but eloquent prayer. It was considered rather presumptuous in those days for a woman to pray in public, but as Miss Brown was a graduate of Oberlin College, had gone through the theological department, was a regularly ordained preacher, and installed as a pastor, she felt quite at home in all the forms and ceremonies of the church.[32]

Even the *Cleveland Journal* in a report on the convention took note of Brown Blackwell's participation, stating, "She has one distinction, she is the handsomest woman in the Convention. Her voice is silvery, and her manner pleasing. It is generally known that she is the pastor of a Congregational church in South Butler, N.Y."[33] The reports at the time failed to convey, however, the monumental significance of Brown Blackwell's ordination and pastoral service. This was remedied to some extent by a later report on woman's rights activities in the state of New York, which noted her ordination and the fact that it had occurred in the state in which "the pulpit made the first demand for the political rights of woman."[34]

Antoinette Brown Blackwell worked hard to meet the needs of her congregation, but by the summer of 1854, less than a year after her unprecedented ordination, she left her church in poor physical and mental health as well as in debilitating spiritual doubt. She found parish ministry more demanding than she had anticipated, and she failed to meet the theological and professional expectations of many of her parishioners. Once again she returned to her family's farm for solace and rest. After several months' rest she took up public speaking again for antislavery and woman's rights groups, but her call to preach continued to tug at her and rendered her new life of strictly political oratory unsatisfactory. In a letter to *New York Tribune* editor Horace Greeley concerning his earlier offer to assist her in hiring a hall in New York City where she would preach each week, Brown Blackwell confessed:

32. *History of Woman Suffrage*, I:124.
33. Ibid.
34. Ibid., 473, 472.

> Of course I can never again be the *pastor of a Church*; but must be a *preacher for the people.* . . . My present religion is a free one—all its truth are revelations from Nature's God to the soul; and one must be outside of all sectarian pressure to speak it freely.[35]

This "preacher for the people" took advantage of every opportunity to preach or speak on behalf of her social convictions and her evolving theological vision of human equality under the cope of divine love. Throughout the 1850s she preached frequently, often every Sunday, in pulpits in various places and different denominations despite the fact that marriage and motherhood shaped her life during the second half of the decade. After marrying Samuel Blackwell, brother of abolitionist and woman's rights activist Henry Blackwell and brother-in-law of Lucy Stone, she continued to preach and speak until the demands of motherhood and the exigencies of the Civil War forced her to curtail her public speaking activities.

After the war, two national suffrage associations were organized,[36] but Brown Blackwell did not join either group. She set out, instead, on an intellectual quest for truth, believing that only by means of the philosophical enlightenment of all humankind would moral progress leading to equality for women and to other social reforms come about. She published books in the areas of metaphysics (*Studies in General Science*, 1869), gender (*The Sexes Throughout Nature*, 1875), philosophy (*The Physical Basis of Immortality*, 1876), and theology (*The Philosophy of Individuality*, 1893) as well as a novel (*The Island Neighbors*, 1871) and a book of poetry (*Sea Drift*, 1902). A self-described "woman who chooses to go off on so many tangents," Brown Blackwell expanded her organizational involvement beyond local and national suffrage groups. She was one of the first women admitted to the American Association for the Advancement of Science and a founding member and leader of the Association for the Advance-

---

35. Recorded in Cazden, *Antoinette Brown Blackwell*, 94–95.

36. Following the war, woman's rights activists and abolitionists joined forces to form the American Equal Rights Association (AERA) in 1866 with the goal of securing universal suffrage. After the Fourteenth and Fifteenth Amendments were passed with the deliberate exclusion of women, several feminist leaders, feeling angry and betrayed by their male colleagues, broke from the AERA in 1869 to form the National Woman Suffrage Association (NWSA). Led by Stanton and Anthony, the group denied membership to men and lobbied for national suffrage legislation. The NWSA increasingly became associated with radical ideologies and individuals, leading to the founding of the American Woman Suffrage Association (AWSA) led by Stone, Julia Ward Howe, and Mary Livermore shortly thereafter. The AWSA concentrated on securing the ballot for women on a state-by-state basis. It was considered to be the more conservative of the two organizations in approach and ideology.

ment of Women. The AAW, founded in 1873 and modeled on the Science Association, was organized "to receive and present practical methods for securing to Woman higher intellectual, moral, and physical conditions, and thereby to improve all domestic and social relations."[37] Brown Blackwell delivered papers to both associations "on such subjects as Cross Heredity, the heredity from father to daughter and from mother to son, and the Longevity of the Sexes."[38]

While these affiliations and her success as a writer provided Brown Blackwell with a sense of accomplishment, especially during the years when she was preoccupied with raising her family, the call of ministry reclaimed her life in late middle age. During her year with the South Butler congregation, she had grown increasingly distanced from the orthodoxy of her youth and her Oberlin years. Her philosophical studies had only confirmed her more liberal theological views, and for twenty-five years she avoided affiliation with any denominational group. By 1878, however, she felt drawn once again to the fellowship of the church and to the work of ministry. She explored the possibility of joining the Unitarian Church, perhaps influenced by her husband and three sisters-in-law who had joined that denomination some years earlier. Brown Blackwell wrote to the Reverend Rush R. Shippen, secretary of the American Unitarian Association, expressing her "need of advice or rather of clear information" concerning Unitarian beliefs and confessing her own need for the fellowship of a religious yet liberal community of believers:

> The feeling may be largely personal or it may belong rather distinctively to my sex. At any rate, having grown up in the midst of those who shared common beliefs, aims, sympathies and work religiously, I have greatly missed the moral support which that class of associations can give. In studying others, I am more and more convinced that many become lax and inefficient if not hopeless from need of the same bracing influence.[39]

Soon after her correspondence with the Reverend Shippen, Brown Blackwell affiliated with the Unitarian Church. Although the denomination recognized her ministerial credentials and welcomed her as a preacher, she

---

37. Cazden, *Antoinette Brown Blackwell*, 185–86.

38. Gilson ms., 323. Some of the papers Brown Blackwell delivered to these two associations were later published as monographs, including her work on the Longevity of the Sexes.

39. Antoinette Brown Blackwell to R. R. Shippen, December 29, 1878, BFP, SL, Fol. 38.

was unsuccessful in finding a permanent position as a parish minister and had to settle for preaching opportunities as they arose. In her seventies, however, she returned to her true religious calling as a "preacher for the people" when she served as supply pastor for a Unitarian society organized in Elizabeth, New Jersey, in 1902 that met in a rented hall. When the society grew to the point that it needed a permanent building, Brown Blackwell donated a portion of the property she owned in Elizabeth for the building. Then she wrote:

> A year or two after the death of my husband, I returned to the old home in Elizabeth and when the little church was completed in 1908 as a most unexpected surprise to me I was asked through the minister, Mr. Arthur H. Grant, to accept the more or less honorary position of Minister Emeritus, preaching once a month, which I was happy to accept.[40]

She preached her last sermon in the Elizabeth church on Easter Sunday, 1915, when she was ninety years old.

"The female Beecher of the rostrum": Olympia Brown (1835–1926)

One of the few longer trips Antoinette Brown Blackwell took at the end of the 1850s when she was preoccupied with domestic concerns was to Antioch College in Ohio, where she had been invited to speak to a group of women students about her experiences as a minister. The invitation came as a result of the frustration of several Antioch women students led by Olympia Brown who resented the fact that the guest lecturers brought to campus were always men. "When we girls ventured to inquire why no women had been invited we were told that there were no women comparable to the men they had secured." That institutional response became a gauntlet thrown down before Brown and her spirited women colleagues, who raised private funds to bring a well-known female speaker to the Antioch campus. They chose Antoinette Brown Blackwell and arranged for her to lecture on a Saturday night and preach in a local church on Sunday morning. Brown Blackwell's visit was a success, and a large audience gathered for her Sunday service. "It was the first time I had heard a woman

---

40. Gilson ms., 220.

preach," Olympia Brown recalled, "and the sense of victory lifted me up. I felt as though the Kingdom of Heaven were at hand."[41]

Long before Brown encountered the Reverend Antoinette Brown Blackwell, she had come under the influence of Lephia Brown, her mother, another strong woman with progressive ideas about gender, whom Brown referred to as "the earliest reformer I ever knew."[42] Following their marriage in 1834, Lephia and Asa Brown had moved with the nineteenth-century western frontier from Vermont to Michigan. Their first child, Olympia, arrived on January 5, 1835. From the beginning, Lephia determined that Olympia and her siblings would acquire not only the household skills needed by frontier families but a classical education as well. Lephia herself taught her children at home before a public school system was approved when Michigan obtained statehood in 1837. "She was a remarkable woman, of unbounded energy, of great optimism, and of keen appreciation of the best in literature," Olympia noted years later. "She now took the place of library and school teacher for her children for whom she had great ambitions, and for whose education she was ready to spend and be spent."[43] The actual establishment of schools in Michigan, however, was left to local municipalities, many of which, including the one in which the Brown farm was located, saw no need for public education. With the encouragement of his wife, Asa Brown took it upon himself to build a schoolhouse on his own property and hire a teacher. The commitment of Lephia and Asa Brown to the education of their children was demonstrated in the time and money they invested in books and discussions with their children, investments unique among frontier families.

The Browns, led by the convictions of Lephia, were also unique in their equal treatment of their three girls and one boy, assuring that all would have access to the same educational opportunities. In the interstices of the demands of frontier life, the child Olympia observed that her mother seized "every opportunity to read and her mind was well stored with

---

41. Olympia Brown, *An Autobiography*, ed. Gwendolen B. Willis, *Annual Journal of the Universalist Historical Society* 4 (1963): 23, 24. The original unpublished manuscript of Olympia Brown's autobiography, which was edited and completed by her daughter Gwendolen B. Willis, can be found in the Olympia Brown Papers (A-69), Schlesinger Library, Radcliffe Institute for Advanced Study, Harvard University, Fol. 2. Subsequent citations to this collection of Olympia Brown's papers will read "OBP, SL" with the appropriate folder number(s).

42. Olympia Brown, *Acquaintances, Old and New, Among Reformers* (Milwaukee, Wis.: Press of S. E. Tate Printing, 1911), 7.

43. Brown, *Autobiography*, 9.

knowledge. She was abreast of the times on every question."[44] One of the contemporary questions on which Lephia Brown was well versed was the "woman question." Her liberal leanings concerning issues of gender surely set the stage for the lifelong feminist passions of her daughter Olympia:

> Long before I had heard of Mrs. Stanton or Miss Anthony, I had grown familiar with the principle of equal rights and of the need of larger liberties and opportunities for women. My mother's conversations on these topics were often most forceful and thrilling and naturally aroused in us a desire to do something to realize her ideals.[45]

Lephia Brown believed that progress and equality for women were rooted in appropriate educational preparation. Books popular at the time and the *New York Weekly Tribune* became standard accoutrements of the Brown household, and discussions on their contents were a regular part of their family life. The *Weekly Tribune* "was our only periodical literature, and indeed our oracle," Brown recalled. "Every word was read and discussed."[46] She remembered fondly family evenings spent engaged in current readings and conversations on new ideas:

> Among my earliest recollections are the evening readings in the home of my childhood on our little farm in Michigan. These readings were sometimes from the standard books of the time, but a share of the evening was always given to the New York Weekly Tribune. Horace Greeley was then the farmer's authority for everything from grains and soils to religion and reform. Greeley was then the representative of progress. In his paper might be found accounts of and discussions upon Fourierism, Woman's Rights, Dress Reform, Antislavery, Water-cure and all the ideas and theories then new but now either accepted and adopted or exploded and forgotten.[47]

Brown remembered vividly one particular evening when the family read an account of the first annual Woman's Rights Convention held in Worcester, Massachusetts, October 22–23, 1850. The ideas promoted at the convention struck a chord in the heart of the young Olympia:

44. Brown, *Acquaintances*, 7.
45. Ibid.
46. Brown, *Autobiography*, 12.
47. Brown, *Acquaintances*, 8–9.

Young as I was, the idea seized upon me. The speeches stirred my soul; the names of the participants loomed up before me as the names of great heroes often inspire young boys. They seemed to me like prophets of a better time.[48]

The gender realities of mid-nineteenth-century America, however, caught up with Brown when she began, after some resistance from her father, to study at the high school in town and found that the equality so assiduously cultivated and maintained by her mother at home did not exist at higher academic levels. Brown was shocked to discover that girls were not to question, debate, or deliver speeches in class as the boys were required to do. Her first feminist crusade involved an assault on those customary restrictions upon the female students:

We had a "Literary Society" in the school, of which teachers as well as pupils were members. The teachers made our program, and I soon noticed that only boys had been given recitations and debates, while the girls were restricted to reading. We girls instigated cousin Addison Carter to present a resolution at a regular meeting providing that girls as well as boys should be appointed for declamations and debates. Upon this the teachers all arose en masse, and declared that they would leave the society if we persisted in our resolution. One teacher spoke of it with especially contempt, saying "I guess Addison just wanted a little fun." We were thus suppressed, and my first effort for the equality of the sexes was unsuccessful.[49]

Brown was more successful in her academic pursuits than in her feminist pursuits, and after a few years of secondary school, at the age of fifteen, she was considered able to teach in a school herself. She taught for a term and then returned to school at a local seminary. "But my mother had been anxiously planning for a broader education than this could afford," she acknowledged. "She aimed at the best of which she knew. She had heard of Mary Lyon, and her great work for women's education, and was already contriving the daring plan of sending her daughters to Mt. Holyoke Female Seminary."[50]

48. Ibid., 9.
49. Brown, *Autobiography*, 12.
50. Ibid., 13.

After again overriding her father's skepticism, Olympia and her sister Oella went off to the school at South Hadley, Massachusetts, in September 1854. Mary Lyon's Mount Holyoke Female Seminary was considered to be a radical experiment in women's education. Many years later, Olympia conceded that Mary Lyon "had accomplished a work which entitled her to be remembered among the heroines of history. She was inspired with the great idea of building an institution where women could secure an education which would at least approximate that then open to men, and in time equal it."[51] During Brown's tenure at Mount Holyoke, however, the education was far from equal to that offered to young men at comparable institutions. The curriculum at Mount Holyoke excluded subjects such as Latin and mathematics that were considered improper for women to study, although Brown had already studied them. She recalled a chemistry professor from Amherst who was brought in to lecture to the young women. He concluded his presentation by saying, "You are not expected to remember all this, but only enough to make you intelligent in conversation." His attitude did not reflect that of the regular Holyoke teachers, Brown admitted, who truly were interested in developing the minds of their students. But the experience provoked in Brown a sense of indignation that led to a lifelong commitment to women's education:

> The Amherst professor's remark did in fact open up to me the whole subject of education and its purpose. Women need education and needed it still more at that time in order to become an essential part of that great body of men and women who are, by reason of their trained minds, capable of great undertakings in politics, and in society at large.[52]

Later in her life, during her career as a public speaker, Brown's concern for women's education was second only to her concern for woman suffrage, and she always regarded the two as inextricably related. In an essay on "Female Education," she equated the limitations attributed to women with their lack of educational opportunities:

> If the women of today are feeble and inefficient and trifling there must be a cause for this and we must look for that cause chiefly in

51. Ibid., 14.
52. Ibid., 17.

female education since human character is so moulded and fashioned by that agent. We must seek a remedy for this in a new system.[53]

In a later essay on "The Higher Education of Women," she sounded a similar conviction, declaring that character was best cultivated by means of education:

Higher education looks to the supremacy of all that is noblest and best in human nature; it means that quickening of the moral sense, that opening of the spiritual eye which makes one not merely an efficient worker in the business of the world, but one of the immortals, a companion of the angels. In the higher education of women we seek that which shall make them noble characters.[54]

Brown, her sister, and the other young women at Mount Holyoke were also prohibited from debating and speaking publicly. As Antoinette Brown Blackwell and Lucy Stone had done several years earlier at Oberlin, Brown and a few other iconoclastic female students responded to the prohibition by organizing their own literary society, invoking the wrath of the Mount Holyoke administration. After attending one of the women's debates, a committee of the administration offered no criticism, "but when the end of the term arrived the members of the Literary Society were sent for and informed that if they wished to return to the school they must understand that there would be no Literary Society."[55]

Mount Holyoke's ultimate challenge to Brown's convictions, however, was theological. Along with a thorough knowledge of history, literature, other classical subjects and contemporary events, Lephia Brown instilled in her children the doctrines of the Universalist tradition. "I was a Universalist by inheritance," Brown remarked, "my mother being a very zealous follower of Hosea Ballou [one of the founders of Universalism]."[56] Mary Lyon, the founder of Mount Holyoke, on the other hand, was steeped in Protestant orthodoxy and required each student to define herself as a "professing Christian," "hopefully pious," or "hopeless" upon her

---

53. Olympia Brown, "Female Education—The Admission of Women to the University of Michigan," ca. 1870, OBP, SL, Fol. 26.

54. Olympia Brown, "The Higher Education of Women," as recorded in Dana Greene, ed., *Suffrage and Religious Principle: Speeches and Writings of Olympia Brown* (Metuchen, N.J.: Scarecrow Press, 1983), 89.

55. Brown, *Autobiography*, 17.

56. Brown, *Acquaintances*, 27–28.

enrollment in the seminary.[57] She also instituted a procedure for provoking conversion experiences among the nonconverted by inviting a guest preacher to spend several weeks among the students, inquiring into each student's "state of mind" and holding daily services for the purpose of conversion. "At [Mount Holyoke]," Brown recalled, "the strictest orthodoxy was taught not only by the teachers, but by the occasional visits of the Rev. Dr. Kirk, of Boston, a minister with a beautiful strong voice and pleasant personality, but, as it seemed to me, quite destitute of logic."[58] She and her sister

> were considered suitable objects for this zealous missionary, and we were invited to evening meetings at which we were confronted with embarrassing questions as to our religious convictions, which we were not prepared to answer. When a young girl, who has never given any thought to such questions, is asked to define her "state of mind" she does not know how to express herself. However, even this proved profitable to us for we were now obliged to study our Bibles, and to read and investigate in order to form our own opinions. We managed to evade the religious persecution, privately sent to Boston for books, and set to work to find out for ourselves whether we were to believe in such uncongenial doctrines, and if not, how to give reasons for our non-belief.[59]

Like Antoinette Brown Blackwell, Olympia Brown had been raised with a liberal theological understanding that was grounded in a belief in a kind and gracious God. The evangelical bombast that characterized God as vindictive and capricious, which Brown encountered for the first time at the religious meetings held at Mount Holyoke, was disturbing and unwelcome. She sought help from her mother and from the Universalist headquarters in Boston in order to respond to the repeated and coercive overtures from the evangelists brought to campus. In an astute and accurate assessment of the situation, Lephia shared her fears that Olympia would be corrupted by the harshness of orthodoxy and perhaps even "fooled into the presbyterian church":

57. Charlotte Coté, *Olympia Brown: The Battle for Equality* (Racine, Wis.: Mother Courage Press, 1988), 31.

58. Brown, *Acquaintances*, 28.

59. Brown, *Autobiography*, 18.

Allow me to say, my dear, that under the influence that surrounds you there, it would be impossible for you to come to any just conclusion upon a subject so mystified by creeds and theologians, particularly a person of your enthusiastic and impressible temperament.

While there is no faculty of the human soul so elevating, so delightful, as pure devotion of feeling, there is nothing so benumbing, so deadening, so baneful, as a narrow, soul-contracting creed. It is absurd to judge of the Almighty and his disposal of the human race from some text of scripture or peculiar wording of some phrase.[60]

After a frustrating year at Mount Holyoke, Brown returned to Michigan to gain her parents' support for enrolling in a college that granted full opportunities to women, although she later acknowledged her gratitude for what Mount Holyoke had taught her:

That I went to Mt. Holyoke Seminary I am thankful. There I learned to think for myself, and adopted, through the stimulus of opposite views, the great principles which I have taken as my guide through life, and which, if consistently followed by our government, would furnish a solution of many perplexing problems of the present time.[61]

After her experience at Mount Holyoke, her father felt "so much sympathy for me because of my disappointment in the character of that institution that in burst of generosity and of real pride in my persistence, he told me that I might go to any school that I chose."[62] She chose Antioch over Oberlin because of Oberlin's infamous treatment of Antoinette Brown Blackwell and Lucy Stone, and traveled to Yellow Springs, Ohio, where Antioch was located, in the autumn of 1856.

Educator Horace Mann's Antioch College was liberal in its ideology and curriculum and "imposed no doctrinal teachings upon its students," which appealed to Brown. Mann had recently declared that the college, in keeping with the ideas of the founders, "was to try 'a great experiment,' namely, the education of women on the same terms with men."[63] The school's intentions, however, were not always matched by the realities of the classroom, and Brown continued to encounter discrimination because

60. Lephia Brown to Olympia Brown, April 12, 1855, OBP, SL, Fol. 127.
61. Brown, *Autobiography*, 18.
62. Ibid., 19.
63. Ibid.

of her gender. She responded by defying imposed limitations whenever possible and by beginning her lifelong practice of thinking, writing, and speaking about woman's rights.

One of the traditions of Antioch College that Brown challenged was that of bringing only male guest lecturers to campus. When the lecture committee refused to invite a woman to speak, claiming "that there were no women at all comparable to the men employed," Brown organized her own committee of women students who raised money to bring women lecturers to campus. The committee chose the Reverend Antoinette Brown Blackwell as their first speaker, and Olympia Brown herself had the honor of extending the invitation to Brown Blackwell. Brown later reflected:

> It now seems incredible that there should have been such opposition to this lecture as made it necessary to scheme and contrive to secure it and especially that it was with some difficulty that we obtained the Christian Church for her to preach in on Sunday. However, we were all delighted with the result. Even those who had been opposed were converted by her quiet and ladylike demeanor and words of wisdom.[64]

While she did not need conversion to the idea of the capabilities of women, Brown herself acknowledged that this first experience of hearing a woman preach confirmed in her a "sense of victory" in the achievements of women and made her feel "as though the Kingdom of Heaven were at hand."[65] She never explicitly linked this experience of meeting and hearing Brown Blackwell with the confirmation of her own sense of call, but her description of the moving nature of the experience makes the assumption of such a connection quite obvious.

While Brown was at Antioch, Frances Gage, at that time a leader of the woman's rights movement, visited Yellow Springs to give a lecture. Again, while her autobiographical materials and papers make no explicit connection between Gage's inspiring lecture and Brown's own lifelong work for woman's rights, the admiration with which she wrote of Gage's presentation indicates the impression Gage must have made on the young feminist. Brown later would recall:

64. Brown, *Acquaintances*, 16, 17.
65. Brown, *Autobiography*, 24.

She opened the work of the evening by reading the description of the virtuous woman in the last chapter of Proverbs. It has since been a favorite chapter with me and I often read it at Suffrage meetings as it really contains the gist of the whole matter. "Give her of the fruit of her hands and let her own works praise her in the gates." That is just what the advocates of Woman's Suffrage ask. "Aunt Fanny" Gage was really one of the ablest women we have ever had in this country. She was strong and true and original, but she had lived a hard life battling with the prejudices of the age and seeing the wrongs done to women so plainly, and feeling her helplessness to right them so forcibly that it made her too earnest, if such a thing were possible.[66]

By the time she graduated from Antioch in 1860, Brown knew she was called to pastoral ministry. "My mind was not only full of the excitement of the day," she wrote after finishing her course and returning to her family, "but also with the plans for my own personal future, for I had already conceived the idea of studying with a view to entering the ministry, and was planning to take this step in the following year."[67] Securing a theological education proved to be as difficult as securing an undergraduate education, however. She received numerous rejection letters from theological schools asserting the inappropriateness of women in ministry and, by implication, the uselessness of a theological education for a woman. Even Antoinette Brown Blackwell, to whom Brown had looked for confirmation of her conviction that women could succeed in ministry, disappointed her, for by then Brown Blackwell had left parish ministry, married, and disaffiliated herself from her denomination. "Her example thus had been in a measure lost," Brown lamented. Eventually Brown was accepted into the theological program of St. Lawrence University Theological School in Canton, New York, the Universalist theological institution. She entered St. Lawrence in the fall of 1861 as the only female student. In a letter sent following her acceptance, however, Ebenezer Fisher, the school's president, warned her that she "may have some prejudices to encounter in the institution from the students and also in the community."[68]

Brown encountered the predicted prejudices primarily among her fellow students. In an ironic twist of expectations, she noted that those

66. Brown, *Acquaintances*, 10–11.
67. Brown, *Autobiography*, 25.
68. Ebenezer Fisher to Olympia Brown, June 21, 1861, OBP, SL, Fol. 127.

students who advocated abolition and were ardent supporters of the liberal principles of the Republican Party were the ones most opposed to her presence at the school:

> One would have expected that the "Liberal" and "Progressive" party would be most favorable to the advancement of women, but such was not the case. Young men who could scarcely find words sufficiently strong to express their feelings on the subject of liberty for all were the ones who led the way in the effort to drive out the first woman who had dared to invade the sacred precincts of the Divinity School, while the "Copperheads" [those less supportive of or opposed to the prevailing political course] were kind and friendly and apparently willing that all should have a fair chance.[69]

Nevertheless, her two years at St. Lawrence were relatively pleasant and free from discrimination. She found abundant opportunities to preach and found support and encouragement for her ministry from the congregations she served, but the goal of ordination remained elusive. The St. Lawrence faculty, despite their acknowledgment of Brown's excellent work, refused to ordain her. Like Antoinette Brown Blackwell, her ecclesiastical predecessor, Brown was forced to go outside her theological school to request ordination from the Northern Universalist Association, which met in nearby Malone, New York, in the spring of 1863. To everyone's surprise and with the support of a member of the ordaining council who had heard her preach the week before, the Northern Universalist Association voted to ordain her on June 25, 1863, making her, according to most historians, the second woman ordained by a Protestant church in the United States.[70]

Following her ordination, Brown filled pulpits in Vermont, spent several months with her family in Michigan, and studied elocution in Boston until her installation in July 1864 as pastor of a church in Weymouth Landing, Massachusetts. During her tenure in Weymouth Landing, she became

---

69. Brown, *Acquaintances*, 29.

70. Historians debate whether Antoinette Brown Blackwell or Olympia Brown was the first woman ordained to ministry. Brown Blackwell's ordination, conducted by a local congregation of the Congregational Church, occurred according to Congregational rules of governance but was protested and not recognized by the Congregational General Conference. Brown's ordination, however, was conducted and recognized by the Northern Universalist Association, an official body of the Universalist Church.

involved in the New England movement for woman's rights. She attended the 1866 Equal Rights Convention in New York City, her first woman's rights convention, where she met Susan B. Anthony, Elizabeth Cady Stanton, Lucy Stone, and other reformers and became a charter member of the American Equal Rights Association, the organization formed after the Civil War with the purpose of securing universal suffrage. Brown's ability as a preacher captured the attention of suffrage leaders who requested that she represent the Republican central committee as an itinerant speaker during the 1867 Kansas campaign for woman suffrage. She arranged for other pastors to care for her church in her absence and traveled through Kansas for four months in support of a state constitutional amendment to enfranchise women. Reflecting on that grueling time she wrote:

> In those four months I traveled over the greater part of Kansas, held two meetings every day, and the latter part of the time three meetings every day, making in all between two and three hundred speeches, averaging an hour in length; a fact that tends to show that women can endure talk and travel as least as well as men.[71]

Brown's eloquence made an impression despite Republican efforts to undermine her work and defeat the proposition the party at first had supported. She left Kansas feeling gratified that "by her eloquent appeals, she had so educated public sentiment that the result showed more than one-third of the voting citizens in favor of the change."[72]

Brown returned to Weymouth to continue her successful pastorate. She moved on from there to a church in Bridgeport, Connecticut, which she served for several years. During her years in Bridgeport she married John Henry Willis, who had been a member of the board of trustees at the Weymouth church, and had two children.[73] The call of a Racine, Wisconsin, church prompted Brown to move her family to the Midwest in

71. Brown, *Autobiography*, 58.
72. "Olympia Brown," in Frances E. Willard and Mary A. Livermore, eds., *American Women*, vol. I (New York: Mast, Crowell and Kirkpatrick, 1897), 130.
73. Olympia Brown continued to use her family name after marrying Willis. "In this I followed the example of Lucy Stone (Blackwell)," she wrote, "who had given, as I felt, cogent reasons for the practice. The retaining of my own name was fully understood and approved by my husband at the time of our marriage" (Brown, *Autobiography*, 63). Her decision was noted in the following way in the March 21, 1874, issue of the *Woman's Journal* under the column "Concerning Women": "Rev. Olympia Brown is the wife of John Henry Willis, but retains her maiden name."

1878. She had been successful in all her pastorates, due in no small part to her pulpit eloquence. A Racine parishioner recalled, "Her sermons interested the indifferent, called many of the wanderers back and furnished food for thought to the most advanced thinkers."[74] A reporter for the *Superior Daily Leader* called her "the female Beecher of the rostrum,"[75] comparing her to Henry Ward Beecher, the best-known preacher in late-nineteenth-century America.

While in Racine, Brown felt increasingly drawn to suffrage work and helped to organize the Wisconsin State Woman Suffrage Association. She was elected president of the association in 1884 and served in that position for twenty-eight years. For three years she worked as both a pastor and a suffragist. Antoinette Brown Blackwell visited Olympia Brown in Racine and found Brown "able to run her own household and take care of her two little children, preach regularly on Sunday and doing a considerable amount of lecturing in addition."[76] In 1887, however, after twenty-five years in parish ministry, she decided to leave and devote her efforts to suffrage. She appears to have considered suffrage work an extension of her ministry and continued to preach in various contexts for the remainder of her life. A reconciliation of both commitments was possible, according to Dana Greene, her biographer, "because in her mind there was no discontinuity between the general goals of spreading Universalist principles as a minister and the realization of a particular goal, the equality and liberty of women, through suffrage work."[77]

When the National Woman Suffrage Association and the American Woman Suffrage Association were organized in 1869, Brown joined the former, based on her close association with Elizabeth Cady Stanton and Susan B. Anthony, its founders. She maintained a good relationship with both associations, however. When the two associations merged in 1890, however, Brown refused to support the new association. She believed that women's full equality depended on the passage of a suffrage amendment to the U.S. Constitution. That goal might be jeopardized, she feared, by the AWSA approach of seeking amendments to state constitutions at the expense of a federal amendment. In response, Brown joined with others to found the Federal Suffrage Association of the United States in 1892. She endured what she referred to as "the Great Desert of woman suf-

---

74. "Olympia Brown," in Willard and Livermore, *American Women*, 131.
75. See "Press Notices" in OBP, SL, Fol. 5.
76. Gilson ms., 283.
77. Greene, *Suffrage and Religious Principle*, 4.

frage" during the early 1900s without losing hope. Even through that "Great Desert," she remained a popular figure on suffrage platforms, in churches, and before legislators, using "incisive arguments," as she put it, to help bring about "those changes in the laws which have so greatly ameliorated the condition of women."[78]

Queen of the Suffrage Platform:
Anna Howard Shaw (1847–1919)

Anna Howard Shaw heard her call to preach as a child growing up in the Michigan wilderness. She was born in Newcastle-on-Tyne, England, on Valentine's Day in 1847. In search of a better life for his family, Thomas Shaw, Anna's father, moved Anna along with her mother and five siblings to New England in the spring of 1851. After a brief stay in New Bedford, Massachusetts, the Shaws moved in 1852 to Lawrence, Massachusetts, where they would reside for the next seven years. Shaw recalled the years in Lawrence as "interesting and formative ones." It was in Lawrence that she first encountered the abolition movement, having accidentally discovered a slave hiding in the coal bin of their cellar whom her parents were protecting as supporters of the Underground Railroad. Shaw's formative years in Lawrence also fostered her theological openness. Her family had belonged to the Unitarian Church in England, a commitment for which they "paid the penalty of being outside the fold of the Church of England." In her autobiography, Shaw related the poignant story of her mother's twenty-mile "dreary journey alone" by stagecoach in 1845 to bury an infant in the nearest Unitarian churchyard. The baby "could not be laid in any consecrated burial-ground in her neighborhood" due to the family's Unitarian faith.[79]

In 1859, Thomas Shaw joined with several fellow Englishmen in purchasing tracts of land in the northern forests of Michigan. After her father and brother had cleared the land, Shaw and her mother and siblings made the "journey through the wilderness," as she called it, to Grand Rapids, Michigan, and then on to the desolate stretch of land that would be their new home. Settlement on the frontier for a family used to urban life proved to be extremely trying, especially when Thomas left the family and

78. Olympia Brown, "Reminiscences of a Pioneer," *Suffragist* (September 1920), OBP, SL, Fol. 36.

79. Anna Howard Shaw with Elizabeth Jordan, *The Story of a Pioneer* (New York: Harper & Brothers Publishers, 1915), 12, 7.

returned to Lawrence for a year to earn enough money to establish the Michigan farm. Frontier life demanded unrelenting labor and sacrifice from children and parents alike, and Shaw was often sent into the woods to do her share of the chores. Whenever she could, she would hasten or neglect the work at hand, spending her time instead in the enchanting world of the few books they had managed to bring from Massachusetts. Her father also regularly sent the family the *New York Independent*, "and with this admirable literature," Shaw recalled, "after reading it, we papered our walls. Thus, on stormy days, we could lie on the settle or the floor and read the *Independent* over again with increased interest and pleasure."[80]

At some point, perhaps inspired by her bucolic surroundings, Shaw realized that she "had begun to feel the call of my career. For some reason, I wanted to preach—to talk to people, to tell them things," she recalled. "Just why, just what I did not yet know—but I had begun to preach in the silent woods, to stand up on stumps and address the unresponsive trees, to feel the stir of aspiration within me."[81] Even at that young age, however, Shaw recognized the unconventional nature of her call, as she later related to her biographer, Ida Husted Harper:

> The soul within me refused to beat out its life against a barred door, and I rebelled. I would not submit to the untrained life of an ignorant girl of the old time type. I knew in my soul the earth and all things in it were my heritage and I had a right to share in their power to build me up and make me worthy to be part of the world's fighting force for better things, which I believed even then God intended for His children. That night sealed my determination. I would go to college. I would live my life, not the life which had been urged as the destiny of all women but the life which face to face with my Creator I believed was my right and His will.[82]

Shaw knew of no woman who had gone to college, let alone entered the ordained ministry. Nevertheless, she accepted the persistent feeling within her and gradually prepared herself for the long and difficult road

---

80. Ibid., 40.
81. Ibid., 44.
82. Ida Husted Harper, "Biography of Anna Howard Shaw," unpublished manuscript, 9, Anna Howard Shaw Papers (Series X of the Mary Earhert Dillon Collection), Schlesinger Library, Radcliffe Institute for Advanced Study, Harvard University, Fol. 357. Subsequent citations to this collection will appear as "AHSP, SL" with the appropriate folder number(s).

of education that lay ahead. Most of her knowledge had been self-taught after her family's move from New England to the Michigan frontier, acquired by reading whatever books or journals she could find, but it proved to be substantial enough to enable her to pass college entrance examinations years later.

Despite Shaw's deliberate efforts to prove herself worthy of acceptance to a college, her family had neither the resources nor the will to finance higher education for a daughter. In addition, the timing of her decision to pursue a college education was not good since the Civil War was well under way, drawing all able-bodied men, including Shaw's brothers and father, away from their farms and family responsibilities. Anna, now age fifteen, her mother, and her fourteen-year-old brother were left to maintain the family farm. Her mother took in work as a seamstress as she had done before in financially difficult times, and Anna accepted a position as a teacher. She was given a teaching certificate signed by four "inspectors" upon satisfactory completion of a series of examinations and promised two dollars a week and "board round." The job "often necessitated walking from three to six miles to end from the little log school house and often carrying in the fuel and building the fire, while the place where she boarded frequently consisted of one room in a log cabin."[83] After the war, her employment as a teacher enabled her to accumulate money for her education, but Shaw still saw "a long, arid stretch ahead of me before the college doors came even distantly into sight."[84]

Those doors were pushed open with the help of a fortuitous encounter. Shaw had given up teaching and moved to the town of Big Rapids to live with her sister and learn a "money-making" trade. She found the possibilities for women quite limited in "a small pioneer town" in the 1860s:

> The fields open to women were few and unfruitful. The needle at once presented itself, but at first I turned with loathing from it. I would have preferred the digging of ditches or the shoveling of coal; but the needle alone persistently pointed out my way, and I was finally forced to take it.[85]

From her youth, Shaw had resisted—and loathed—the expectations of a defined domesticity that were imposed upon women in the nineteenth

83. Ibid.
84. Shaw, *Story of a Pioneer*, 54.
85. Ibid., 55.

century. "I could not endure to have the world look on and tell me it was Nature and the Divine Will for women to lead a domestic life," she later wrote of those years; "it was too absurd to be longer tolerated."[86] She did not have to endure for long, for "fate, however, as if weary at last of seeing me between her paws, suddenly let me escape."[87] While working in Big Rapids, Shaw learned that the Reverend Marianna Thompson, a Universalist minister, was to preach in town on Sunday morning, and she eagerly went to hear her:

> It was a wonderful moment when I saw my first woman minister enter her pulpit; and as I listened to her sermon, thrilled to the soul, all my early aspirations to become a minister myself stirred in me with cumulative force. After the services I hung for a time on the fringe of the group that surrounded her, and at last, when she was alone and about to leave, I found courage to introduce myself and pour forth the tale of my ambition. Her advice was as prompt as if she had studied my problem for years.
>
> "My child," she said, "give up your foolish idea of learning a trade, and go to school. You can't do anything until you have an education. Get it, and get it *now*."[88]

Like countless women before her and since, Shaw discovered the needed inspiration and courage for acting on her own long-perceived sense of call by way of a fortuitous encounter with another individual. For Olympia Brown, it was meeting Antoinette Brown Blackwell when she came to speak at Antioch College. For Anna Howard Shaw, it was hearing and speaking with Marianna Thompson. On Thompson's advice, Shaw entered a college preparatory school in Big Rapids. There she met another woman who would shape the direction of her life, Lucy Foot. Foot, the preceptress of the school, quickly recognized Shaw's oratorical ability and placed her in speaking and debating classes where she learned—painfully at first—the art of public speaking. Her rhetorical and theatrical performances attracted the interest of the presiding elder of the Big Rapids district of the Methodist Episcopal Church, Dr. H. C. Peck, who at the time was leading the movement to license women preachers in the Methodist Church. Peck approached Shaw following a social evening

---

86. Harper, "Biography of Anna Howard Shaw," 9.
87. Shaw, *Story of a Pioneer*, 55.
88. Ibid., 55–56.

and surprised her with an invitation to preach at the district's quarterly meeting. As Shaw reported:

> "Why," I stammered, "*I* can't preach a sermon!" Dr. Peck smiled at me. "Have you ever tried?" he asked. I started to assure him vehemently that I never had. Then, as if time had thrown a picture on a screen before me, I saw myself as a little girl preaching alone in the forest, as I had so often preached to a congregation of listening trees. I qualified my answer. "Never," I said, "to human beings." Dr. Peck smiled again. "Well," he told me, "the door is open. Enter or not, as you wish."[89]

Before walking through that open door, however, Shaw had to resolve a personal crisis of faith. While she was considering Dr. Peck's offer, it suddenly occurred to her that she had never been "converted" according to "the old-time idea of conversion, which now seems so mistaken." She had been raised in her parents' Unitarian tradition, a tradition that did not embrace the prevalent Protestant understanding of conversion as a "struggle with sin and with the Lord until at last the heart opened, doubts were dispersed, and the light poured in." In order to preach with integrity, Shaw sought such an identifiable experience of faith and enlisted Lucy Foot to help her obtain it. Foot advised her "to put the matter before the Lord, to wrestle and to pray; and thereafter, for hours at a time, she worked and prayed with me, alternately urging, pleading, instructing, and sending up petitions in my behalf."[90] Their efforts culminated in an all-night session of prayer after which Shaw "seemed to see the light, and it made me very happy." "With all my heart I wanted to preach," she stated, "and I believed that now at last I had my call." The next day Shaw and Foot sent word to Dr. Peck that Shaw would accept his offer and preach at the quarterly meeting of his district in Ashton.[91] Her sermon was based on John 3:14–15—"And as Moses lifted up the serpent in the wilderness, even so must the Son of Man be lifted up; that whosoever believeth in him should not perish, but have eternal life"— and it reflected an evangelical zeal that remained characteristic of Shaw's fiery preaching throughout her life:

89. Ibid., 59.
90. Ibid., 60.
91. Ibid.

And what are the effects of evil? You see it in the haggard counte-
nance, that emaciated and sinking frame, that loathsome train of dis-
ease and want and all the numberless forms of wretchedness which
guilt has created. . . . The fiery serpent saved the Hebrews from the
effect of the serpent's bite. Jesus Christ saves us from our sins—not
in our sins—from our sins. There is this difference, the serpent saved
from the effect of the evil, Jesus Christ from the evil itself.[92]

The opportunity to preach, which Shaw had dreamed of since childhood, was bittersweet, however, for it brought Shaw face to face with the
reality of her family's rejection of her call. It took her several weeks to
muster the courage to tell her sister of the impending preaching engagement, "and if I had confessed my intention to commit a capital crime she
could not have been more disturbed."[93] Her unconventional pursuits had
always troubled her family, but after her public appearance in the pulpit,
they denounced her. The morning after she delivered her first sermon, a
notice appeared in the local newspaper, placed there by her brother-in-
law: "A young girl named Anna Shaw, seventeen years old,[94] preached at
Ashton yesterday. Her real friends deprecate the course she is pursuing."
Their final attempt at reconciliation was to offer to finance her college
education in exchange for the relinquishment of her preaching activity.
Tempted by the educational opportunity, she nevertheless held on to her
"childish dreams" of a pulpit ministry. After a long and anguished
evening, she recalled, "I was given twenty-four hours in which to decide
whether I would choose my people and college, or my pulpit and the arc-
tic loneliness of a life that held no family circle. It did not require twenty-
four hours of reflection to convince me that I must go my solitary way."[95]
Shaw accepted Peck's invitation to preach in the churches of his ministerial district. She was licensed to preach by the District Conference of
the Methodist Episcopal Church on August 26, 1873. When doubts once
again threatened to eclipse her sense of determination, another chance
encounter with a progressive woman inspired her to go on. This time the
inspiration came from Mary A. Livermore, a Unitarian preacher and leading suffrage lecturer whom Shaw heard lecture in Big Rapids. When she

92. The text of Shaw's first sermon is found in Harper, "Biography of Anna Howard Shaw,"
13–20.
93. Shaw, *Story of a Pioneer*, 61.
94. Shaw was actually twenty-three years old at the time. See Shaw, *Story of a Pioneer*, 62.
95. Ibid, 62, 63.

and a friend went to speak to Livermore after the lecture, the friend confided Shaw's dilemma to the speaker. Shaw recorded the conversation:

> "My dear," [Livermore] said quietly, "if you want to preach, go on
> and preach. Don't let anybody stop you. No matter what people say,
> don't let them stop you!"
>
> For a moment I was too overcome to answer her. These were
> almost my first encouraging words, and the morning stars singing
> together could not have made sweeter music for my ears. Before I
> could recover a woman within hearing spoke up.
>
> "Oh, Mrs. Livermore," she exclaimed, "don't say that to her!
> We're all trying to stop her. Her people are wretched over the whole
> thing. And don't you see how ill she is? She has one foot in the grave
> and the other almost there!"
>
> Mrs. Livermore turned upon me a long and deeply thoughtful
> look. "Yes," she said at last, "I see she has. But it is better that she
> should die doing the thing she wants to do than that she should die
> because she can't do it."

In response to the conversation with Livermore, Shaw became more
determined than ever to pursue her call to preach: " 'So they think I'm
going to die!' I cried. 'Well, I'm not! I'm going to live and preach!' " She
preached in various churches and lectured for the local temperance society to support herself as she pursued her education at Albion College,
where she had matriculated in the autumn of 1873 at the age of twenty-
six. Shaw recalled the adventures of her days as an itinerant preacher and
lecturer. Among her most interesting congregations were those composed of Indians who inhabited the Michigan wilderness. The squaws
brought their infants to church with them, Shaw marveled:

> The papooses, who were strapped to their boards, were hung like a
> garment on the back wall of the building by a hole in the top of the
> board, which projected above their heads. Each papoose usually had
> a bit of fat pork tied to the end of a string fastened to its wrist, and
> with these sources of nourishment the infants occupied themselves
> pleasantly while the sermon was in progress.

This arrangement made for constant excitement in the church since the
infants frequently managed to get the pork stuck in their throats, resulting in much choking and struggling. But the squaws left them alone in

their struggles, for "in that assemblage," Shaw noted, "the emotions were not allowed to interrupt the calm intellectual enjoyment of the sermon."[96]

Shaw's most dramatic experience during those years occurred in the summer of 1874, she recalled, when she was asked to preach at a Northern lumber camp where the minister was away on his honeymoon. Because of the camp's isolation, the stagecoach could take her only within twenty-two miles of her destination. She finally found a driver with a wagon who offered to take her through the woods to the camp. She accepted his offer despite her reservations about his appearance and "forbidding expression." It was dark and desolate as they traveled alone, and Shaw sensed impending danger from the driver, who began telling her gruesome tales peppered with "shocking vulgarities." He stopped the wagon to continue his diatribe and, Shaw recounted, "ended by snarling that I must think him a fool to imagine he did not know the kind of woman I was." As it turned out, he really *did not* know the kind of woman Shaw was, for she was fully prepared to defend herself with a revolver she had long before learned to use but rarely carried. When the driver continued to threaten her, she slipped her hand into her satchel and touched the revolver. "No touch of human fingers ever brought such comfort," she recalled. She pulled it out of her bag and cocked it, its sudden click recognized by the driver:

> "Here! What have you got there?" he snapped.
> "I have a revolver," I replied, as steadily as I could. "And it is cocked and aimed straight at your back. Now drive on. If you stop again, or speak, I'll shoot you."
> For an instant or two he blustered.
> "By God," he cried, "you wouldn't dare."
> "Wouldn't I?" I asked. "Try me by speaking just once more."
> Even as I spoke I felt my hair rise on my scalp with the horror of the moment, which seemed worse than any nightmare a woman could experience. But the man was conquered by the knowledge of the waiting, willing weapon just behind him. He laid his whip savagely on the backs of his horses and they responded with a leap that almost knocked me out of the wagon.

The rest of the journey was uneventful if silent. She made it safely to the lumber camp and preached in the morning. The rough building "was

96. Ibid., 65, 74–75.

packed to its doors with lumbermen who had come in from the neighboring camp," and "the collection was the largest that had been taken up in the history of the settlement," Shaw noted. She later learned that her driver of the night before was one of the lumbermen, and when he reported his experience to his pals, "the whole camp had poured into town to see the woman minister who carried a revolver."[97]

After two years at Albion and at age twenty-eight, Shaw decided not to complete her college course but to move on to the theological education she always desired. During summers spent visiting her brother in Vermont, she had learned of the Boston University School of Theology. She entered the school in February 1876. Her class "was composed of forty-two young men and my unworthy self, and before I had been a member of it an hour I realized that women theologians paid heavily for the privilege of being women." More pressing than the prejudice she faced from fellow students, however, was the impoverishment that marked those years of her life. "I went through some grim months in Boston," she admitted, "months during which I learned what it was to go to bed cold and hungry, to wake up cold and hungry, and to have no knowledge of how long these conditions might continue."[98] Several times she questioned her call when her meals consisted of a few biscuits and her shoes had burst open at the seams.

Despite the challenges of impoverishment and prejudice, Shaw completed the theological course in 1878 and the following October accepted an appointment as pastor of a church in East Dennis, Cape Cod. Because she was not ordained, she could not administer the sacraments of baptism and the Lord's Supper, but the congregation welcomed her preaching and pastoral care. Those pastoral care skills were quickly tested as the congregation, she soon discovered, was "in the hands of warring factions." She entered the new field "as trustfully as a child enters a garden; and though I was in trouble from the beginning, and resigned three times in startling succession, I ended by remaining seven years."[99] In addition to serving as pastor of a feuding congregation, Shaw accepted a "temporary" charge that lasted more than six years as preacher for a nearby Congregational church and completed a medical degree at Boston Medical School. Her years in Boston had awakened her to the desperate plight of the poor that, she came to realize, required not only a spiritual remedy

97. Ibid., 77, 78, 80.
98. Ibid., 82–83.
99. Ibid., 107.

but a physical remedy as well. "These were, therefore," Shaw reflected, "among the most strenuous as well as the most interesting years of my existence, and I mention the strain of them only to prove my life-long contention, that congenial work, no matter how much there is of it, has never yet killed any one!"[100]

Even with her theological qualifications and pastoral success, Shaw could not function fully as a minister without being regularly ordained. "I could perform the marriage service, but I could not baptize. I could bury the dead, but I could not take members into my church. That had to be done by the presiding elder or by some other minister. I could not administer the sacraments."[101] She applied for ordination to the New England Spring Conference of the Methodist Episcopal Church in 1880 and, along with another woman, Anna Oliver, was examined and approved by the Conference board as "fitted for ordination." When their names were presented to the Conference, however, the presiding bishop refused to accept them. Deeply disappointed, Shaw and Oliver confronted the bishop only to be told calmly "that there was nothing for us to do but to get out of the Church." Oliver resolved to stay and fight for her ordination in the denomination, but Shaw was wearied from years of fighting.

> I said: "I shall get out. I am no better and no stronger than a man, and it is all a man can do to fight the world, the flesh, and the devil, without fighting his Church as well. I do not intend to fight my Church. But I am called to preach the gospel; and if I cannot preach it in my own Church, I will certainly preach it in some other Church!"[102]

At the suggestion of a sympathetic minister in the Methodist Protestant Church, she applied to that denomination for ordination and was accepted and ordained on October 12, 1880, after days of conference debate and not without a fight.[103]

Even as she ministered to both body and soul as a pastor and physician,

---

100. Ibid., 119.

101. Ibid., 122.

102. Ibid., 123–24. Not only did the 1880 Conference forbid women's ordination, but it voted to revoke the preaching licenses previously granted to women.

103. The Methodist Protestant Church was formed in 1830 by a group of self-proclaimed "Reformers" who left the Methodist Episcopal Church over issues of episcopal administration

Shaw realized the limitations of her effectiveness, especially in her work on behalf of the impoverished women who made their homes on the streets of Boston. "One could do little for these women," she concluded. "For such as them, one's efforts must begin at the very foundation of the social structure. Laws for them must be made and enforced, and some of those laws could only be made and enforced by women." She felt within her a compelling new call that rendered her Cape Cod environment "almost a prison where I was held with tender force."[104] That call was to work on behalf of woman suffrage.

During the busiest period of her life, when she was both a pastor and a medical student, Shaw also accepted invitations to lecture for the Massachusetts Woman Suffrage Association, in which she had become involved through her friendship with Mary Livermore, who had, many years earlier, inspired Shaw's career. "In a few years," Harper noted in her biography, "she began meeting the advocates of woman suffrage" and was particularly influenced by the work of Lucy Stone and her husband, Henry B. Blackwell.[105] Shaw's belief in the suffrage cause grew steadily for years, as she noted,

> until it became the dominating influence in my life. I preached it in the pulpit, talked it to those I met outside of the church, lectured on it whenever I had an opportunity, and carried it into my medical work in the Boston slums when I was trying my prentice hand on helpless, pauper patients.[106]

In 1885, Shaw sent her resignation to the two churches she had served since 1878 and moved to Boston to begin full-time work for suffrage. It was a critical time for the movement, Shaw noted, as industrialization had created new opportunities for women but also new hardships as women were "overworked and underpaid" because of their gender. She recalled:

---

and the representation of lay men and local preachers in denominational conferences. The General Judiciary Committee of the denomination later declared Shaw's ordination unlawful, according to the archives of the Methodist Protestant Church, but "she continued to enjoy recognition in her annual conference. The issue of ordination remained in a sort of constitutional limbo" (Frederick A. Norwood, *The Story of American Methodism: A History of the United Methodists and Their Relations* [Nashville: Abingdon Press, 1974], 352).

104. Shaw, *Story of a Pioneer*, 141–42.

105. Harper, "Biography of Anna Howard Shaw," 42.

106. Shaw, *Story of a Pioneer*, 141.

Again, too, I studied the obtrusive problems of the poor and of the women of the streets, and, looking at the whole social situation from every angle, I could find but one solution for women—the removal of the stigma of disfranchisement. As man's equal before the law, woman could demand her rights, asking favors from no one. With all my heart I joined in the crusade of the men and women who were fighting for her. My real work had begun.[107]

For the next three decades, Shaw was known as the Queen of the Suffrage Platform. She traveled across the United States and Europe, captivating congregations and audiences with her wit, insight, and powerful oratorical style. Her suffrage colleagues honored her abilities and her commitment by electing Shaw president of the National American Woman Suffrage Association in 1904, a position she held for ten years. Attempts were made to oust Shaw from the position as some members were alienated by "her personal style and lack of administrative acumen."[108] Even her detractors, however, had to acknowledge the successes of her administration as membership in the NAWSA increased from 17,000 to more than 200,000 accompanied by a proportional increase in the number of auxiliary suffrage societies. The number of states granting woman suffrage increased from four to twelve. She presided over the national organization through years of tremendous growth but also tremendous contentiousness as suffragists grew tired and quarrelsome from the protracted struggle for their elusive goal. "But long or short," Shaw declared,

the one sure thing is that, taking it all in all, the struggles, the discouragements, the failures, and the little victories, the fight has been, as Susan B. Anthony said in her last hours, "worth while." Nothing bigger can come to a human being than to love a great Cause more than life itself, and to have the privilege throughout life of working for the Cause.[109]

Making Their Homes in Strange Lands

Although the particular obstacles encountered and decisions made along the paths of their lives differed in many ways, Antoinette Brown Black-

107. Ibid., 151–52.
108. Wil A. Linkugel and Martha Solomon, *Anna Howard Shaw: Suffrage Orator and Social Reformer* (New York: Greenwood Press, 1991), 9.
109. Shaw, *Story of a Pioneer*, 337.

well, Olympia Brown, and Anna Howard Shaw were, more often than not, "strangers in a strange land," as Brown Blackwell once described herself. Nevertheless, all three women made places for themselves in their respective "strange lands" by means of their tenacity, abilities, convictions, and faith.

These three pioneers of ecclesiastical and political rights for women reveal remarkable similarities in their backgrounds and experiences. All three women were raised not in Eastern, urban areas from which most leaders of nineteenth-century progressive movements emerged but in rural and/or frontier communities. Upstate New York and the then-territory of Michigan appear to be unlikely places for the rearing of feminists. Perhaps those communities, however, were less hampered by conventional expectations—including gender expectations—than larger, more cosmopolitan communities. The very decision to move beyond the settled boundaries of Eastern civilization and the hardships encountered and endured in rural areas manifested an openness to something new on the part of their families and neighbors.

Brown, Brown Blackwell, and Shaw all were nurtured in families that valued education, even education (at least to some extent) for women. Recently accessible periodical literature and classic books were staples in the homes of all three women during their childhood and adolescent years. Their references to the reverence shown to articles in the *New York Weekly Tribune* as it was read and discussed in their homes suggest both the importance of an awareness of current events and an acceptance of progressive ideas within their families. The radical idea of women pursuing higher education, then, while met with some skepticism, was viewed as the natural progression of one's intellectual life. In the process of their educational pursuits, all three women found mentors, supporters, and benefactors, often in unlikely places and through chance encounters. At propitious moments in their lives, someone came along to allay whatever doubts had accrued concerning their own abilities and their unconventional choices. Whether teachers, colleagues, parishioners, or friends, these individuals, their advice, and, often, their ecclesiastical and social connections made the difference between the success and failure of the ventures of these three pioneers.

The common thread in the religious background of all three women was the rejection of religious dogmatism. In her autobiography, Anna Howard Shaw, whose upbringing included little formal religious training, mentioned her mother's staunch Unitarianism and the line of English religious dissenters who preceded her.[110] Olympia Brown attributed her own struggles with the Calvinist orthodoxy she encountered at Mount Holyoke to her mother's zealous adherence to the Universalist doctrine promulgated by Hosea Ballou.[111] Antoinette Brown Blackwell was the only one of the three raised within the bounds of traditional Protestant orthodoxy. Nevertheless, her family rejected the extreme orthodoxy most representative of their Congregational tradition for a more liberal and evangelical expression of faith.[112] Perhaps these less dogmatic manifestations of nineteenth-century American Protestantism made possible the radical notion of a woman pursuing ordination. At the very least they did not carry with them burdensome doctrines concerning strict biblical interpretation or clerical authority.

Perhaps most instructive for the church today, especially its women in ministry, and most predictable were the common struggles of Brown Blackwell, Brown, and Shaw. The resistance they encountered in educational and congregational settings, their struggles for ordination and acceptance as pastors, and their ambivalence concerning the appropriate venues of their calls are not unique to women religious leaders in the nineteenth century. What *was* unique about their experiences was their eventual success in meeting their educational, professional, and ecclesiastical goals despite those who sought to hamper them, and the acceptance and goodwill they encountered once given a chance to prove themselves. No doubt their success was the result of their remarkable abilities, their gracious spirits, and their unyielding belief in the persistent call of God.

110. Ibid., 7.
111. Brown, *Acquaintances*, 27–28.
112. Gilson ms., 71.

Chapter Two

"Neither male nor female":

The Ordination Question Raised and Answered

The decision in 1853 of the Congregational Church of South Butler, New York, to call and, several months later, ordain Antoinette Brown Blackwell to the gospel ministry was only the first of many difficult decisions and heated debates concerning female ordination to follow. According to the polity of the Congregational denomination, each congregation comprised the locus of authority for decisions concerning who would or would not be ordained, but the service of ordination itself required certain liturgical actions by designated clergymen and lay leaders. The traditional act of ordination by means of the laying on of hands required the participation of church leaders. An equally important element of the service in Brown Blackwell's tradition was the delivery of an ordination sermon. The proclamation of the Word through the act of preaching conveyed a sense of divine affirmation and biblical sanction to accompany the ecclesiastical act.

While the decision to ordain Brown Blackwell seemed to be reached without great difficulty, the South Butler congregation *did* find it difficult to secure a clergyman who was willing to participate in an act as ostensibly subversive as the ordination of a woman. Participation in the service could possibly jeopardize the clergyman's own ecclesiastical status if not his own ordination. Today, one hundred fifty years after Antoinette Brown Blackwell's ordination, in an era when women are ordained routinely in all but a handful of Protestant traditions, it is hard to imagine the significance of the South Butler congregation's decision. In the church's eighteen-hundred-year history, no Christian woman had until then been set apart for liturgical and pastoral service by ecclesiastical sanction and ordination to all the rights and privileges of the clergy.[1]

The ecclesiastical and theological implications of ordaining a woman were significant. Equally significant, however—and, to many, equally disturbing—were the implications of Brown Blackwell's ordination for the social and political worlds of mid-nineteenth-century America. The harmonious and smooth functioning of American society depended upon certain assumptions shaped by rules—de jure and de facto rules—concerning gender roles. Any perceived threat to the delicately woven system of social and gender relationships that characterized the era was greeted with scorn and ominous invective by those who shaped and benefited from the social system, particularly white men. The incipient movements for rights for both African Americans and women had proved that to be true. Thus, the ordination of a woman would become emblematic of a whole complex of challenges to assumptions that underlay not only the order of Christian communities but the structure of all of nineteenth-century American life.

Despite the implications of Brown Blackwell's ordination for both church and society, and despite the implications for those who would participate in and thus sanction such an action, a Wesleyan Methodist preacher was secured to deliver the sermon at her ordination in South Butler. The Reverend Luther Lee was well known in western New York as an outspoken and spirited Methodist revivalist. Nicknamed "Logical Lee," he never hesitated to engage in debates concerning theological or social issues. He became an active abolitionist in the late 1830s, lecturing against slavery, defending himself and other clergymen brought up on ecclesiastical charges as a result of their abolitionist work, and helping to form the antislavery Liberty Party. He joined with other Methodist abolitionists to form the Wesleyan Methodist Connection in 1843 and became a leader of the new denomination.[2]

Lee's participation in Brown Blackwell's ordination appears to have represented not only his commitment to female equality but his deliberate challenge to the whole social structure of the United States. He was

1. As noted earlier, there is some evidence that women were among those set apart for special service in early centuries of the church's history. But in terms of modern understanding of ordination to a ministry of Word and sacrament, Brown Blackwell appears to be the first woman ordained. See Torjesen, *When Women Were Priests* (San Francisco: HarperSanFrancisco, 1993), and Ruth A. Tucker and Walter Liefeld, *Daughters of the Church: Women and Ministry from New Testament Times to the Present* (Grand Rapids: Zondervan Publishing House, 1987).

2. Luther Lee, *Five Sermons and a Tract*, ed. Donald W. Dayton (Chicago: Holrad House, 1975), 9, 10.

known for his public support of divisive social issues such as temperance and woman's rights in addition to his abolitionism. He did not hesitate to mix politics with religion, convinced that "the Gospel is so radically reformatory, that to preach it fully and clearly, is to attack and condemn all wrong, and to assert and defend all righteousness," including the wrong and righteousness found in secular political life. In a sermon on "The Radicalism of the Gospel," Lee declared, "A large portion of the evils are connected with civil government, and the Gospel will never remove them until it is preached as to have something to do with politics."[3] Like Brown Blackwell, Brown, and Shaw, Lee discerned in the gospel message a call to political action toward the goal of a society that more nearly reflected the biblical portrayal of the kingdom of God. "He insisted in his *Autobiography*," writes historian Donald Dayton, "that 'I never had any politics which was not a part of my religion, and I urged men to vote the Liberty ticket as a religious duty.' "[4]

Given Lee's history of activism in western New York and his demonstrated support for woman's rights, "Logical Lee" was a logical choice for the preacher on the auspicious occasion of Brown Blackwell's ordination even though he was from the Methodist rather than the Congregational tradition.[5] He already knew Brown Blackwell through their common work for temperance. His sermon was titled "Woman's Right to Preach the Gospel" and was based on the apostle Paul's words in Galatians 3:28: "There is neither male nor female; for ye are all one in Christ Jesus." After noting the unusual nature of the text and the occasion, Lee acknowledged the significant action of the South Butler congregation that afternoon:

> The ordination of a female, or the setting apart of a female to the work of the Christian ministry, is, to say the least, a novel transaction,

3. Ibid., 11.

4. Ibid.

5. Luther Lee became a hero among woman's rights advocates for his participation in Brown Blackwell's ordination. Twenty years later, after moving to Michigan, Lee became president of the newly organized Michigan Suffrage Association. A report appeared in the *Woman's Journal*: "We are extremely proud of our President, Rev. Luther Lee, D.D., a well-known veteran in the anti-slavery cause, and one of the first Orthodox clergymen in the country who admitted a woman into his pulpit. He assisted at the ordination of Antoinette Brown Blackwell, and preached the sermon on that occasion. . . . And now, Dr. Lee, crowned with the snows of seventy-four winters . . . gives the great weight of his influence, gained by a long, useful and noble life, in favor of the enfranchisement of Woman" ("The Michigan Campaign—Mrs. Stanton in Northville," *Woman's Journal*, June 6, 1874).

in this land and age. It cannot fail to call forth many remarks, and will, no doubt, provoke many censures.

For myself, I regard it in the light of a great innovation upon the opinions, prejudices and practices of nearly the whole Christian world. There have been some Christian communities who have allowed females to preach the gospel, but so far as I know, they have not ordained their ministers, male or female, or by any solemn form or service, set them apart to the work of the ministry, as I suppose is intended to be done at the conclusion of this discourse.[6]

Lee's sermon was essentially a treatise in support of women's full participation in the church based on exegetical study of several Old Testament and New Testament texts involving or about women. His major argument, however, rested on his primary text of Galatians 3:28:

Without even presuming to discuss, on this occasion, the questions of civil and political rights, the text amply sustains me in affirming that in a Christian community, united upon Christian principles, for Christian purposes; or, in other words, in the Church, of which Christ is the only head, males and females possess equal rights and privileges; here there is no difference, "there is neither male nor female; for ye are all one in Christ Jesus." I cannot see how the text can be explained so as to exclude females from any right, office, work, privilege, or immunity which males enjoy, hold or perform. If the text means anything, it means that males and females are equal in rights, privileges and responsibilities upon the Christian platform.[7]

"The overthrow of the monopoly of the pulpit"

Luther Lee was correct in his assertion that no Christian community, even among those that had permitted women to preach, had ordained a woman to the work of ministry. Five years before Luther Lee's declaration of "Woman's Right to Preach the Gospel," the visionary women who organized the Seneca Falls Convention also recognized the glaring absence of women in church leadership. And so, when they put on paper their demands for equal rights for women in the form of the Seneca Falls Declaration of Sentiments and Resolutions, the loci of equality for women

6. Lee, *Five Sermons and a Tract*, 79.
7. Ibid., 80.

included not only the secular, political realm but the ecclesiastical realm as well. As noted earlier, the final resolution adopted unanimously at the convention expressed the realization that women had been too long excluded from ministry as well as other professions:

> *Resolved,* That the speedy success of our cause depends upon the zealous and untiring efforts of both men and women, for the overthrow of the monopoly of the pulpit, and for the securing to woman an equal participation with men in the various trades, professions, and commerce.[8]

Anne Hutchinson (1591–1643)

Although at the time of the Seneca Falls Convention in 1848 women did not have equality in most Christian traditions and men did, indeed, maintain on the pulpit a "monopoly" that needed to be overthrown, there were a significant number of women preachers in the United States. In fact, a venerable tradition of "preaching women" extends back to the earliest days of the American colonies. If one defines preaching as a public and oral exposition of scripture or theological doctrine, the long line of women preachers in America begins with the work of Anne Hutchinson in Boston. Hutchinson and her husband became faithful followers of the Reverend John Cotton, an English Puritan, and followed Cotton from England to the Massachusetts Bay Colony in 1634. Hutchinson's interest in theology had been nurtured by her clergyman father, who also instilled in her a critical eye toward the church and its teachings as a result of his own disputes with the Church of England. She continued her interest in theology by reading and listening to sermons and eventually taught others by gathering women in her Boston home to study Cotton's sermons.

As a result of her religious activity, Hutchinson was accused of a variety of transgressions against the Massachusetts Bay church and society. The clergy and magistrates branded her an Antinomian for her advocacy of a doctrine of salvation based on grace rather than on obedience to the laws of church and state. She continued to "preach" her beliefs to larger and larger gatherings and attracted men as well as women to her teachings. In 1637 she was tried by both the civil magistrates and the church

8. Elizabeth Cady Stanton, Susan B. Anthony, and Matilda Joslyn Gage, eds., *History of Woman Suffrage*, vol. I (6 vols.; Rochester, N.Y.: National American Woman Suffrage Association, 1881–1922), 73.

on charges of disturbing the social order. Rather than back down, however, Hutchinson used her trial as an opportunity to preach her convictions to the whole community. In the course of the trial it became clear that Hutchinson's greatest offense was not the content of her preaching but that, as a preaching woman, she had done something more heinous than preach heresy: she had transgressed sacred and established gender boundaries. In the opening statement of charges, John Winthrop, governor of the Massachusetts Bay Colony, made it clear that it was not only Hutchinson's theology that was on trial but her subversive gender activities as well:

> *Mr. Winthrop governor:* Mrs. Hutchinson, you are called here as one of those that have troubled the peace of the commonwealth and the churches here; . . . you have spoken divers things as we have been informed very prejudicial to the honour of the churches and ministers thereof, and you have maintained a meeting and an assembly in your house that hath been condemned by the general assembly as a thing not tolerable nor comely in the sight of God nor fitting for your sex.[9]

Hutchinson was excommunicated from the church and banished from the Massachusetts Bay Colony in 1638. She moved first to Rhode Island and then to New York where she was killed by Mohegans in 1643. The remarkable extant transcript from her trial stands as testimony to her incisive theology and her skill as a preacher and theological debater.

Mary Dyer (c. 1611–60)

Other early American women who, like Hutchinson, were so bold as to transgress social prohibitions against women's public speaking and preaching also provoked censure and severe punishment, including death. One of those women, Mary Dyer, had supported Hutchinson throughout her trial and escorted her out of the courtroom after the pronouncement of judgment.

Dyer was a Quaker who had her own history of conflict with the Puritans of Massachusetts Bay. Her Quaker religion, rooted in the belief in God's guidance through an "inner light" within each person, challenged

---

9. David D. Hall, ed., *The Antinomian Controversy, 1636–1638: A Documentary History* (Middleton, Conn.: Wesleyan University Press, 1968), 312.

traditional Puritan understandings of authority (as vested in clergy and magistrates) and threatened, as did Hutchinson's reputed antinomianism, the stability of the society. Also like Hutchinson, Dyer violated the boundaries proscribing women's place and role in seventeenth-century New England by testifying publicly—preaching, for all intents and purposes—about her spiritual convictions, something Quakers felt called and compelled to do. Despite skirmishes with the Massachusetts authorities and banishments from the colony, Dyer defied the authorities and regularly returned to Boston to preach. She was eventually sentenced to death for these actions and hanged in 1660, becoming one of many Quakers, both male and female, executed by the New England Puritans because of their continued missionary activity and defiance of Puritan authority.

As in the case of Anne Hutchinson, it is difficult from a historical distance of more than three centuries to separate the theological, social, and gender issues that resulted in the death of Mary Dyer. The historical record bears witness to many men (the Baptist Roger Williams, for example) who were banished from the Massachusetts Bay Colony or put to death because of their public criticism of the Puritans and the Puritan intolerance of any challenge to their beliefs and practices. From sources such as the transcript of Hutchinson's trial, however, it is clear that the women who preached in Puritan New England were considered to be doubly subversive and thus more dangerous than men because they defied not only theological but gender norms.

These theological and gender norms began to fracture, however, as the natural changes inherent in the march of time and the evolution of societies left their mark on the American colonies. Puritan intolerance crumbled under the weight of the new ideas brought by immigrants who flooded into New England and other established American communities around the turn of the eighteenth century.[10] Perhaps the greatest challenge to New England Puritanism, however, came in the form of new religious ideas rooted in Puritanism itself. The Great Awakening that washed like waves over the American colonies through the middle decades of the eighteenth century infused the prevailing Protestant doctrine with a new emphasis on "heart" over "head." The nonemotional Puritanism of the seventeenth century, characterized by protracted struggles over the state of one's soul and intellectual assent to established doctrines, was

---

10. See Jon Butler, *Awash in a Sea of Faith: Christianizing the American People* (Cambridge, Mass: Harvard University Press, 1990) for a study of the "religious eclecticism" that characterized the first three centuries of America's history.

challenged by an appeal to the "religious affections," as the most successful Awakening preacher, Jonathan Edwards, described it.[11] The revival
emphasis on conversion, preceded by the acknowledgment of one's sin-
fulness, guilt, and need for salvation, required an appeal not only to the
intellect but to the emotions as well. Once the believer had passed
through the travails of conversion and been delivered into the joyous state
of redemption, he or she could not help but testify publicly to the goodness of God, inviting others into the same glorious state. It was this
emphasis on public testimony that opened the doors to public proclamation by those—including women, African Americans, and lay men—
whose voices had not been heard due to social constraints proscribing
their activities. As historian Susan Hill Lindley notes,

> The central experience of God's grace in conversion not only assured
> the individual of salvation, it also propelled him or her to witness of
> that experience to others and to join a community of like-minded
> persons where the new life in Christ could be shared and cultivated.
> Significantly, it was the experience of grace that gave authority, not
> formal theological training, thus opening a door for women as well
> as black men. Few Christians in the eighteenth century approved of
> women's preaching in public, and even the acceptance of black men
> as preachers was relatively rare, but there were other ways a person
> could testify to her or his faith, even in semipublic settings.[12]

The new theological emphases and practices introduced by the Great
Awakening created previously unknown opportunities for women to participate in religious life. While the majority of church members in colonial America were women, their participation was limited to nonpublic,
nonleadership roles of passive worshiper or spiritual autobiographer.
Women were encouraged to listen and learn and to read and write about
theological matters, but other than perhaps teaching or leading small all-
female gatherings for pietistic study, they were prohibited from engaging
in public religious dialogue. As a result of the spiritual revivals of the eighteenth century, however, women became more public and assertive in

11. See Jonathan Edwards, "A Treatise Concerning Religious Affections" (1746) in John E.
Smith, Harry S. Stout, and Kenneth P. Minkema, eds., *A Jonathan Edwards Reader* (New Haven,
Conn.: Yale University Press, 1995), 137–71.

12. Susan Hill Lindley, *"You Have Stept Out of Your Place": A History of Women and Religion
in America* (Louisville, Ky.: Westminster John Knox Press, 1996), 43.

their religious activities. These newfound opportunities for women, rather than representing an intentional expansion of women's roles sanctioned by ecclesiastical authorities, were an accidental by-product of the theological and ecclesiastical revolution that became known as the Great Awakening. The Awakening coincided with cultural changes that engendered greater fluidity in the social structure as well as innovative religious practices—most notably in the form of the new Methodist movement brought from England, with its acceptance of women and laity in leadership roles—that broke Puritanism's unbending hold on American society. As a result of this coincidence of influences, preaching by women and women's public religious leadership that had once been considered aberrant, dangerous, or evil became accepted and even encouraged.

Sarah Osborn (1714–96)

Many women, both named and unnamed in the historical record, took advantage of the religious doors opened to them in the mid-eighteenth century. They prayed and gave testimonies in revival meetings; they opened their homes for small groups that gathered for study and worship; they wrote on spirituality and theology and interpreted Scripture; and they served as examples of piety and faith for male religious leaders. There is even evidence of women "preaching" in more recognizable ways in religious gatherings. One such woman whose activities and writings have received much attention from historians in recent years is Sarah Osborn. An English immigrant first to Boston and then to Newport, Rhode Island, Osborn became enamored of the Calvinist preacher Nathaniel Clap. Although she had experienced conversion before the Great Awakening, she was drawn to the preaching of George Whitefield, Gilbert Tennent, and other theological luminaries of the day. "For Sarah Osborn the Awakening was her reawakening," suggests Charles Hambrick-Stowe.[13]

Osborn's reawakening and piety were demonstrated by her organization of a Religious Female Society in First Church, Newport. The group was influential in the calling of Jonathan Edwards's protégé Samuel Hopkins as pastor of the church in 1769.[14] Hopkins later wrote a biography of Osborn in which he praised her exemplary piety and religious activities.

---

13. Charles E. Hambrick-Stowe, "The Spiritual Pilgrimage of Sarah Osborn (1714–1796)" in *Religion in American History: A Reader*, ed. Jon Butler and Harry S. Stout (New York: Oxford University Press, 1998), 131.
14. Ibid.

Not all of her contemporaries, however, were as unequivocal in their praise of Osborn's work. The Religious Female Society was an early example of what occurred repeatedly in communities of faith from the days of Anne Hutchinson to the Second Great Awakening. What began as an innocent gathering in Osborn's home of women "who were awakened to a concern for their souls" for the purposes of education and spiritual growth moved unintentionally toward forbidden activities. Osborn's teaching and religious nurture became so popular that her gatherings attracted men and African Americans. By 1765, she was hosting a group of free blacks on Tuesday evenings and a group of slaves on Sunday. According to historian Barbara J. MacHaffie,

> Word of her compassion for people spread rapidly in Newport, and white people, children and adults, males and females, began crowding into her home on other evenings during the week. In January 1767 the number had reached an extraordinary 525 people in one week.[15]

Even a close friend and confidant, the Reverend Joseph Fish, warned Osborn that these gatherings of men and women and African Americans threatened the social order. Her behavior also provided ammunition for critics of the Great Awakening. Charles Chauncy, minister of First (Congregational) Church of Boston and leader of the "old lights" who opposed the revivals of the Great Awakening, grumbled, "Indeed young *Persons*, sometimes *Lads*, or rather *Boys*: Nay, *Women* and *Girls*, yea *Negroes*, have taken upon them to do the Business of Preachers."[16] But the success of Osborn's "ministry" and the many testimonies to her effectiveness as a teacher and perhaps even preacher confirm her important role in the Great Awakening of New England and demonstrate the growing power of women's vocations and voices in American religion.

Preaching Women of the Second Great Awakening

Sarah Osborn lived until almost the end of the eighteenth century and thus witnessed the evolution of religion in America from the dawn of the

---

15. Barbara J. MacHaffie, *Herstory: Women in Christian Tradition* (Philadelphia: Fortress Press, 1986), 87.

16. Charles Chauncy, *Seasonable Thoughts on the State of Religion in New England* (Boston, 1743) as quoted in Albert J. Raboteau, *Slave Religion: The "Invisible Institution" in the Antebellum South* (New York: Oxford University Press, 1978), 129.

Great Awakening to the dawn of the Second Great Awakening, the renewed revival of religious fervor that defined American Protestantism and greatly shaped American culture through the first half of the nineteenth century. Between the two Awakenings, a few other women preached in various contexts with notable success. Mother Ann Lee brought her reformed version of Quakerism from England to America in 1774 and founded the United Society of Believers in Christ's Second Appearing (known popularly as the Shakers because of their ecstatic worship practices). Lee portrayed herself as the conveyer of divine wisdom and the completion of the revelation of Christ. Besides being the founder of the Shaker community, Lee remained its undisputed leader and primary preacher until her death in 1784. With a similar appeal to revelatory experience emerging from an encounter with death, Jemima Wilkinson, the Public Universal Friend, as she called herself, traveled throughout America during the last quarter of the eighteenth century as an itinerant preacher proclaiming the imminence of the last days before the final judgment of God. Her preaching met with great success, and she attracted a significant following of believers among both men and women, three hundred of whom followed her to a colony in Seneca Lake, New York, where they lived until her death in 1819. At the same time, Quaker women continued their missionary preaching in an effort to bring new members into their tradition.

All of these preaching women commonly defended their "unfeminine" behavior by appealing to divine authority. They claimed to have been blessed with unique revelatory experiences or guided by the presence of an "inner light," as the Quakers defined it, through which God directly communicated to them divine sanction for their activities.

New Roles for Religious Women

Despite these instances of preaching women who left their marks on early American religion, religious leadership did not open up significantly for women until the middle decades of the nineteenth century. The decades of revivals and the emergence of new—and renewed—religious traditions that made up what is now regarded as the Second Great Awakening represent a turning point in the acceptance of women's expanded participation in religious activities. A plethora of opportunities for benevolent service and for the expression of spiritual commitment developed in the midst of the abundant growth and consequent needs of the young United States. And as had occurred in the mid-eighteenth century, once again the irrepressible march of time and acceptance of new ideas fractured what were once considered to be immutable truths of church and society. Women found new roles as guardians of the moral virtue of the nation. The growth of benevolent organizations, Sunday schools, tract and Bible societies, maternal associations, moral reform societies, and other organizations of women for pietistic and charitable work gave middle-class (primarily white) women new avenues for meaningful service. They also enabled women to create and lead what in many cases became wealthy and powerful organizations, giving women new experiences in leadership.

While much of the religious work of women during the middle decades of the nineteenth century was confined to independent, all-female organizations that accomplished their benevolent work behind the scenes, women were also encouraged to assume more public roles in religious gatherings. The theological principle of a necessary testimonial to one's experience of religious transformation that had propelled many women into uncharacteristic public roles during the Great Awakening once again opened new doors of opportunity for women a century later. New theological and cultural ideas converged to allow women access to public religious participation in ways previously forbidden to them. Once those ideas were fostered by respected male religious leaders of the day such as Charles G. Finney, they became accepted in many Protestant evangelical circles.

Phoebe Palmer (1807–74)

Perhaps the most influential woman to emerge from the opportunities generated by Finney's "new measures" was Phoebe Palmer. Raised in the Methodist Episcopal Church, Palmer sought solace and a deeper spirituality in response to the deaths of her first three infants. She and her husband, Walter Palmer, a physician, attended a series of revival meetings near their New York City home in 1837. The meetings proved to be the catalyst for Palmer's own spiritual transformation and led her to build on Wesley's doctrine of entire sanctification in order to develop her own "altar theology." She expounded this Holiness doctrine through weekly gatherings that her sister, Sara Lankford, had begun in their home in 1835. These "Tuesday Meetings for the Promotion of Holiness" were gatherings of women—and eventually, women and men—in which Palmer and other participants would expound on Holiness theology and testify to their experiences of sanctification. The Tuesday Meetings continued for forty years and gave Palmer an effective forum for her theological views. In 1865, the Palmers bought a Methodist journal called *The Guide to Holiness*, which was published for more than a century and served as the foremost periodical promoting Methodist Perfectionism.

Palmer's subversive act of holding and speaking to "promiscuous" gatherings was not, as has been demonstrated above, unique within early American Protestant history. What *was* unique about Palmer's work was her systematic development of the theological doctrine of Holiness *and* her extensive writing in defense of that doctrine and its obligations, most notably the obligation to testify to one's experience of sanctification. While the obligation of personal testimony had opened the doors earlier in American religious history to public speaking and teaching by women (as well as African Americans and lay men of all social classes), no one had written extensively or defensively about the resultant new practice of women's public speech in religious gatherings. Palmer's 1859 treatise in defense of women's preaching, *The Promise of the Father; or, A Neglected Spirituality of the Last Days*, was prompted, Palmer herself declared, by the experience of witnessing a distraught young woman who was torn between testifying to her experience of sanctification and respecting the boundaries circumscribing women's public speaking.

Because of her encounter with that one young woman Palmer provided inspiration for countless women, including well-known preacher/reformers Catherine Booth and Frances Willard, who acted on their calls to preach in the second half of the nineteenth century. Palmer made it clear that her support for women's preaching emerged not from any intentional challenge to the social order but from her belief in the spiritual obligation of those who had received the gift of sanctification. At the beginning of the first chapter of *The Promise of the Father* she stated that she did not "intend to discuss the question of 'Women's Rights' or of 'Women's Preaching,' technically so-called."[17] Rather, she and other women who have been identified as "evangelical feminists" operated out of what historians Rosemary Ruether and Eleanor McLaughlin have termed a "stance of radical obedience" from which women who defend their orthodoxy can nevertheless challenge the normative practices of the church and the culture.[18] Thus, in response to the call to testify to their own regeneration in order to prompt the regeneration of others in a

17. Phoebe Palmer, *The Promise of the Father; or, A Neglected Speciality of the Last Days* (Boston: Henry V. Degen, 1859), 1.

18. Rosemary Ruether and Eleanor McLaughlin, eds., *Women of Spirit: Female Leadership in the Jewish and Christian Traditions* (New York: Simon & Schuster, 1979), 19.

quest to transform society, nineteenth-century women felt compelled and justified to defy social dicta by transgressing their ascribed sphere through public speaking. Female preachers became a not uncommon sight in the last half of the nineteenth century, especially on the revival circuit. In addition to Phoebe Palmer (Holiness), women such as Clarissa Danforth (Free Will Baptist), Lucretia Mott (Quaker), Sojourner Truth (independent), and Amanda Berry Smith (Holiness) were among the most powerful and popular preachers of the century. They traveled internationally, attracting large and enthusiastic crowds as they preached in church and revival settings.

African American Preaching Women

Several of the best-known and most influential women preachers of the nineteenth century were African American.[19] Some of these women, including Jarena Lee and Julia A. J. Foote, emerged from African American churches and were endorsed, at least to some extent, by their congregations and denominations. Lee, who preached throughout the United States during the 1830s and 1840s, was recognized by the hierarchy of the African Methodist Episcopal Church as an official traveling exhorter (although they denied her the more significant role of licensed preacher).[20] Julia Foote, who had a successful career as an itinerant evangelist throughout New England and the Middle Atlantic states during the second half of the nineteenth century, maintained ties with the African Methodist Episcopal Zion Church. On May 20, 1894, she was ordained a deacon in the A.M.E. Zion Church, the first woman to be so recognized, and before her death in 1900 she was ordained to the higher office of elder.[21] The first woman to achieve the office of elder in the A.M.E. Zion Church (1898) was Mary J. Small, who worked in parishes with her husband, a pastor and later bishop in the denomination, through the last quarter of the nineteenth century. Although denied pastorates of her own following her husband's death in 1905, she continued serving as an itinerant evangelist.[22]

---

19. Bettye Collier-Thomas states that more than twenty African American women are known to have preached in the nineteenth century. See Collier-Thomas, *Daughters of Thunder* (San Francisco: Jossey-Bass Publishers, 1998), 41.

20. William L. Andrews, ed., *Sisters of the Spirit: Three Black Women's Autobiographies of the Nineteenth Century* (Bloomington: Indiana University Press, 1986), 6.

21. Ibid., 10.

22. Collier-Thomas, *Daughters of Thunder*, 91.

Other African American women preached with less formal ties to denominations or congregations. Two of the most well known and widely traveled African American women preachers, Amanda Berry Smith and Sojourner Truth, maintained tenuous if any ties to the A.M.E. and A.M.E. Zion churches, respectively. Smith found her spiritual home in the Holiness tradition, the Spirit-centered, evangelistic tradition that emerged from Phoebe Palmer's theological work. Her call and her connection to the Holiness movement came through her attendance at the 1870 National Camp Meeting Association for the Promotion of Holiness. For the next several decades, she traveled nationally and internationally as a Holiness evangelist and social reformer.[23] Sojourner Truth's career followed a similar path. After years of association with the Methodist, A.M.E., and A.M.E. Zion churches as well as a utopian community through the middle decades of the nineteenth century, Truth became an independent evangelist and a popular speaker for woman's rights and abolition.[24]

Whether they worked for change as recognized preachers within denominational structures or acted on their calls to preach as itinerant evangelists, African American preaching women of the nineteenth century contributed significantly to the inevitable discussion concerning the ecclesiastical rights and roles of women. Their lives and experiences reveal their belief in the power of the Holy Spirit and the Spirit's ineluctable call that enabled them to overcome the forces of gender and race that otherwise would have thwarted them. They preached salvation and empowerment through the Spirit even as they modeled those gifts in their ministries and "implicitly affirmed women's ministerial work by emphasizing the inclusiveness of God's call."[25]

In Defense of Preaching Women

As the lives and work of both African American and white preaching women attest, women preachers came into prominence through the "back door" of the church in the nineteenth century. They evolved naturally out of new and free church traditions that either had no designation of ordained clergy (such as the Quaker tradition) or did not have a high

23. Ibid., 52–53.
24. Ibid., 53–55. See also Nell Irvin Painter, *Sojourner Truth: A Life, A Symbol* (New York: W. W. Norton, 1996).
25. Collier-Thomas, *Daughters of Thunder,* 5.

regard for ordained clergy (such as the Holiness tradition in which one's spiritual authority to preach transcended any authority bestowed by ecclesiastical, thus human, action). Nevertheless, their presence generated significant debate in religious and secular circles in the nineteenth century. The content and contexts of the debates varied, but most of the arguments supporting expanded ecclesiastical roles for women could be categorized as spiritual, biblical, or pragmatic.

The spiritual argument was used most frequently to defend women's preaching. It claimed that God could choose anyone, even a woman, to proclaim the gospel. Support for that contention came by reviewing those who had been called by God and given special gifts of the Holy Spirit to do God's work in biblical times and through the centuries of Christian history. The spiritual argument was perhaps best articulated by Phoebe Palmer in *The Promise of the Father*, in which she presented an extensive study of biblical and historical women who were recognized by their communities for their unique spiritual gifts. Palmer spoke "of that consistently pious, earnest, Christian woman, whose every-day life is an ever-speaking testimony of an indwelling Saviour, and on whose head the tongue of fire has descended." Who would place "the seal of silence on those Heaven-touched lips?" Palmer asked. "Who would restrain the lips of those whom God has endued with the gift of utterance, when those lips would fain abundantly utter the memory of God's great goodness?"[26] The work of the Spirit can be neither thwarted nor constrained by gender or other human characteristics, as demonstrated by the number of surprising individuals—men and women—called and used for divine purposes in the history of the church. Those who believe in the continued presence and work of the Spirit in their own age must, then, acknowledge the efficacy of even unexpected bearers of the Spirit's message. If the Spirit blows where it will and chooses whom it wishes, one must accept and affirm those whom the Spirit appoints; otherwise, by disavowing the spiritual call of those who claim it, the believer would usurp divine authority and interfere with divine intentions.

The spiritual argument necessarily presumed a biblical argument in favor of women's preaching. The ultimate authority for the Spirit's activity rested on biblical texts that witnessed to the powerful, transformative work of the Spirit within individual believers and within the community of faith. Particularly authoritative for women seeking a greater ecclesias-

---

26. Palmer, *The Promise of the Father*, 4.

tical role were those texts in which women were empowered by the Spirit for extraordinary service, Old Testament texts such as the leadership of Deborah and Esther and New Testament texts such as the story of Pentecost, the day on which men and women received spiritual gifts of equal measure. Other texts featuring women in leadership roles also figured significantly in defenses of women's public ecclesiastical activity, as we will see in the arguments for women's ministry used by Brown Blackwell, Brown, and Shaw.

Pragmatic arguments in support of preaching by women accompanied the spiritual and biblical arguments. The mid-nineteenth-century American revival fervor was precipitated in large part by the rapid expansion and consequent secularization of the United States. Although some prominent women preachers remained in settled, urban areas, most of the women preachers who gained prominence did so as a result of grueling itinerant ministries, especially on the emerging frontier of the United States. Even when sanctioned by denominations, they were often consigned to revival circuits and mission outposts in sparsely settled areas. Women preachers were often willing to go where ordained and lay men would not go simply for the opportunity to fulfill their calls to preach. Most traveled thousands of miles annually on their preaching tours across the United States and even abroad. Testimonies to the impact of their ministries, even from secular observers, were abundant.

During this era of religious decline in American history, nineteenth-century religious leaders could hardly argue with the obvious effectiveness of women preachers in bringing women and especially men back to the churches. Their case was bolstered by the enormous growth and efficacy of the denominational and interdenominational organizations established by women for reform and mission work. The female leaders of those powerful organizations found themselves, like the women who testified to their experiences of faith, in the unintentional and once-prohibited role of public proclaimer as they did nothing more than that which they felt divinely called to do. No matter how the weighty ecclesiastical doors opened to them, nineteenth-century church women took advantage of every opportunity to assert their religious convictions. It was only a matter of time, then, before the ultimate question of women's full ecclesiastical participation as ordained ministers of Word and sacrament was raised and answered.

While the historical record reveals a significant number of preaching women and at least some public debate concerning the role of women in public religious gatherings (most notably, revivals) by the mid-nineteenth century, it reveals little public debate on the ordination question. As Susan Hill Lindley asserts, "formal ordination was not the dominant concern of women religious leaders in the nineteenth century. . . . Women's preaching was a greater concern than formal ordination." The acceptance of women's preaching, however, was "a necessary foundation for the cause of women's ordination."[27] Thus, the two issues—women's preaching and women's ordination—developed on separate but parallel tracks. At times the issues, and thus those tracks, converged; at other times the issues, due mostly to differences in denominational theologies and polities, could remain quite distinct. Therefore, the issue of ordination was resolved in many different places and ways.

By the time Brown Blackwell, Brown, and Shaw pursued their theological educations in the mid-nineteenth century, women public speakers were prepared to defend their right to speak before they moved on to their real subject matter, usually abolition, temperance, moral reform, or woman's rights. Early-nineteenth-century women preachers and speakers such as the Grimké sisters, Lucretia Mott, and Abby Kelley Foster had to present rationales—usually biblical and theological as well as pragmatic— for what was viewed as audacious public behavior. Like women preachers of earlier decades, they appealed to the kinds of arguments I noted above in defense of their religious activity, including spiritual affirmation of their calls, the success of their work, and the reinterpretation of traditional biblical and theological prohibitions against women. It is not surprising, then, that the writings of Brown Blackwell, Brown, and Shaw include defenses of their ecclesiastical goals.

Antoinette Brown Blackwell

The challenge to Brown Blackwell's ministry that prompted a formal defense of her claim to sacred space occurred early in her theological career. To spite Brown Blackwell, a professor required her to write an essay on 1 Corinthians 14:34–35 and 1 Timothy 2:11–12, the New Testament texts that commanded women's silence in church. She took the assignment to heart, regarding it as her chance to make a claim for women's right to a public role in the church, and worked on the essay through the winter and spring of 1848, mentioning her work to Lucy Stone in a letter at the end of March:

27. Lindley, *"You Have Stept Out of Your Place,"* 117.

I have been examm[in]ing the bible position of women a good deal this winter—reading various commentaries comparing them with each other & with the bible, & hunting up every passage in the scriptures that have any bearing on the subject either near or remote. My mind grows stronger & firmer on the subject & the light comes b[ea]ming in, full of promise. Lately I have been writing out my thoughts to see if they will all hang together but have not finished yet. It is a hard subject & takes a long time to see through it doesn't it. But "no cross no crown."[28]

Brown Blackwell's thoughts eventually did "hang together" well enough that Charles G. Finney chose her essay for an issue of the *Oberlin Quarterly Review*.[29] In the essay, Brown Blackwell followed a line of argumentation established by earlier feminist exegetes, asserting that Paul, the attributed author of the texts, did not intend his words to be applied in the way subsequent interpreters had applied them to church practice. Rather than intending his comments to be proscriptive for all Christian communities to come, Brown Blackwell argued, Paul meant his radical injunctions against women to serve as warnings against possible abuses of leadership in the church. As a result of her exegesis, she concluded that the passages had "nothing whatever to do with the question of public teaching. The females were not forbidden to take part in the work of instructing the church, of speaking 'either by revelation, or by knowledge, or by prophesying, or by doctrine,' or of doing anything else which they had the wisdom and ability to do."[30]

Women who had been "taught by the Spirit of the mighty God" did indeed take part in the public activities and proclamation of the New Testament church, Brown Blackwell believed, based on evidence inherent in the Pauline texts themselves. The ultimate questions raised by the texts concerned not whether women exercised public leadership in worshiping communities but the content of their proclamation and how their leadership was exercised:

28. Antoinette Brown Blackwell to Lucy Stone, March 28, 1848, BFP, LC.

29. Brown Blackwell's essay, "Exegesis of I Corinthians, XIV, 34, 35; and I Timothy II, 11,12," appeared in the July 1849 issue of the *Oberlin Quarterly Review*. Ironically, the same issue featured an article by James H. Fairchild, one of the Oberlin professors most opposed to Brown Blackwell's presence in the theological program. Fairchild's essay was titled "Woman's Rights and Duties."

30. Memoirs told by Brown Blackwell in 1909 to Mrs. Claude U. (Sarah) Gilson, 99, BFP, SL, Fols. 3–14.

> But in what portion of the inspired volume do we find any com-
> mandment forbidding woman to act as a public teacher, *provided* she
> has a message worth communicating, and will deliver in a manner
> worthy of her high vocation? Surely nowhere. . . . This was too sacred
> a subject to be coldly decided by the voice of law, and they left it,
> where it must ever remain, at the portal of the individual conscience
> of every moral agent.[31]

For those who knew Brown Blackwell and her theological interests in
1850, it was no surprise that her first speech in support of woman's rights
was an exegetical one, a reworking of her Oberlin paper. The speech
occurred at the convention that was declared the First National Woman's
Rights Convention, in Worcester, Massachusetts, in the fall of 1850. It
was also the first national woman's rights gathering Brown Blackwell
attended. "Antoinette L. Brown," reported the secretary of the convention, "a graduate of Oberlin College, and a student in Theology, made a
logical argument on woman's position in the Bible, claiming her complete
equality with man, the simultaneous creation of the sexes, and their moral
responsibilities as individual and imperative."[32] Brown Blackwell's presentation received enthusiastic support and assured her a place in the
growing circle of woman's rights speakers. Two years later at the national
convention held in Syracuse, New York, in 1852, Brown Blackwell again
distinguished herself by offering a resolution and making "a few good
points on the Bible argument":

> *Resolved*, That the Bible recognizes the rights, duties, and privileges
> of woman as a public teacher, as every way equal with those of man;
> that it enjoins upon her no subjection that is not enjoined upon him;
> and that it truly and practically recognizes neither male nor female
> in Christ Jesus.

Brown Blackwell began her defense of women's equality in church and
society with an assertion of the equality into which man and woman had
been created: "God created the first human pair equal in rights, possessions,
and authority. He bequeathed the earth to them as a joint inheritance; gave
them joint dominion over the irrational creation; but none over each other."
The first man and first woman also sinned jointly, she argued, and were con-

31. Ibid., 104.
32. *History of Woman Suffrage*, I:224.

signed to live with the consequences of their sin. But through her own translation of the text from Hebrew into English, she concluded that the curse of sin was not upon woman alone but upon both of them jointly:

> The results [of God's announcement] are the effects of sin. Can woman then receive evil from this rule, and man receive good? Man should be blessed in exercising this power, if he is divinely appointed to do so; but the two who are one flesh have an identity of interests, therefore if it is a curse or evil to woman, it must be so to man also. We mock God, when we make Him approve of man's thus cursing himself and woman.

She then went on to address the problematic New Testament texts that mandate the submission and silence of women. She interpreted the texts commanding the submission of women to men in the larger context of the mutual "Christian submission due from man towards man, and from man towards woman." In support of her argument, she quoted several texts from the epistles in which help, subjection, and submission are expected of those participating in Christian community. And, she asserted, any interpretation of the letter to the Ephesians (5:22–24) that suggests that man is literally the head of the woman is "blasphemous," for man would then be exercising over woman "all the prerogatives of God Himself." Instead, "the mystical Head and Body, or Christ and His Church, symbolize oneness, union."[33]

Brown Blackwell's earlier work on 1 Corinthians and 1 Timothy appeared in her resolution as well. She denied that women are commanded in either text not to teach in the church. In fact, she maintained, when interpreting the text from 1 Corinthians, "woman is merely told not to talk unless she does teach"; the rule of the chapter is, "Let all things be done unto edifying":

> Their women, who had not been previously instructed like the men, were very naturally guilty of asking questions which did not edify the assembly. It was better that they should wait till they got home for the desired information, rather than put an individual good before the good of the Church. Nothing else is forbidden. There is not a word here against woman's teaching. The apostle says to the whole Church, woman included, "Ye may all prophesy, one by one."[34]

33. Ibid., 535, 536.
34. Ibid, 536.

In 1 Timothy, Brown Blackwell stated, "the writer forbids woman's teaching over man, or usurping authority over him; that is, he prohibits dogmatizing, tutoring, teaching in a dictatorial spirit. This is prohibited both in public and private; but a proper kind of teaching is not prohibited." The reference to Eve in 1 Timothy 2:13–14 she dismissed as "merely such a suggestion as we would make to a daughter whose mother had been in fault. The daughters are not blamed for the mother's sin, merely warned by it; and cautioned against self-confidence, which could make them presume to teach over man." In conclusion, she offered a positive portrayal of women in the Bible and an interesting prolepsis of the text that would serve as the centerpiece of her ordination service one year later: "The Bible tells us of many prophetesses approved of God. The Bible is truly democratic. Do as you would be done by, is its golden commandment, recognizing neither male nor female in Christ Jesus."[35]

Brown Blackwell's exegetical proficiency came to be respected and depended on by her colleagues in the woman's rights movement. The spokespersons of the movement continually found themselves on the defensive against biblical arguments countering their vision of gender equality. The presence of an articulate, theologically trained speaker on the woman's rights platform became a significant weapon in the war against the religious rhetoric that threatened the progress of the movement.

Olympia Brown

Olympia Brown served a function for the woman's movement similar to that of Antoinette Brown Blackwell in that she was an articulate religious spokesperson who was able to bridge the worlds of ecclesiastical and political reform. Her theological education, her ordained status, and her experience as a pastor commanded respect from those who otherwise would have dismissed her ideas as merely philosophy. She developed a reputation as a powerful orator and was at least heard if not affirmed in a wide array of public venues.

Brown's most cogent essay in defense of women in ministry was delivered to the interdenominational Ministerial Union meeting in Boston on May 10, 1869. She argued for the primacy of Christianity in granting to women their rightful place in the religious community:

35. Ibid.

It was for Christ, first in the history of the world, to recognize woman as worthy of the respect, the liberty, and the obligations that belong to a human being. He saw her capability of grasping those great principles which lie at the basis of the absolute religion, and of applying those principles to the needs of the world.

In this essay, Brown foreshadowed what would become a major theme in her suffrage rhetoric: the uniqueness of the Christian faith in transcending all other systems of belief in its concern for "the humble, the poor, and the oppressed" and in breaking "the shackles which the old barbarous law of might makes right had imposed upon woman." Christianity represented a new way of organizing society and shaping human relationships, and those who claimed to live under its principles would be recognized by their embrace of new ideals and redefined human qualities. The test of excellence as initiated by Christ "should be no longer physical strength, but moral power and spiritual discernment."[36]

Among the innovations of the Christian dispensation, Brown argued, was the emancipation of women. In her later writings in support of woman suffrage, she would identify the vote as one aspect of this general emancipation of women that was incumbent upon a nation that claimed to be Christian. But in this speech, she focused on the ecclesiastical emancipation of women, which, she stated, was another important manifestation of a Christian society. Consistent with the direction of liberal theology in the nineteenth century,[37] Brown set forth a portrait of a "feminized" Christ, a figure "possessing all feminine characteristics, ushering in the reign of gentleness and peace, [who] was at once the representative of man and woman." Christ, "like the great, infinite Being whose vicegerent he was," combined "all the excellences of male and female character in himself, and his system made no distinction of sex in respect to sphere of labor or moral obligations."

Brown then turned to the usual biblical texts quoted to support the ministries of women, including the prophecy of Joel (anticipating an outpouring of the Spirit on all flesh, and the prophetic abilities of sons *and* daughters), the last chapter of Proverbs (describing the wise woman), and, especially, the New Testament references to the partnership of women with men in proclaiming the gospel. The way in which Christ related to the women among his disciples should be particularly instructive for the

---

36. Olympia Brown, "Woman's Place in the Church," OBP, SL, Fol. 25.
37. See Ann Douglas, *The Feminization of American Culture* (New York: Avon Books, 1977).

modern church, Brown advised, citing the numerous significant ways in which women supported the work of Christ according to the gospel accounts:

> Christ first revealed himself as the promised Messiah to a woman; it was at a woman's request that he performed the first miracle; he admitted women to listen to his instructions, and to cooperate with him in carrying the glad tidings of salvation to a sorrowing world. It was Mary who sat at Jesus' feet and conversed with him of the lofty themes which engaged his attention. It was women who were last at the cross and first at the sepulchre.

Although she acknowledged that no woman was among the twelve disciples named in Scripture as called by Jesus, that, she maintained, was due to the "peculiarities of the times" rather than "to any unfitness in woman herself." She offered a compelling argument in response to those who would claim that church leadership must be restricted to men since only men were numbered among the twelve:

> We do not seek in our ministers and church-members a likeness to the disciples in merely personal matters; we do not ask that they shall be all Jews, all fishermen, or tax-gatherers; that they shall correspond in color of hair or eyes with the teacher,—it was not these little particulars, nor yet the fact that they were *men*, which fitted the original twelve to be Christ's disciples; but it was that they were earnest and loyal to the truth, and filled with the Holy Spirit; and wherever there is man or woman, bond or free, Jew or Gentile, who has received this spirit, there is one whom Christ has chosen, and who is worthy to go forth to labor in his cause.[38]

Rather than argue as Antoinette Brown Blackwell had over the nuances of the Greek words used in the Pauline passages that prohibited women's public leadership in the church, Brown pointed to New Testament materials that demonstrated the extensive and crucial roles women *did* play in the early church, becoming "a part of all public congregations" and "entering into public discussions." She acknowledged Paul's rebuke of "those [women] who were ignorant and not accustomed to so much lib-

---

38. Brown, "Woman's Place in the Church."

erty, and were taking up the time with foolish questions," but she quickly moved on to point to other women commended by Paul for their faithful service to the church, especially Phoebe, to whom Paul referred using the same term for "minister" that he applied to himself. Brown quoted church historians who concluded that women participated fully in the worship life of the early church, even speaking in the gatherings as they felt moved. Evidence of women who served in the early church as deaconesses, those engaged in "all that we mean by the pastoral labor of the preacher," is abundant, as are indications that they "were formally set apart for the Christian work, consecrated by the imposition of hands, a ceremony in all respects similar to the ordination ceremony of the present day." In her own time, Brown argued, those traditions that "most availed themselves of woman's earnest religious spirit and ready cooperation in the cause of truth" were most successful. Noting the acceptance of the gifts of women among the Catholics, Methodists, and Quakers—an interesting list of wide-ranging Christian traditions that reflected Brown's liberal and ecumenical stance—Brown concluded that, indeed, "woman has rightfully, by every law of God, a place in the church."[39]

Brown's defense of women in ministry was based on an assumption of natural, essential differences between men and women, another argument that figured largely in her suffrage rhetoric. The church in particular and the world in general needed the complementarity of the uniqueness of men and women working together for good:

> God has placed man and woman together in the world in families and in society; they modify each other, and the great facts of human experience, the great needs of the world, cannot be comprehended until man's observation and reason are supplemented and made complete by woman's perception and ready inference. . . . let us have the strongest, bravest, best thought of which the masculine mind is capable, and, too, the loftiest inspiration, and the clearest vision, which has been given to woman; and then, if we have sentiment, it will be genuine healthful, life giving.

And the churches, Brown maintained, should not attempt to limit the good influence of women to particular places of ministry. It should not be up to tribunals of the church to "ascertain her sphere of labor." With a

39. Ibid.

note of resentment, she pointed out the common practice of allowing women to do the work of the church without proper recognition:

> There are those who seem to think that woman's place in the church is to carry on the Sunday school, to conduct the sewing society, to raise money for missionary enterprises, to add life to the prayer and conference meetings, to get good dinners for the ministers, in fact, to do anything and everything pertaining to ministerial work, except to receive the recognition and take the salary.

By right and revelation, Brown concluded, woman "has some place in the Christian church, it remains only to give her freedom of choice as to what that place shall be." She conceded that "there are some portions of the pastoral labor which man can perform better than woman," but argued "there are also some which woman can perform better than man." The time was right for the acceptance of the gifts of women by the church.

> The hour draws nigh when the gospel shall find its most efficient preachers, Christianity its most devoted laborers, among women. . . . Woman, long time waiting amid oppression and ignorance, is, ere long, to arise from her darkness, and, girded with strength and honor, to go forth to speak words of wisdom for the regeneration of the people, and her own works shall praise her in the gates. And when we shall see women calling the people by thousands to lives of purity and holiness, when through their instrumentality churches shall be established, and the glad tidings of salvation carried to sorrowing hearts, then will the prophecy be verified, "The seed of the woman shall bruise the serpent's head. In her shall all the nations of the earth be blest."[40]

In her autobiography, Brown related her experiences, good and bad, from twenty-five years in parish ministry and concluded, "There is certainly room for women in the ministry." Her depth of experience in serving congregations made her less concerned about the biblical justification for women's place in the church than for the good work women could do as pastors. As we will see also in Anna Howard Shaw's writings on women in ministry, the pragmatic argument dominated Brown's defense. She sug-

40. Ibid.

gested that the ideal church staff configuration, frequently seen in the church today, would consist of a man and a woman putting their individual gifts to best use in the work of the church:

> It is often said of a preacher "he is a good preacher but no pastor. He does not call upon his people." This is because one man cannot do everything, and the same person is not usually suited to both pastoral work and pulpit service. Many of the larger churches now have two ministers for this reason. One of these should be a woman.[41]

The problem in securing good women pastors was not the lack of qualified women, Brown concluded, but the lack of sufficient encouragement of their gifts for ministry and the lack of welcome offered to them by the church. "Our church papers are always calling for preachers," she reasoned, "and if women were welcome and made efficient preachers as they would be in that case, many women would come into the ministry. But women are not encouraged to enter the ministry." She defended her argument with the example of an incident at a Universalist convention she had attended in La Crosse, Wisconsin. The audience was composed primarily of women, yet the speaker, a male minister, addressed only the young men present when encouraging them to attend coeducational Lombard University.

> I called out, "What about young women, Doctor?" He replied that no church had ever asked that a woman pastor be sent so far as he knew. He then described the difficulties which a woman would encounter; but, said he, "if a woman accepts these difficulties Lombard is hers." I afterwards showed him that such a talk as he had given created a public sentiment against women's preaching.[42]

Brown maintained that ministers themselves were primarily "responsible for the limited number of women who enter the ministry." The sentiment perpetuated by people like the speaker at the Universalist convention discouraged churches from seeking women pastors. She noted, however, that in spite of the discouragement and small remuneration offered to women, many had succeeded in obtaining theological

41. Olympia Brown, *An Autobiography*, ed. Gwendolen B. Willis, *Annual Journal of the Universalist Historical Society* 4 (1963): 43–44.
42. Ibid., 44.

educations and church positions. A new attitude of acceptance toward women ministers and intentional efforts to direct women toward careers in ministry would only enhance the work of the church:

> Our women's colleges are filled with young women, many of whom, with proper encouragement, would make good ministers. We must present the needs of the church and the fitness of the profession for women to these students. The difficulties and discouragements in their way must be overcome by the indefatigable efforts of individual women, so that prejudices will be conquered and church rules, where necessary, amended.[43]

Olympia Brown's life experiences proved her final statements. Through her own efforts, she overcame the difficulties and discouragements placed in her way by skeptical family members, uncooperative mentors, and intransigent institutions. As a result, more than any other individual woman in the Universalist tradition, she managed to conquer and even amend church rules. In the process, Brown was forced both to justify her own place in the church and to ensure that other women would have a place. She was not the biblical exegete that Brown Blackwell was, although she used biblical arguments in support of women in ministry and women's equality in general. Perhaps her most significant contribution to the rhetorical debate over women in ministry was to examine and explain the relationship between woman's nature and her suitability for ministry. By twenty-first-century standards her argument is decidedly unfeminist and even detrimental to the progress of women, but in the 1860s, Brown's argument created a way of acknowledging what traditionalists held dear, that is, a belief in the essential differences and unique natures of men and women, while using that same, otherwise conservative, argument to support a radical new idea.

Anna Howard Shaw

Like her predecessors, Anna Howard Shaw was forced to justify her claim to ecclesiastical leadership early in her ministerial career. As she was often the only woman in a class full of young men, she had to be prepared to defend her place. She recalled an amusing exchange with a seminary pro-

43. Ibid.

fessor who was adamantly opposed to her presence in his classroom and to the philosophical idea of women preachers. Like other preaching women, Shaw relied on the text from Acts 2 describing the events of the day of Pentecost as biblical evidence of women's equality in the church. She questioned the professor about a crucial verse in the text (v.17) that states, "In the last days . . . I will pour out of my Spirit upon all flesh: and your sons and your daughters shall prophesy."

> And I innocently said to the professor, "What does prophesy mean?" "Well," he said, "it depends on where it is used; in the Old Testament they use it in a double sense, in the sense of foretelling or in the sense of preaching, but in the New Testament it is used wholly in the sense of preaching. When the word prophesy is used in the New Testament it means that they shall preach." "Oh," I said, "then women did preach, did they not, at the time of Pentecost?" He was bitterly opposed to women preaching—didn't want me there. He said, "No, oh no, the women talked to each other." I said, "Yes, and what did the men do? Talk to each other?" He said, "Oh no they preached." And I said, "But the two are connected by a conjunction, 'men and women,' and when women talk they talk, and when men talk they preach; is that the way it was?" He said, "We will resume."[44]

That early exegetical battle proved to be only the first of many Shaw fought to secure her right to serve in ministry. Like other preaching women, she mined the Bible for examples and images of strong and faithful women. In her first sermon, for example, she referred to Vashti, the deposed queen in the book of Esther. Her first formal essay on "Women in the Ministry" opened with this statement of the place of women in Judeo-Christian history:

> From the earliest history of the Hebrews women were teachers, prophetesses and servants of the church. The recorded ministry of Miriam the prophetess and joint leader with her brother of the hosts of Israel; of Deborah who became the theocratic ruler and judge of her nation; of the little Hebrew maid whose evangelistic fervor led Naaman to bow before the true God; of Anna the prophetess who "departed not from the temple"; with scores of other illustrious

44. Anna Howard Shaw, "Testimony Before New Jersey Legislature, January 25, 1915," also referred to by the title "We Demand Equal Voting Qualifications," AHSP, SL, Fol. 463.

names will remain forever famous in the history of the Hebrew nation.[45]

In 1898, Shaw set forth her mature thoughts on the ecclesiastical service of women in an article also titled "Women in the Ministry." By then, almost a generation after her own ordination, a significant number of women were serving in a variety of ecclesiastical roles. It has proved impossible for historians to calculate the precise number of women who served as pastors, lay and licensed preachers, professional exhorters and itinerants, deaconesses, Christian Science readers, and Salvation Army officers, and in other recognized roles in the many traditions that constituted American Protestantism by the turn of the twentieth century.[46] There was, however, both statistical evidence of women's ministries and common knowledge of their work. Therefore, Shaw was correct when she opened her essay with the following assertion: "It is impossible, with the limited data obtainable, to make an exact statement of the number of women ministers or the value of their services." She might have been a bit optimistic in her next statement, however: "Judging from the rapid increase of the past ten years it is safe to say that the dawn of the twentieth century will see not less than two thousand women preaching the gospel in the United States."[47]

The history of women in ministry compiled by Shaw testified to the changing ecclesiastical climate of the second half of the nineteenth century. She listed the names and service of several of the earliest ordained women in America, such as Antoinette Brown Blackwell, Olympia Brown, Lydia Sexton of the United Brethren Church, and Unitarian Mary Augusta Safford. Shaw also explored the denominations that remained opposed to women's ordination and even, as in the case of the Presbyterian Church, opposed to women's preaching. "The Presbyterian Church," Shaw declared, "refuses to ordain women, and a clause in the 'blue book' prohibits ministers of that denomination from inviting women into their pulpits, but this rule is constantly and wisely violated."[48] Her former denomination, the Methodist Episcopal Church, refused to ordain

---

45. Anna Howard Shaw, "Women in the Ministry" (1879), AHSP, SL, Fol. 420.

46. See the discussion of the difficulty of obtaining accurate figures concerning ordained and preaching women at the end of the nineteenth century in Carl J. and Dorothy Schneider, *In Their Own Right* (New York: Crossroad Publishing, 1997), 99, n.105.

47. Anna Howard Shaw, "Women in the Ministry," *Chautauquan* 18 (August 1898): 489.

48. Ibid., 490. The "blue book" to which Shaw referred was the constitution of the Presbyterian Church that governed the activities of Presbyterian churches and clergy.

women yet recognized their service in nonordained capacities. Shaw did not conceal her frustration with such denominations, nor did she hesitate to gloat about the obvious effectiveness of women engaged in various ministries:

> There are several hundred women evangelists doing a work which is not surpassed by that of the pulpits, and which is indisputable proof that they are God-ordained even though refused ordination by man. A large part of the missionary work, home and foreign, of all the churches is in the hands of women.[49]

After recounting the good work accomplished by women in ministry, Shaw resorted to the pragmatic argument that figured prominently in the rhetoric supporting women's preaching and ordination in the debates of the nineteenth century. "It is difficult," she lamented, "to understand the attitude of a denomination which will refuse to ordain the inspired women whose evangelistic work has brought thousands into a religious life, and yet which gladly ordains every young stripling of a boy fresh from the theological seminary."[50]

Shaw moved on to address the arguments raised against women in ministry, realistic about the unrelenting problems and struggles that would hinder women pastors:

> Notwithstanding women pastors have demonstrated their fitness for the work, most churches which avail themselves of their services are not quite ready to accept them on the same grounds as men. There is still a sensitiveness on the part of these denominations that the admission of women ministers is a tacit acknowledgment of weakness. The prejudice of the past and the conservatism of the present hinder them from receiving the same open, generous welcome which is extended to men. This reacts upon the women themselves and they are conscious of an unexpressed, and it may be unacknowledged, antagonism. This restrains the freedom of their thoughts, expressions, and actions, necessarily cripples their powers, and prevents their giving the best service of which they are capable.

49. Ibid., 491.
50. Ibid.

The appropriate resolution to this situation required a change of mind and heart that would foster full acceptance of women's work:

> Until women are received with the same cordial welcome as men, have the same representation on official boards, are accorded the same rights in the ministerial office, and are as heartily urged and assisted to enter it, there can be no fair comparison between their work and that of men pastors.

Perhaps that lack of welcome was why Shaw discouraged young women from entering the ministry despite her own generally positive experience as a pastor:

> Many young women come to me for counsel in regard to entering the ministry as a life work, but I am unable to encourage them, because I know how unwelcome they will be to the orthodox churches and how difficult every step of the way will be made. Men find it hard to contend with "the world, the flesh, and the devil," and it is asking too much of women to add to these the church also.

In the end, Shaw believed, the church would be incomplete without the gifts of women in ministry, and, she concluded, "it would be as undesirable to have only women ministers as it is now to have only men in that position. The church needs the two, and both can do better work together than either can do alone."[51]

Like Olympia Brown, Anna Howard Shaw's apologetic for women in ministry contains glimpses of the argument that characterized her suffrage rhetoric. And like Brown, her argument assumes that the essential nature of women is more suited than that of men to the pastoral responsibilities of ministry and more capable of uplifting individual souls and entire congregations to higher spiritual and moral ideals. The role of the clergy had changed, Shaw asserted, making the participation of women in the ministry more appropriate than ever before:

> Since the office of minister is no longer that of school-master, and he is not so much a propounder of theological dogmas as a persuader of mankind toward a life of purity and righteousness, woman seems particularly adapted to the ministry. Her superior persuasive powers

51. Ibid., 493, 494, 495.

render her especially effective in leading men to higher thoughts and purer lives.[52]

By the time Shaw wrote this defense of women in ministry, late-nineteenth-century industrialization was being held responsible for the moral and spiritual climate of America. The emphasis on work and the accumulation of wealth became primary targets of religious and political spokespersons who perceived a connection between economic progress and social decay, and Shaw explored that connection in her defense of women ministers who, she claimed, had the potential to restore the moral standards of the nation:

> Men, wearied with the turmoil of life, harassed by the rush and clamor of the market-place, attend religious services to be soothed and comforted, fed on holy thoughts, and encouraged by the inspiration of a diviner life. They seek to be shown that they are not mere human machines, but carry in themselves a spark of the divine which may be kindled into a sacred flame. Who so well as woman can bring rest to these tired hearts, peace to these sinful souls, and at the same time arouse the moral and spiritual nature to noble action?[53]

Who, indeed, but a woman minister, when "untrammeled and allowed the fullest use of her highest powers," will be "most successful in drawing men into the church"? Women ministers could certainly do no worse than their male counterparts, Shaw concluded, for men were already conspicuous by their absence "in the congregations of our large churches to-day where male preachers of unquestioned ability have officiated for years." Any logical mind, she reasoned, was "forced to conclude that a change of some kind is an imperative necessity." And, of course, besides drawing men who were preoccupied with the business world back to the church, women pastors could more effectively minister to the women and children who made up the majority of church participants.

As if to anticipate feminist criticism of her argument and its acceptance of woman's essential nature, Shaw concluded her essay with appeals to the divine rights and human equality of women. She admitted that it was impossible to predict the ultimate result of women's ministerial work. But, she believed,

52. Ibid.
53. Ibid.

their power in the pulpit and their especial fitness for the pastorate will be developed and shown in proportion as the church makes them free. So long as they are permitted to officiate only in small and poor parishes; so long as many denominations continue to oppose their preaching as contrary to the Scriptures and antagonistic to the best interests of the church; and so long as both internal and external influences combine to limit and dwarf to its greatest possible insignificance all that women do in this office—just so long will their real value as pastor and preacher remain unknown.[54]

Such restrictions on the use of women's gifts for ministry were not only unfair but dangerous in that "the spiritual advance of the kingdom of Christ will be hindered and delayed." In the meantime, women ministers could only continue to labor in "barren and untried fields," working to prove their capabilities for ministry to "cold and skeptical denominations." Shaw realized at the turn of the twentieth century what continues to be the case in the twenty-first century: women in ministry not only have to do their work as well as men,

but they will be compelled to prove themselves superior before just recognition will be accorded them. They have had to stand this crucial test in every other department of the world's work, and the church will prove no exception to the rule. The last of the learned professions to accord to women equal opportunities with men will be the ministry; and yet the church is founded upon the sublime declaration, "God is no respecter of persons," and, "There is neither male nor female, for ye are all one in Christ Jesus the Lord."[55]

"In the light of a great innovation": The First Female Ordinations

Antoinette Brown Blackwell

For three years after her graduation from the theological program at Oberlin, Brown Blackwell traveled around the country lecturing on behalf of the newly organized woman's rights movement, preaching in churches, and, above all else, seeking a congregation that would ordain

54. Ibid., 496.
55. Ibid.

her and provide a settled place where she could serve as a pastor in fulfillment of her call to ministry. She was well received as a preacher and
lecturer, but she did not succeed in having what she perceived as a divine
call to ministry acknowledged by human ecclesiastical authority. In 1852,
Horace Greeley and Charles Dana of the *New York Tribune* offered to rent
a hall in New York City where Brown Blackwell could preach regularly
for a year. The offer was quite remarkable and surely affirmed Brown
Blackwell's gifts for preaching and speaking, but her youthful insecurities
and the persistent sense of call to congregational ministry caused her to
reject the offer. Her continued requests to the faculty at Oberlin College
for ordination by the community in which she was educated as a theologian were denied, prompting this expression of frustration in a letter to
Lucy Stone in the summer of 1852:

> I am not ordained yet either, so you may rejoice and welcome; but
> what a milk sop you must take me to be, if I can be manufactured over
> in to a "would-be-but-can't-priest" by so simple a ceremony as ordi-
> nation. It is well that certain grave divines should have drawn back
> just in time, for they were on the very brink of the fatal spring over
> the great wall of custom. A little more and I should have been a man
> acknowledged minister, but somebody happened to think that
> though a woman might preach she ought not to administer the sacra-
> ment, &c. Others thought this and that, so they joined hands and
> turning around walked backwards together, and I took up my bundle
> and walked home.[56]

By the spring of 1853, Brown Blackwell at last found the situation for
which she had looked so long. The congregation in South Butler, New
York, that had first heard her speak while she was on a preaching tour of
upstate New York invited her to be their pastor. After considering the
offer for several months, Brown Blackwell accepted it and moved to South
Butler in the spring of 1853. Her responsibilities were typical for pastors
in the mid-nineteenth century: preaching twice on Sunday and caring for
the congregation. She also continued lecturing and traveling for woman's
rights and other causes, making her life busy and full. By June, she wrote
to Stone:

56. Antoinette Brown Blackwell to Lucy Stone, August 4, 1852, BFP, LC.

Have hardly got settled here yet. Have a good boarding place in the village with a firm of doctors. Had an overflowing house Sunday last, have two Sermons to prepare for Sunday next, and its now Friday afternoon.[57]

Pastoral ministry fit the abilities and interests of Brown Blackwell. In a letter to Gerrit Smith, her colleague in the abolitionist movement, she remarked, "The pastoral labors at S. Butler suit me even better than I expected & my heart is full of hope."[58] As she reflected years later in her autobiography:

My little parish was a miniature world in good and evil. To get humanity condensed into so small a compass that you can study each individual member opens a new chapter of experience. It makes one thoughtful and rolls upon the spirit a burden of deep responsibility.[59]

During her first several months at South Butler, Brown Blackwell functioned fully as the pastor, preacher, and liturgical leader of the congregation and even administered the sacraments, the one aspect of ministry usually reserved for ordained clergy. The congregation was well pleased with her work, prompting the church board to move toward her ordination. Since she had been, in fact, functioning as an ordained minister, the ordination would represent no alteration in her activities or responsibilities but would, instead, represent a significant alteration in and major statement of the congregation's regard for her.

What is notable about the process leading to Brown Blackwell's ordination—something that will be noted in relation to the ordinations of Brown and Shaw as well—is the lack of significant debate and angst that accompanied the monumental act of ordaining a woman. Unlike the debates concerning women's ordination that raged for decades in many Protestant denominations in the twentieth century (and continue to rage in some traditions into the twenty-first century), Brown Blackwell's ordination occurred with little discussion or fanfare. It grew quite naturally out of her faithful service in the ministerial role. The members of the board of the Congregational Church in South Butler knew that, accord-

57. Antoinette Brown Blackwell to Lucy Stone, June 10, 1853, BFP, LC.

58. Antoinette Brown Blackwell to Gerrit Smith, August 16, 1853, as recorded in Elizabeth Cazden, *Antoinette Brown Blackwell* (Old Westbury, N.Y.: Feminist Press, 1983), 75.

59. Gilson ms., 158.

ing to the polity of their denomination, it was within their purview to ordain Brown Blackwell without the approval of any higher ecclesiastical authority. They also knew, however, that their action would be unprecedented and attract much attention and even more criticism from voices within and beyond the church. Gerrit Smith, by then a congressman from the state of New York, was invited to speak at the ordination ceremony to, as one deacon of the church put it, make them "all feel stronger."[60] In a communication with Smith about the event, Brown Blackwell made clear her understanding of the symbolic importance of the ordination:

> We do not care whether the ceremony is performed in the usual way or not. We only want something done to show the world that we believe in a woman's being initiated into the ministry and something which will answer without questioning as a legal ordination in the eyes of the Law & Public Opinion. . . . Every person present may express himself opposed to all ordination & welcome, if he will only be willing in addition to put woman upon the same platform with man, & recognise me as much a minister as others. I already take part in administering the Sacraments &c. . . . It will do them good, and me good, & good to the cause of woman.[61]

Smith did attend and speak at the ordination, unlike Brown Blackwell's fellow Congregational clergymen from the area. Whether those other ministers disagreed with the action of the South Butler congregation or simply feared for their reputations were they involved in such a radical act as the ordination of a woman will never be known. Even Brown Blackwell's liberal colleagues from the woman's rights movement such as Unitarians William Henry Channing and Samuel J. May chose not to attend the ordination for fear of branding Brown Blackwell herself as a liberal Protestant rather than an orthodox Congregationalist.

As if a portent of the challenges to come, September 15, 1853, the ordination day, brought with it a violent rainstorm. Nevertheless, the members of the South Butler Congregational Church and many visitors, including a reporter sent from the *New York Tribune*, gathered at two in the afternoon for the historic event. The service had to be held in the building of the local Baptist Society due to the size of the crowd expected.

60. Antoinette Brown Blackwell to Gerrit Smith, August 23, 1853, as recorded in Cazden, *Antoinette Brown Blackwell*, 77.
61. Ibid.

After a choir anthem, an opening prayer, and a hymn, one of the church's deacons, Mr. Caudee, spoke to the reason for the gathering. After stating that their church did not believe in the necessity of ordination as a qualification to preach the gospel, he asked:

> Why then have an ordination? The church needs to be instructed, and it is well, for pastors and for people, to be reminded of their duties to each other, therefore we have invited a few friends to be with us and to recognize with us the relationship between ourselves and pastor.[62]

The Reverend Luther Lee delivered the ordination sermon, recounting the gifts of ministry given to women throughout the history of the church and acknowledging the validity of Brown Blackwell's call by God to this extraordinary work. He concluded:

> We are here assembled on a very interesting and solemn occasion, and it is proper to advert to the real object for which we have come together. There are in the world, and there may be among us, false views of the nature and object of ordination. I do not believe that any special or specific form of ordination is necessary to constitute a gospel minister. We are not here to make a minister. It is not to confer on this our sister, a right to preach the gospel. If she has not that right already, we have no power to communicate it to her. Nor have we met to qualify her for the work of the ministry. If God and mental and moral culture have not already qualified her, we cannot, by anything we may do by way of ordaining or setting her apart. Nor can we, by imposition of our hands, confer on her any special grace for the work of the ministry, . . . All we are here to do, and all we expect to do, is, in due form, and by a solemn and impressive service, to subscribe our testimony to the fact, that in our belief, our sister in Christ, Antoinette L. Brown, is one of the ministers of the New Covenant, authorized, qualified, and called of God to preach the gospel of his Son Jesus Christ. This is all, but this even renders the occasion interesting and solemn.[63]

Gerrit Smith also addressed the congregation and confirmed their choice of pastor and the gifts that Brown Blackwell brought to ordained

---

62. "Ordination of the Rev. Antoinette L. Brown," *New York Tribune*, September 19, 1853.
63. Lee, *Five Sermons and a Tract*, 99.

ministry. Smith "spoke not only for the cause of womanhood, fully endorsing the equality of the sexes," Brown Blackwell recalled, "but his charge to the church was fine and timely and his remarks to the minister were sympathetic, encouraging and strengthening."[64] He congratulated the South Butler congregation on choosing a pastor "who is wise, and strong, and good, and faithful, and trusting, and full of love." He also commended their boldness in hiring a woman and predicted, "The day is coming—and is not that a happy future?—when merit and capability will be the ground of choice. Will it not be a day of common sense, when powers and ability will be the tests for any station?"[65] Perhaps to balance the solemnity of the occasion, later in the ceremony Smith sneaked a note to Brown Blackwell with a poem he had penned:

> This pouring rain doth make it clear,
> That silly woman must not teach;
> When will you learn, my sister dear,
> That noble man alone should preach?
> So now, Miss Brown, just stay at home,
> Tend babies, knit, and sew, and cook;
> And, then, some nice young man will come
> And on you cast a loving look.[66]

In a coincidental display of female professional progress, Boston physician Harriot Hunt, one of the first women medical doctors in the United States, attended the ordination. She happened to be in Syracuse visiting abolitionist friends and, hearing of the event, she

> went thence to South Butler to attend the ordination of Antoinette L. Brown. The storm raged, but even an equinoctial tempest could not detain me from being present, on an occasion so monumental to the cause of woman; there was something grand and elevating in the idea of a female presiding over a congregation, and breaking to them the bread of life—it was a new position for woman, and gave promise of her exaltation to that moral and intellectual rank, which she was designed to fill.

64. Gilson ms., 156.
65. "Ordination of the Rev. Antoinette L. Brown," *New York Tribune*.
66. Gerrit Smith to Antoinette Brown Blackwell, September 15, 1853, BFP, SL, Fol. 54.

Hunt was particularly drawn to the celebration, she admitted, because

> the subject of woman in the ministry had occupied much thought,
> and the more I pondered it, the more convinced I was that her love
> nature and the strength of the religious element in her, fitted her
> peculiarly to bind up the broken heart, to sympathize with the peni-
> tent, to strengthen the weak, to raise the fallen, and to infuse hope
> and trust in the Divine.[67]

The following Monday, the *New York Tribune* carried an extensive report
titled "Ordination of the Rev. Antoinette L. Brown" written by the paper's
editor, Horace Greeley, who commented:

> Heaven bless this society [the South Butler congregation]! and surely
> it is blessed. Composed mostly of farmers, whose thoughts have
> room to range 'neath the broad sky, whose opinions conservatism
> cannot trammel; the assemblage on the Sabbath fills the little brown
> meeting house to overflowing. Nor will it be to its disadvantage that
> in the growing favor of its pastor this people have deemed it wise to
> remove every restriction that custom or legal statute impose, on her
> performing the various religious and civil ordinances devolving on a
> Gospel minister.[68]

In her memoirs, Brown Blackwell reflected on the momentous event:
"It seemed to me a very solemn thing when our three deacons and these
clergymen all stood around me each placing a hand upon my head or
shoulder and gravely admitting me into the ranks of ministry."[69] While
Brown Blackwell seemed to sense the gravity of the occasion, her recol-
lection of the ordination was not unlike that of anyone who has been similarly recognized. Like the other women who were among the pioneers of
female ordination, she seemed unaware of the monumental nature of her
ordination. She and her early sisters in ministry gave evidence of a naïveté
born of the certainty of their convictions.

As noted above, Brown Blackwell's ordination was unaccompanied by
any rancorous debate, at least within the congregation she served and

---

67. Harriot K. Hunt, *Glances and Glimpses; or Fifty Years Social, Including Twenty Years Professional Life* (Boston: John P. Jewett, 1856), 304.

68. "Ordination of the Rev. Antoinette L. Brown," *New York Tribune*.

69. Gilson ms., 156.

which served as the ordaining body. The Congregational context certainly was a significant factor in bringing about this momentous "first." The fact that Brown Blackwell was doing an admirable job as pastor of the South Butler congregation proved more influential in the decision to ordain her than the theological and biblical arguments that could have prohibited the ordination. The church's location in New York also meant there was a favorable climate for such a departure from tradition, for the state had become known for its progressive stances, particularly in terms of woman's rights and other social reforms. A report in the *History of Woman Suffrage* recounts the many "firsts" attributed to New York:

> In this State, the preliminary battles in the anti-slavery, temperance, educational, and religious societies were fought; the first Governmental aid given to the higher education of woman, and her voice first heard in teachers' associations. Here the first Woman's Rights Convention was held, the first demand made for suffrage, the first society formed for this purpose, and the first legislative efforts made to secure the civil and political rights of women; . . . Here too the pulpit made the first demand for the political rights of woman. Here was the first temperance society formed by women, the first medical college opened to them, and woman first ordained for the ministry.[70]

Surely the history of openness to new ideas and support for liberal causes that came to characterize the state of New York had something to do with the willingness of the South Butler congregation to ordain Antoinette Brown Blackwell before a congregation in any other region of the nation. Although that openness resulted in very different ecclesiastical and religious expressions, ranging from the evangelistic triumphs of Charles Grandison Finney to the founding of utopian communities and the Mormon Church to unprecedented public leadership opportunities for women, all those expressions appear rooted in the same penchant for religious innovation.

Olympia Brown

Interestingly, New York state was also the location of the next ordination of an American Protestant woman, that of Olympia Brown in 1863. The

---

70. *History of Woman Suffrage*, I:472.

circumstances that led to Brown's ordination by the Northern Universalist Association were both similar to and different from the circumstances leading to Brown Blackwell's ordination ten years earlier. Like Brown Blackwell, Brown found no support for her call to ordained ministry among the theological educators who had admitted her to their degree program. Ebenezer Fisher, the president of the St. Lawrence University Theological School in Canton, New York, had tried to discourage Brown from entering his institution. While agreeing to admit her and provide her with all the opportunities afforded the other students, all male, he made it clear in his response to her initial inquiry that "he did not think women were called to the ministry. 'But,' he said, 'I leave that between you and the Great Head of the Church.'" "This, I thought," Brown later reflected, "was just where it should be left, and I could not ask anything better." Her arrival at St. Lawrence, however, surprised President Fisher, who thought his discouraging words would be enough to turn her away. Nevertheless, he accepted her presence on campus, never discriminating against her "until I began to take steps looking toward ordination."[71]

Despite unrelenting challenges from her male teachers and colleagues in divinity school, Brown's commitment to ordination grew during her two years of theological education. She found herself continually ridiculed, mimicked, and mocked by her fifteen classmates. Every student was required to write and read a sermon before the class each week, and the other students were particularly critical of her work. "The young men usually indulged in very derogatory remarks about my sermons," Brown recalled, "which I found hard to bear. The mildest of these criticisms was this frequent one: 'Well, it was very good, but I should hardly call it a sermon.'"[72]

It is not surprising that, of all the work involved in theological education, Brown's preaching was most vulnerable to criticism. More than any other pastoral activity, preaching has been historically most representative of the pastoral office for those traditions (including Universalism) that do not place a significant emphasis on the sacraments. In addition, as noted above, preaching became a subversive act when done by women since they transgressed both biblical and cultural norms by speaking publicly to mixed audiences and interpreting Scripture for proclamation. Brown, however, must have felt a great sense of vindication later in her career when she was described as "the female Beecher of the rostrum."

71. Brown, *Autobiography*, 27.
72. Ibid.

She noted with some irony in her autobiography that her two greatest detractors among the student body both left ministry within a year of their entrance, "for I think they could not have had the right spirit, and their ministry would only have been a make-believe."[73]

Considering the prejudice and frustrations she endured to achieve ordination, Brown's ministry certainly could not be called a "make-believe." She had no difficulty finding preaching assignments in churches in New York and Vermont. In fact, by the second year of her theological program, she had the confidence to begin the process of ordination. Since the Universalist tradition did not require her to have a "call" or invitation from a church to serve as pastor before being ordained, she was able to pursue the credential of ordination while still studying and serving as an itinerant preacher. Like Antoinette Brown Blackwell, Brown realized that the faculty and administrators of her own school would not ordain her despite their power to do so and their repeated affirmation of her work, including praise for her sermons from President Fisher.

When she learned in the spring of 1863 that the Northern Universalist Association was to hold its annual meeting in nearby Malone, New York, she decided to make application to the ordaining council for ordination. President Fisher warned Brown of his opposition to her request for ordination, "speaking in a significant manner which seemed to say that I would be sorry for he would oppose me."[74] What Fisher did not reckon with was the support and good will that Brown had generated through her pulpit work in Universalist churches throughout the northern New York area. Fortuitously, she had preached the week before the association's meeting in a church at Heuvelton and had been invited to serve as pastor of the church. Even more fortuitously, Brown recalled,

> a delegate from Heuvelton was a member of the ordaining council, so I went into the presence of that body feeling quite confident, and although there was much discussion and opposition, I spoke for myself, and when the vote was taken, it was in my favor.[75]

The Northern Universalist Association set the date of June 25, 1863, for Olympia Brown's ordination. There is no extant information on the service of ordination, no sermon text or newspaper accounts such as there

73. Ibid.
74. Ibid., 29–30.
75. Ibid., 30.

are for Brown Blackwell's earlier ordination service. Even Brown's own recollections of the event are scant. The one thing she does note in her autobiography concerns President Fisher's change of heart. "Mr. Fisher," she stated, "had so far overcome his feelings that he took part in the exercises." Apparently, however, his wife did not have a change of heart and warned, just after the ordination ceremony, " 'You will see now the consequences of this. Next year there will be fifteen women in the class, and then women will flock to the ministry.' " Another observer feared that " 'the profession would soon be swamped with women who would bring down the price of preaching.' " Years later Brown wrote, "Such comments seem laughable to us now." Indeed, writing more than sixty years later, she noted with some regret that those fears were unfounded as not more than sixty women were, at that time (1925), preaching in Universalist churches:

> How slight an understanding of the value and importance of the ministerial service comments like those quoted above imply. If there really were women truly prepared for the ministry, and sincerely called to that service, could there be too many of them? Surely no one could think so who was actuated by no smaller motive than to spread the teachings for which the church stood.[76]

Shortly after her ordination, Brown completed the degree and graduated from St. Lawrence on July 9, 1863, now confronting the next hurdle of acceptance as she sought a church position. To her surprise, and "in spite of the prophecy of an opposing student that 'if she sought an appointment to preach there would be a gradual turning up of noses,' I found a pastorate immediately and have never once met the appalling reception predicted by the student."[77] An invitation came from a church in Marshfield, Vermont, not far from her extended family. It was made clear to Brown, however, that her first Sunday "was to be a trial. If they liked it I was to go on; otherwise not."[78] The "trial" went well, and she stayed on at the Marshfield church and added the responsibility of another small church in East Montpelier. She remained at the churches until the fall of 1863 when family circumstances caused her to leave the two churches and return to Michigan.

76. Ibid.

77. Olympia Brown, *Acquaintances, Old and New, Among Reformers* (Milwaukee, Wis.: Press of S. E. Tate Printing, 1911), 30–31.

78. Brown, *Autobiography*, 31.

Anna Howard Shaw

It was in the "silent woods" of Brown's home state of Michigan that Anna Howard Shaw first acknowledged her own call to preach, standing on stumps to address "the unresponsive trees."[79] In fact, at about the same time that Brown returned to her Michigan home before seeking a permanent parish position, Shaw was preaching to the trees in the woods of the same state. Shaw's family had been less willing to entertain the idea of a college education for a woman than either Brown Blackwell's or Brown's families had been. She herself admitted that, as a young teenager, so far as she knew no woman had gone to college. Family opposition, financial constraints, and the intrusion of the Civil War delayed her pursuit of a college education until she garnered the courage to repudiate her family's warnings and set off on her own to pursue her call to ministry.

More than a decade after Brown's graduation from St. Lawrence and more than two decades after Brown Blackwell's completion of the theology program at Oberlin, Shaw still faced opposition to her presence in the Boston University School of Theology from both faculty members and classmates. If experiencing prejudice and isolation as the only woman in her theological class were not enough, Shaw faced poverty and hunger that threatened to destroy her physically. The men in the theological program received room and board, but a misplaced woman was given nothing. When she received a rare invitation to preach, she did not know what or even if she would be paid. Eventually, a weekly stipend from an anonymous benefactor through the Woman's Foreign Missionary Society of Boston enabled her to complete her theological degree and alleviated her financial concerns.

After her graduation from the Boston School of Theology and a trip to Europe as part of a bequest from a woman whom she had befriended during her first summer supply pastorate, Shaw was invited to serve as pastor of the First Wesleyan Methodist Society of East Dennis and Brewster on Cape Cod. The congregation had been affiliated with the Free Methodist denomination, but by the time of Shaw's arrival, it was independent of any connectional church. This independent history and spirit might account for the willingness of the congregation to accept Shaw's leadership. Also, the congregation had come to know Shaw during her summer supply work on Cape Cod, another factor that surely convinced them to take the unusual

---

79. Anna Howard Shaw with Elizabeth Jordan, *The Story of a Pioneer* (New York: Harper & Brothers Publishers, 1915), 44.

step of calling a woman pastor. She began her ministry in October 1878 with great enthusiasm for her first full-time pastorate. "My previous occupation of various pulpits," she later recalled, "whether long or short, had always been in the role of a substitute. Now, for the first time, I had a church of my own, and was to stand or fall by the record made in it."[80]

While the congregation was united in its support for Shaw and welcoming of her ministry, she did not realize that members were divided by a long-standing dispute, the origin of which no one could any longer recall:

> The ink was barely dry on my diploma from the Boston Theological School, and, as it happened, the little church to which I was called was in the hands of two warring factions, whose battles furnished the most fervid interest of the Cape Cod community. But my inexperience disturbed me not at all, and I was blissfully ignorant of the division in the congregation. So I entered my new field as trustfully as a child enters a garden; and though I was in trouble from the beginning, and resigned three times in startling succession, I ended by remaining seven years.[81]

After two tumultuous years and three tendered (but refused) resignations, Shaw settled down to several more years during which "the relations between my people and myself were wholly harmonious and beautiful."[82] Shaw earned a reputation as a strong and capable leader, much of that reputation having been honed in the process of mediating congregational disputes. Early in her tenure at East Dennis, she and the women of the church repainted and refurbished the building, doing much of the work and all of the fund-raising themselves. Several months after she began her work at the First Wesleyan Church, a Congregational church in Dennis asked her to serve as their pastor as well. For the next six years, she served both churches, preaching for her original congregation in East Dennis on Sunday mornings and traveling to Dennis to preach for the Congregational congregation on Sunday afternoons.

Despite the obvious fulfillment and success that Shaw achieved through her pastoral work, she realized the limitations imposed on her due to her lack of formal ordination:

80. Ibid., 107.
81. Ibid.
82. Ibid., 121.

But I was in the ministry, and I was greatly handicapped by the fact that, although I was a licensed preacher and a graduate of the Boston Theological School, I could not, until I had been regularly ordained, meet all the functions of my office. I could perform the marriage service, but I could not baptize. I could bury the dead, but I could not take members into my church. That had to be done by the presiding elder or by some other minister. I could not administer the sacraments.[83]

After her unsuccessful attempt, with Anna Oliver, to obtain permission for ordination from the New England Spring Conference of the Methodist Episcopal Church in 1880, Shaw took her request, on the suggestion of a ministerial colleague who had witnessed her rejection by the Methodist Episcopal Conference, to the Methodist Protestant Church. The "celebrated contest," as Shaw referred to it, over her ordination took place at the Methodist Protestant Conference held in the Methodist Protestant Church of Tarrytown, New York, in October 1880. Shaw acknowledged,

For three days I was a storm-center around which a large number of truly good and wholly sincere men fought the fight of their religious lives. Many of them strongly believed that women were out of place in the ministry. I did not blame them for this conviction.[84]

Nevertheless, Shaw argued that she already was in the ministry and serving quite effectively although significantly "handicapped," as she described it, by her lack of ordination.

When Shaw's petition to the Conference came up for consideration, the usually perfunctory discussion over a candidate's fitness for ordination brought the procedures of the Conference to a halt. Shaw waited outside the meeting room for what turned from hours into days. Two days after the request was presented, the opponents of women's ordination had found their loophole: they declared that because she was not a member of the denomination to which she had applied for ordination, her request must be denied. Undaunted, the pastor of the church where the Conference was meeting and a supporter of Shaw gathered the trustees of the congregation late that Saturday night to act on Shaw's application for church membership. Within five minutes, she was a member of the

83. Ibid., 122.
84. Ibid.

Methodist Protestant Church in Tarrytown. Unfortunately, it was too late for her request to be considered by the Conference participants. "I was now a member of the Church," Shaw recalled, "but it was too late to obtain any further action from the Conference. The next day, Sunday, all the men who applied for ordination were ordained, and I was left out."[85]

The persistence of Shaw and her supporters paid off, however, as her case was reopened on Monday morning at the final session of the Conference. As she had done all of her life, she had to fight for human—and especially ecclesiastical—recognition of what she believed she was called by God to do. The Conference members subjected her to a period of intensive, often ridiculous questioning. Shaw responded to their queries with her characteristic sense of humor. While the session was grueling and annoying, Shaw confessed that "several of the episodes that occurred [that morning] were very amusing." One particularly agitated elderly gentleman "led the opposition by racing up and down the aisles, quoting from the Scriptures to prove his case against women ministers," and in the process revealing the strings of his flannel undergarment.

> "Paul said, 'Wives, obey your husbands,'" shouted my old man of the coat-tails. "Suppose your husband should refuse to allow you to preach? What then?"
>
> "In the first place," I answered, "Paul did not say so, according to the Scriptures. But even if he did, it would not concern me, for I am a spinster."
>
> The old man looked me over. "You might marry some day," he predicted, cautiously.
>
> "Possibly," I admitted. "Wiser women than I am have married. But it is equally possible that I might marry a man who would command me to preach; and in that case I want to be all ready to obey him."[86]

The line of questioning continued in this vein, with Shaw meeting both biblical and practical arguments with intelligence and good humor. The most satisfactory exchange, she admitted, occurred with "the downfall of three pert young men" who tried to argue that Shaw might become a financial burden to the denomination if it proved impossible to find a pas-

85. Ibid., 125.
86. Ibid., 126–27.

toral position for her, a responsibility incumbent upon the Conference according to the Methodist system of government. A friend of Shaw's quickly responded to the concern:

> "I have had official occasion to examine into the matter of Miss Shaw's parish and salary," he said, "and I know what salaries the last three speakers are drawing. It may interest the Conference to know that Miss Shaw's present salary equals the combined salaries of the three young men who are so afraid she will be a burden to the Church. If, before being ordained, she can earn three times as much as they now earn after being ordained, it seems fairly clear that they will never have to support her. We can only hope that she will never have to support them."[87]

With that said, Shaw's opponents tempered their remarks but continued the barrage of questioning throughout the day. The prolonged debate enabled her to "gain ground," and by the end of the final business session of the Conference, the delegates voted to ordain her by a large majority. The battle for ordination was contentious and seemed for Shaw to rage "for days." Her ordeal *was* longer and more intense than the debates over the ordinations of Brown Blackwell and Brown (at least as far as the historical records reveal), but it bore no resemblance to many of the wrenching denominational debates over women's ordination that followed in the twentieth century. Perhaps because she was the "storm-center," as she described it, of the battle and because she was physically present for and very much engaged in the battle herself due to the procedural exigencies of the Methodist Protestant Conference, Shaw reflected much more extensively and emotionally on her ordination than did either Brown Blackwell or Brown.

The ordination took place on Tuesday, October 12, 1880, the evening following the Conference's monumental decision, at the Tarrytown Church. Word of the denominational debate and the unique event had spread quickly, ensuring a large crowd. The hope of a good attendance at the ordination prompted the members of the Conference, many of whom had opposed Shaw, to take up a special collection for the support of retired ministers. "The three young men who had feared I would become a burden were especially active in the matter of this collection," Shaw recalled

87. Ibid., 127–28.

with great irony, "and, as they had no sense of humor, it did not seem incongruous to them to use my ordination as a means of raising money for men who had already become burdens to the Church."[88]

A crowd did appear for Shaw's ordination, and she noted that even her opponents took part in the event with grace. The wife of the Conference superintendent, "a dear little old lady of seventy, with a big, maternal heart," rose and escorted Shaw to the altar. Once she had reached the altar, Shaw was overwhelmed by the reality of her accomplishment:

> The ordination service was very impressive and beautiful. Its peace and dignity, following the battle that had raged for days, moved me so deeply that I was nearly overcome. Indeed, I was on the verge of a breakdown when I was mercifully saved by the clause in the discipline calling for the pledge all ministers had to make—that I would not indulge in the use of tobacco. When this vow fell from my lips a perceptible ripple ran over the congregation.[89]

Some years later, she reflected on her accomplishment with her characteristic honesty and good humor:

> So that's how I was ordained. It wasn't very glorious. It was rather like sneaking into the ministry by the back door. But if they won't open the front door to you, what else can you do? Some day they'll open all the front doors and make it a proper use of the enthusiasm for service that women have got—not only in the ministry but everywhere. But until then we've got to keep climbing in the best ways we can. And there's a good deal of fun to be got out of it if you can keep from being bitter and angry.[90]

Shaw returned home to East Dennis immediately after her ordination to once again enter into the work of ministry, arriving there on Saturday night. The next morning, when she entered her church to prepare for the Sunday service, she was greeted with a surprise:

> There I found the communion-table set forth with a beautiful new communion-service. This had been purchased during my absence,

---

88. Ibid., 128–29.
89. Ibid., 129.
90. Anna Howard Shaw, "Ordination," AHSP, SL, Fol. 354.

that I might dedicate it that day and for the first time administer the sacrament to my people.[91]

The "monopoly of the pulpit" Overthrown

Considering the rancorous debates over women's ordination that have challenged—and in some cases, even split—denominations over the past century, the relative ease with which these three women were ushered into the ranks of the ordained clergy is remarkable. The doors to ministry opened for them in ways that they all probably would have admitted had the marks of divine intervention as well as individual determination.

This is not to suggest that their paths were not strewn with obstacles to their ecclesiastical service both before and after their ordinations. All three related painful experiences of discrimination from faculty, administrators, and fellow students throughout their pursuit of theological education. And they all had to endure questions and, in Shaw's case, even alienation from their families because of their chosen profession. Nor would the discrimination end with the pronouncement of their official ordained status. While these women were supported, appreciated, and even deeply loved by members of their congregations, there were constant reminders that they would always be "strangers in strange lands." Their churches included members who were quick to criticize any pastoral decisions with which they disagreed, often turning administrative and leadership issues into issues of gender.

Perhaps most discouraging for them was the lack of support from fellow clergy. After her installation as pastor of the Weymouth Landing church, Olympia Brown joined other clergy in the area to organize an ecumenical memorial service following Lincoln's assassination. Several of the ministers claimed to have changed their minds about participating in the service and left the meeting. It became clear to Brown that the men did not wish to share in a service with a woman minister.[92] Even Luther Lee, the progressive minister who proclaimed that there is "neither male nor female in Christ Jesus" at Antoinette Brown Blackwell's ordination, later refused to sign a certificate testifying to her ordination. "I do not see my way clear to give you such a paper as you ought to have as I did not ordain you," Lee wrote to Brown Blackwell on April 30, 1855. "All I did was to preach a sermon in defense of woman's right to preach the gospel,

---

91. Shaw, *Story of a Pioneer*, 130.
92. See Charlotte Coté, *Olympia Brown* (Racine, Wis.: Mother Courage Press, 1988), 68.

and of that the sermon itself is sufficient proof. But I do not consider that I ordained you by preaching that sermon."[93] He denied any "want of validity in the transaction," but his reaction raises the question of whether he had second thoughts after his participation in the historic ordination.

In spite of the continued challenges to their vocations and qualifications, Brown Blackwell, Brown, and Shaw took great pride in their ordained status. All three used the title "Reverend" throughout their lives, even after they had left full-time parish ministry. Although no one of the three set out to be the first woman ordained in her particular tradition, they all accepted that designation with gratitude, honor, and humility. In addition to the title and honor bestowed by their ordinations, what did ecclesiastical recognition provide for these women that official recognition as preachers and service as pastors could not provide? One practical result of their ordinations was the addition of a sacramental dimension to their ministries. That dimension was perhaps most meaningful to Shaw, who described her frustration in not being allowed to perform all of the liturgical functions of an ordained minister for her congregation.

Less tangibly, perhaps, but more importantly, the ordinations gave these women a sense of affirmation and sanction—both human and divine—of their calls to ministry that enabled them to face the challenges to come. Prior to the mid-1800s, most preaching women rejected the idea that ordained status would change their understandings of the nature of their calls. Most of them described the sense of affirmation they received from God and from the presence of the Holy Spirit that they felt within them as sufficient to justify their unique work. Amanda Berry Smith, an African American Holiness preacher who achieved international fame as an evangelist and missionary during the last quarter of the nineteenth century, expressed the feelings of most of her preaching sisters when she commented on her lack of interest in ordination:

> The thought of ordination had never once entered my mind, for I had received my ordination from Him, who said, "Ye have not chosen me, but I have chosen you, and ordained you, that you might go and bring forth fruit, and that your fruit might remain.". . . I am satisfied with the ordination that the Lord has given me.[94]

93. Luther Lee to Antoinette Brown Blackwell, April 30, 1855, BFP, SL, Fol. 51.
94. Amanda Berry Smith, *An Autobiography: The Story of the Lord's Dealings with Mrs. Amanda Smith the Colored Evangelist* (Chicago: Meyer & Brothers Publishers, 1893), 200, 204.

Early preaching women usually stated that they felt no need for ordination since, as itinerant or licensed preachers, they were able to do what they felt called to do. Another reason for their disinterest in ordination might have had to do with their reluctance to challenge traditional gender roles. "As much as female preachers expanded definitions of womanhood," writes Catherine Brekus, "they also refused to challenge the fundamental sexual inequalities within their churches."[95] There is only one known instance, Brekus adds, of a nineteenth-century woman preacher prior to 1850 asking for ordination or recognition through the laying on of hands.[96]

Perhaps the midcentury shift in ideology that led to the first requests for and granting of ordination to women had to do with what sociologist Mark Chaves describes as the "gender equality frame" that "was brought into religious organizations and thereby changed the meaning of conflicts over women's ordination." As religious women became involved in the growing abolitionist movement—especially the more radical Garrisonian wing of the movement—during the second quarter of the nineteenth century, Chaves argues, a "language of equal rights" came to dominate their rhetoric. Looking at the influence of the Grimké sisters and other religious women, especially Quaker women such as Lucretia Mott, who led the abolitionist and then the early woman's rights movement, one can trace the emergence of ideology and language concerning the equality of women. "It is clear that it was in this urban, educated, abolitionist milieu," Chaves concludes, "that the idea of equal rights for women came prominently together with the idea that women should be permitted access to official religious positions."[97]

Thus, Brown Blackwell, Brown, and especially Shaw came of age and sensed calls to ministry in times and places in which the language of equal rights had already begun to shape the rhetoric of women's religious roles. They had no intention of being limited to preaching ministries, with or without denominational sanction, since the idea of women's equality in all spheres of life—political, legal, and liturgical—had already been introduced to public debate. The "overthrow of the monopoly of the pulpit," suggested as it was by a cadre of liberal but mostly religious abolitionist women in 1848, became, for the first time in history, a realistic goal.

95. Catherine A. Brekus, *Strangers and Pilgrims* (Chapel Hill: University of North Carolina Press, 1998), 224.

96. The request for ordination by Laura Clemens, an evangelist in the United Brethren tradition, was denied by a ministerial conference in 1843. See ibid.

97. Mark Chaves, *Ordaining Women: Culture and Conflict in Religious Organizations* (Cambridge, Mass.: Harvard University Press, 1997), 75, 77.

Chapter Three

"Breaking to them
the bread of life":

Joys and Challenges of Pastoral Ministry

D r. Harriot K. Hunt, who witnessed the ordination of Antoinette Brown Blackwell in September 1853, wrote of her joy "in the idea of a female presiding over a congregation, and breaking to them the bread of life."[1] While Hunt probably had the sacramental ministerial function in mind when she wrote this description, the image of "breaking to them the bread of life" had far more than just sacramental implications for these three early clergywomen. Antoinette Brown Blackwell, Olympia Brown, and Anna Howard Shaw all became sources of the symbolic bread of life for the people they served. Once they had become "man-acknowledged ministers," as Brown Blackwell once put it, through official actions of their churches, they settled into the routine of congregational responsibilities. Inherent in their recollections of their years in parish ministry is the obvious seriousness and commitment with which they pursued their pastoral responsibilities. They exhibited joy even in the relentless task of sermon preparation, good humor in the administrative tasks incumbent with running a church, and sincere empathy with the sorrows and struggles of their parishioners. And they demonstrated patience and resignation—if not always understanding—in the face of ridicule because of the unusual paths they had chosen as nineteenth-century women.

That patience and resignation proved to be essential to their professional success as all three women continually found themselves forced to justify their positions in response to criticisms originating both within and outside their churches. They endured blatant prejudice and subtle—and

1. Harriot K. Hunt, *Glances and Glimpses* (Boston: John P. Jewett, 1856), 304.

not so subtle—reminders that they might be tolerated but certainly not encouraged in their transgression of traditional social and ecclesiastical boundaries. Antoinette Brown Blackwell's warmhearted approach to the needs of her congregation and her nonjudgmental theology were rejected as antithetical to the style of ministry preferred by most people. Olympia Brown was hired with relative ease by a congregation in Marshfield, Vermont, but after her arrival in town, no one would provide a place for her to live. The validity of the first wedding she conducted was questioned, and she was excluded from participation in a community memorial service after the death of Abraham Lincoln. Anna Howard Shaw saw once-prominent members of her congregation leave the church in response to her style of ministry. Nevertheless, they all remained faithful to the people—and more importantly, to the God—who had called them to ministry.

"A pleasant and easy parish": Antoinette Brown Blackwell

Antoinette Brown Blackwell, the first woman ordained, also had the shortest full-time pastorate. After her ordination on September 15, 1853, she settled back into her ongoing ministry among the people of South Butler. "My work through the following winter after my ordination proceeded in the usual way," she recalled. "We had good audiences for the conditions of the surrounding country, and no friction occurred anywhere in the church or the congregation." Brown Blackwell's small church proved to be "a pleasant and very easy parish where not only the church members but the village and surrounding neighborhood were apparently friendly and generally sympathetic, ministerial prejudice excepted." She recalled her custom of writing about half her sermons and extemporizing the other half "as we always had two sermons each Sunday."[2]

Along with her pastoral responsibilities, Brown Blackwell continued to do "a good deal of outside lecturing and of attendance on other meetings."[3] Those outside interests at first sustained Brown Blackwell in what otherwise would have been a very isolated and limited existence as pastor of a small rural church, but they also contributed significantly to her frustrations with parish life. For a year she was able to balance her preaching and pastoral ministry with her travel and lecturing for various reform

2. Memoirs told by Brown Blackwell in 1909 to Mrs. Claude U. (Sarah) Gilson, 161, BFP, SL, Fols. 3–14.
3. Ibid.

efforts, especially woman's rights. The reform activity fulfilled her desire to be part of a larger world of important work and interesting colleagues while her parish work fulfilled her call to ministry and her desire to be a pastoral leader. With what appeared to be the cooperation of her congregation, she did the work of a pastor around the growing demand for her services as a platform speaker. Two months after her ordination, she performed her first wedding in Rochester, New York, marking the first time an ordained clergywoman had officiated at a wedding.

Brown Blackwell obviously enjoyed the responsibility of preaching for her congregation for Sunday and midweek services. But she confessed in a letter to Susan B. Anthony written in February 1854 that she had what she termed "the blues," indicating the beginning of what would eventually become a significant emotional crisis. She did not offer much reflection on her year at South Butler. Most of her written work from that time pertains to the reform efforts in which she was engaged. An indication of her loneliness, however, appeared in a letter she wrote to Lucy Stone on May 21, 1854, about a year after she had settled in South Butler:

> Write, Lucy dear, if it is not burdensome to you. When you have been for a year in a place where there is not a mortal person for whom you feel a real affinity, and yet, are *a sort of public property for all*, with the delightful anticipation of a twin year to follow, you will realize how welcome a letter or the face of a *friend* would be.[4]

Brown Blackwell's impending crisis appears to have been precipitated by several factors that eventually resulted in her resignation from her church and her gradual move onto the lecture circuit. One factor was the mark she had already made on the woman's rights and temperance platforms. From her earliest speech at the First National Woman's Rights Convention in 1850, Brown Blackwell was known as an articulate and thoughtful speaker. She supported herself and gained a reputation as a speaker and preacher on behalf of temperance, abolition, and woman's rights between the time of her graduation from Oberlin and her call to the South Butler church. Rather than giving up the lyceum circuit altogether once she accepted the parish position, Brown Blackwell tried to balance both. As a result, she was more entrenched in woman's rights work before her ministry than either Brown or Shaw would be when they

---

4. Antoinette Brown Blackwell to Lucy Stone, May 21, 1854, BFP, LC.

began their work as pastors, and she continued her political work in tandem with her ministry. Thus, when other factors compounded to increase her frustrations in ministry, the temptation to return to full-time work in which Brown Blackwell had already proved her ability was too great.

Among the other factors contributing to Brown Blackwell's restlessness were a sense of alienation from colleagues in both ecclesiastical and reform circles and a theological shift from orthodoxy. Her earlier self-description as "a stranger in a strange land" proved to be apt once again as she discovered her inability to fit in to either of her vocational worlds. The resistance of fellow clergymen to her ministry was obvious from the beginning when the South Butler church had trouble finding ministers who were willing to participate in her ordination. Several liberal clergymen who were active in the reform movements for which Brown Blackwell worked, including Samuel J. May and William Henry Channing, supported her ministry, but they were geographically and theologically limited in the extent of support they could offer. And while her parishioners, at least in the beginning, appreciated her work and welcomed her into their midst, they had deep pastoral needs that demanded all that Brown Blackwell could give them but were able to give her little in return. In her youthful enthusiasm, she had entered into a relationship with the small, rural South Butler congregation with little thought about the intellectual and social isolation she had chosen.

Adding to Brown Blackwell's despair was the alienation she felt from her sisters in the woman's rights movement. Early on, she recognized that her approach to the movement was not always consistent with the approach of its leaders. She feared that efforts on behalf of woman's rights would be tainted by leaders who had emerged from the radical Garrisonian wing of the antislavery movement that pursued abolition by means of more radical tactics than the "voting abolitionists" who sought change through the political system. She also rejected the fragmentation of reform organizations. "Her vision of 'progress' was a broad one," wrote Elizabeth Cazden, "encompassing both spiritual and political issues, which to her were all interrelated."[5] When pressed to consider a position lecturing for a specific abolition, temperance, or woman's rights group, Brown Blackwell expressed her frustration in a letter to Lucy Stone, revealing the independent spirit that would shape—and in many ways hamper—her life's work:

---

5. Elizabeth Cazden, *Antoinette Brown Blackwell* (Old Westbury, N.Y.: Feminist Press, 1983), 64.

For my own part I am glad to be again free from any connection with any one in laboring, for I believe with nobody, & I could not work perfectly well with any one. I will for the present at least, be employed by no society not only, but by no individual in particular either, & will make no engagements for any length of time. Then I shall be free to believe what I please, and to act as I please responsable [*sic*] to my own concience [*sic*] & to God.[6]

While Brown Blackwell disagreed with some of the approaches and philosophies of her woman's rights sisters, her religious commitment created the greatest chasm between them. She became disturbed by the increasing anticlericalism and antiecclesiasticalism of the movement that grew in response to the condemnation of woman's rights by ministers and churches. She thought it best to meet religious criticism on its own ground, as demonstrated by her exegetical defense of women's speaking delivered at the 1850 Woman's Rights Convention. In a bold move indicative of her desire to bring religious sentiment and practice to bear on reform work, Brown Blackwell proposed that all woman's rights conventions be opened with prayer, as she wrote to Lucy Stone in 1852:

There is one thing which I want and have always wanted in our conventions: that they should be opened with prayer, or at least that there might be some vocal prayer at some time during the sessions. I have not felt at liberty to propose this because the control or management of the matter was not at all in my hands, and most of the members I supposed did not approve of any thing of this kind.[7]

To her surprise, her suggestion was well received by woman's rights leaders, and Brown Blackwell herself opened the Fourth National Convention in Cleveland with prayer just weeks after her ordination in October of 1853.[8] Nevertheless, Cazden concluded, her "unique beliefs and her choice of methods would make it difficult for her to work with organized

---

6. Antoinette Brown Blackwell to Lucy Stone, December 19, 1850, BFP, LC.

7. Antoinette Brown Blackwell to Lucy Stone, August 4, 1852, BFP, LC.

8. Elizabeth Cady Stanton, Susan B. Anthony, and Matilda Joslyn Gage, eds., *History of Woman Suffrage*, vol. I (6 vols.; Rochester, N.Y.: National American Woman Suffrage Association, 1881–1922), 124.

groups, either of feminists or of more conservative women."[9] Early on she realized the challenges wrought by her independent spirit as she confessed to Lucy Stone:

> What hard work it is to stand alone! I am forever wanting to lean over on to some body, but no body will support me, and I think seriously of swallowing the yard stick or putting on a buckram corset, so as to get a little assistance some how, for I am determined to maintain the perpendicular position.[10]

She tried valiantly "to maintain the perpendicular position," but the sense of being "a stranger in a strange land" would continue to haunt Brown Blackwell throughout her life, making the already difficult way she had chosen even more difficult. Her ecclesiastical and religious commitments alienated her from many of her woman's rights colleagues. Sadly, they "viewed with suspicion her desire to expand opportunities for women within what they regarded as the corrupt institutional hierarchy of the church. Few feminists saw Brown's work as a minister as part of a common struggle for a change in the status of women."[11] On the other hand, her woman's rights activities made her suspicious in the eyes of many in the church, particularly those in the congregation that had called and ordained her. Even those outside these two groups, including other friends and family members, "viewed her choice [to be a minister] as peculiar."[12] In her autobiography, Brown Blackwell reflected on the overwhelming frustration brought about by her unique and difficult position:

> It was one of my odd experiences to see some of my old intimates of my own age, look at me with a kind of curious incredulity, as utterly unable to comprehend the kind of motive which could lead me to take so peculiar a position in life. No attitude of strangers could have affected me half so much. The novelty of my position in choosing to be a minister seemed to the friends even more peculiar than the choice to be a lecturer on other subjects.
>
> In that earlier day it must have been more or less difficult for any young minister to meet his familiar friends with exactly the same

---

9. Cazden, *Antoinette Brown Blackwell*, 58.
10. Antoinette Brown Blackwell to Lucy Stone, August 4, 1852, BFP, LC.
11. Cazden, *Antoinette Brown Blackwell*, 86.
12. Ibid., 87.

freedom as he did before he had taken up ministerial duties. For a woman minister the situation was even more estranging. It was practically ten years after my ordination before any other woman known to the public was ordained. It was therefore doubly hard for me—a young woman still in the twenties—to adapt myself to the rather curious relationship I must sustain either to home conditions or to those of a pastorate. Personally this was more of an emotional strain than the enduring of any opposition that ever came to me as a public speaker or teacher.[13]

Perhaps the most destructive factor in the undermining of Brown Blackwell's pastoral ministry, however, was her own theological shift away from Calvinist orthodoxy. The assumption of an angry, vengeful God who condemned people to eternal damnation in the absence of a particular pattern of salvation became an untenable doctrine for Brown Blackwell to believe, and, even more, to proclaim to her congregation. Although Brown Blackwell had been raised in the tradition of orthodox Congregationalism, Cazden notes, "her upbringing had been more liberal than orthodox. She had been raised on stories of Heaven, not Hell." In addition, she had come under the strong influence of Charles Grandison Finney at Oberlin, whose own modification of traditional Congregational doctrine "stressed human goodness and the possibility of moral perfection."[14]

While Brown Blackwell probably leaned toward a more moderate interpretation of Congregationalism throughout her early life and education, the ultimate expression of her increasingly liberal theology occurred during her pastorate. One thing a minister cannot hide is her theological perspective. It reveals itself in obvious ways, such as in preaching and teaching, and in less obvious ways, such as in one's theological interpretation of life that is required when relating to parishioners in pastoral settings. Brown Blackwell's beliefs were exposed quickly in all these ways. She portrayed a God of mercy and compassion in her sermons rather than a God of punishment and retribution. She refused to give in to the insatiable appetite of the members of her congregation for the "hell, fire, and brimstone" style that had come to characterize orthodox Calvinist preaching. Brown Blackwell eventually realized that her parishioners had

13. Gilson ms., 161. The "other woman" ordained ten years after Brown Blackwell's ordination was Olympia Brown.

14. Cazden, *Antoinette Brown Blackwell*, 88.

been exposed to such preaching for so long that anything less strident from the pulpit was perceived as not only ineffective but heretical.

An early encounter with the theological orientation of her congregation occurred while she ministered to a dying elderly member of the church known as Mother Dratt. When Brown Blackwell tried to allay Mother Dratt's fears about eternal punishment by reminding her of the atoning work of Christ and God's care for us as the Good Shepherd, Mother Dratt responded, " 'No, Miss Brown, our last preacher told us that God was fierce in His anger. Told us the thunder rolled and the lightning flashed when God looked down upon us, miserable sinners all.' " Visitors to the elderly woman's home reported that they overheard what they described as a blasphemous conversation between Brown Blackwell and the dying woman and reported it to church leaders who took the young minister to task for her theological interpretation. Undaunted, she preached the following Sunday on the goodness of God and the promise of immortality, challenging the congregation's traditional understanding of eternal punishment.[15]

Brown Blackwell's theological differences with her congregation came to the breaking point as a result of the critical illnesses of two children in the church. One was an illegitimate child who died unexpectedly of croup. "I was present to see the last hard sufferings of the poor little thing," she recalled, "and was forced to preach the funeral sermon as the custom then was, with some reference to the mother and the painful conditions surrounding her, while an unusual attendance of curious-minded persons were watching to see in what way I should discharge the painful task."[16] Brown Blackwell's recollections reveal not only her anguish over the suffering she witnessed but also her frustration in having to acknowledge the congregation's theological worldview associating the mother's sin and suffering.

The other child who provoked the theological crisis in Brown Blackwell's ministry was a young boy who, during his dying days, enjoyed many conversations with Brown Blackwell. The conversations occurred at the behest of his mother, "an earnest Christian woman, probably the most conservative member of the little congregation, an intelligent woman, who had done her best (I suspect against her own wishes) to

15. Laura Kerr, *Lady in the Pulpit* (New York: Woman's Press, 1951), 133. Kerr's work is a fictionalized account of actual events that occurred in Brown Blackwell's life as reported in Brown Blackwell's memoirs and other sources.

16. Gilson ms., 171.

accept and befriend the woman minister." Those conversations did not, however, lead to the boy's conversion according to the standard pattern expected by his mother. She implored Brown Blackwell "to hold him as suspended over the brink of eternal suffering and in this way to impel him to a conversion that should bear him in the direction of eternal happiness." To threaten a dying child in such a way was, in Brown Blackwell's words, "cruel." She concluded that "it was impossible to meet in accordance with the mother's wishes. I could only do what could be done conscientiously."[17]

The situation was eerily reminiscent of an event that Brown Blackwell had witnessed as a child and that helped shape her more liberal understanding of God. A neighbor's boy had died suddenly, not long after a series of revival meetings had been held in their community. The boy's mother believed her son had refused to be converted and sought solace in the Brown household. Brown Blackwell remembered what seemed to her "a fearful ordeal" for her whole family as the mother

> sat in a rocking chair, upright, pale and worn, with the saddest expression I have ever seen on the countenance of any mortal. In low steady tones she told the story of her son's life and death, saying in a most sepulchral tone "I have no doubt that he is now suffering the beginning of eternal torture. I cannot doubt it, and, though it break my heart, I will trust in God." The poor woman could not rejoice and I began to wonder whether she would be happy when she reached heaven and looked down upon her suffering son. From that time I more than half disbelieved in a place of eternal torture by literal fire.[18]

Brown Blackwell's experience as a pastor many years later with the dying boy in her church and his spiritually tortured mother no doubt rekindled the resistance to harsh Calvinist doctrine she had developed as a child. Despite her best pastoral efforts, the South Butler boy's family engaged the local Baptist minister to do the funeral, believing that he had died without the benefit of a true conversion and that Brown Blackwell had not done her duty as a minister of the gospel.

Throughout her year of ministry at South Butler, attendance at her church remained steady. But Brown Blackwell felt a growing distance between her own beliefs and ministerial practices and the congregation's

17. Ibid.
18. Ibid., 71.

expectations of her. A number of experiences such as those related above provoked a sense of doubt within her about her beliefs and her ability to function effectively as the leader of a congregation. She realized her increasing discomfort with traditional orthodox doctrines and even questioned the authority of the Bible. "The exclusive inspiration of the entire Bible began to seem uncertain," she recalled. "Part of the Bible seemed to me inspired but other parts definitely not, and discrepancies began to make themselves evident."[19] Her growing doubts, Cazden suggests, were fed by her exposure to a variety of liberal theological beliefs through her friends in the reform movements in which she participated. "Within the network of reformers," Cazden writes, "Brown was constantly exposed to Unitarians, liberal Quakers, and other nonorthodox people who questioned orthodox religion along with traditional social patterns. That questioning strengthened her own doubts."[20] She also read voraciously and became increasingly attracted to philosophical, metaphysical, and scientific writings of the mid-nineteenth century. She admitted:

> Before I had been many months at South Butler I began to be assailed by theological doubts. Undoubtedly I had a strong bent toward speculative topics. This increased by the habit of reading metaphysical books. When traveling with Miss [Susan B.] Anthony I generally carried a heavy volume along some of these lines, studying it as opportunity offered.
>
> During this time I was reading rather extensively on both sides of questions of religious opinion. Darwin and Spencer were beginning their publications. . . . This wide variety of opinion was seething in my mind and to no one was I willing to say anything of the difficulties which began to arise in my earnest endeavor to find my way into real and solid truth where there was so much conflict of opinion.[21]

Her own spiritual crisis left her powerless to deal with the questions and doubts of members of her congregation. "People began to question me about points of doubt and it was extremely difficult to satisfy them without troubling my own conscience," she confessed. In the spring of 1854, she recalled, her "unsettled state of mind" reached a breaking point:

19. Ibid., 169.
20. Cazden, *Antoinette Brown Blackwell*, 88.
21. Gilson ms., 169.

Then suddenly I found that the whole groundwork of my faith had dropped away from me. I found myself absolutely believing nothing, not even in my own continuous personal existence. Was I the same entity now as in my childhood? Was I the same even as six months earlier? Was there any God? To me, it was the complete downfall of confidence in anything possible to know or rely on, necessitating a complete building from the foundation up.

Brown Blackwell continued to minister to her congregation as best she could in this state of despair into the summer of 1854. She admitted that "little by little there seemed to arise a bit of firm ground here and there. The belief in practical service, in justice, and a few moral principles, never quite forsook me and these seemed to make a solid foundation for abstract investigation." She found it possible to go on preaching and lecturing "on the basis of belief in the law of love."[22]

Brown Blackwell's sense of isolation from her congregation, her family, her fellow clergymen, and her colleagues in reform work contributed to her anguish. She feared that no one would understand or have sympathy for her situation since most of them were unsympathetic with her decision to be in parish ministry. It was impossible, she believed, "to appeal to any of my relatives, who all being still orthodox would only be distressed by my doubts." As a result, she confided her feelings to very few individuals, making her burdens even greater to bear. William Henry Channing, a reform colleague, proved to be the only person in whom Brown Blackwell felt she could confide:

> We corresponded very freely and I stated so freely my want of any belief at that time that it seemed wise to destroy the whole correspondence. He did all he could to cheer and encourage me, but told me frankly that no other soul could be a real helper in this personal emergency. Each one must walk over "the burning plough-shares" for one's self.[23]

Channing urged her to be patient with herself and reassured her that her spirit was "a most lively child," threatened not by "rickety dullness" but "endangered by fever in the brain."[24] Brown Blackwell also feared that

22. Ibid., 172, 170.
23. Ibid., 172.
24. William Henry Channing to Antoinette Brown Blackwell, February 2, 1854, BFP, SL, Fol. 43.

since she had "so lately received ordination as a sincerely orthodox believer," her "sincerity at that time might even be called in question."[25] She even asked Gerrit Smith if news of her theological liberalism would cause him to regret his participation in her ordination service.[26]

There is no indication in the extant autobiographical or other materials related to Brown Blackwell's ministry that her failure as a pastor was related to her gender. Historical perspective makes it easy to assume that the first ordained clergywoman failed at, or perhaps was driven from, ministry because of prejudice against her based on gender. The extent to which gender prejudice did or did not play a role in Brown Blackwell's troubled pastorate will never be known. It appears, however, from both Brown Blackwell's own recollections of her year at South Butler and subsequent historical interpretations that the challenges to her ministry emerged more from her own theological evolution, from the circumstances in which she found herself, and from the personal and professional choices she made than from the fact that she was a woman. In retrospect, one wonders if more orthodox personal theological views might have sustained her in ministry—or, for that matter, if she might have succeeded with stronger networks of support or with a life less fragmented by her continuing work for reform. All of these challenges accumulated until they became an unbearable burden on the young minister, compromising her health as well as her confidence.

In July 1854, Brown Blackwell submitted her resignation to the congregation at South Butler and returned to her family's farm to rest and to consider the next stage of her life. A few weeks later she wrote to Lucy Stone, in whom she had confided few of her frustrations in the parish, assuming, perhaps rightly, that Stone would have offered little sympathy in light of Stone's own skepticism about religion and the church. She related nothing of her theological or professional struggles but admitted, "Rest seemed indispensable so I concluded to take it. . . . Is it not good to rest—to lie still and listen to the crickets and grasshoppers."[27] In that peaceful setting Brown Blackwell began to envision a preaching life that would allow her to be true to all she believed and to fulfill all she felt called to do:

> Preaching with me has been deliberately chosen as a life profession
> and will not be lightly abandoned; but I am beginning to feel the need

25. Gilson ms., 172.
26. Cazden, *Antoinette Brown Blackwell*, 89.
27. Antoinette Brown Blackwell to Lucy Stone, August 16, 1854, BFP, SL.

of freer surroundings than can be found even in a very liberal orthodox church. . . . I am stout and brave hearted and mean to preach the
truth as it is revealed to me.[28]

The "gal preacher": Anna Howard Shaw

Anna Howard Shaw's parish career was several years longer and consider-
ably more pleasant that Antoinette Brown Blackwell's. Her greatest battles
occurred during her first two years at East Dennis and prompted Shaw to
resign her position on a regular basis only to be persuaded to remain by a
penitent congregation. The differences in ministerial style between Shaw
and Brown Blackwell were remarkable. While Brown Blackwell seemed to
internalize any opposition and defeat, to the detriment of her physical and
mental health, Shaw met opposition head on. She refused to tolerate the
antics of her conflicted East Dennis congregation.

In her autobiography, she recounted some early challenges to her
authority. One involved criticisms hurled at each other by two warring
factions in the church. Shaw announced publicly

> that I would hear no verbal charges whatever, but that if my two
> flocks would state their troubles in writing I would call a board meet-
> ing to discuss and pass upon them. This they both resolutely refused
> to do (it was apparently the first time they had ever agreed on any
> point); and as I steadily declined to listen to complaints, they devised
> an original method of putting them before me.

The "original method" they devised was to voice their difficulties in
public prayer,

> loudly and urgently calling upon the Lord to pardon such and such
> a liar, mentioning the gentleman by name, and such and such a slan-
> derer, whose name was also submitted. By the time the prayers were
> ended there were few untarnished reputations in the congregation,
> and I knew, perforce, what both sides had to say.

This creative style of prayer persisted for a few weeks until Shaw finally
put an end to it by dismissing the congregation, "telling the members that

---

28. Antoinette Brown Blackwell to Horace Greeley, September 6, 1854, as quoted in Cazden, *Antoinette Brown Blackwell*, 93.

their conduct was an insult to the Lord, and that I would not listen to either their protests or their prayers."[29]

Shaw's refusal to be intimidated by her recalcitrant parishioners created a stir on Cape Cod and resulted in a capacity crowd at her church the following Sunday. The crowd was disappointed, however, when she preached her prepared sermon and avoided any reference to the ongoing congregational disputes. At a meeting that evening, "the leader of one of the factions rose to his feet with the obvious purpose of starting trouble." The troublemaker, a retired sea captain, seemed determined to undermine Shaw's authority and integrity. He began his efforts by attacking the sermon she had delivered earlier that day, contending that it had been

> "entirely contrary to the Scriptures," and for ten minutes he quoted and misquoted me, hammering in his points. I let him go on without interruption. Then he added:
>
> "And this gal comes to this church and undertakes to tell us how we shall pray. That's a highhanded measure, and I, for one, ain't goin' to stand it. I want to say right here that I shall pray as I like, when I like, and where I like. I have prayed in this heavenly way for fifty years before that gal was born, and she can't dictate to me now!"[30]

When other members of the congregation tried to shout down the sea captain, Shaw defended him, declaring that he should be allowed to say all he wanted to say since it would be the last time he would ever speak at a church meeting. The captain, "whose exertions had already made him apoplectic, turned a darker purple." When he demanded to know what Shaw meant, she put her "ultimatum in the one form the old man could understand." She described herself as captain of a ship and asked what he would do with a mutinous or insubordinate member on board. She answered her own question:

> "You would put me ashore or in irons," I reminded him. "Now, Captain Sears, I intend to put you ashore. I am the master of this ship. I have set my course, and I mean to follow it. If you rebel, either you will get out or I will. But until the board asks for my resignation, I am in command."[31]

29. Anna Howard Shaw with Elizabeth Jordan, *The Story of a Pioneer* (New York: Harper & Brothers Publishers, 1915), 108.
30. Ibid.
31. Ibid., 111.

Shaw's bold move paid off in the long run if not immediately. Captain Sears withdrew his support for the church and refused to attend for weeks. The prayers at the prayer meeting the following week were devoid of personal attacks, marking a great victory, and peace reigned at the East Dennis church.

That peace was short-lived, however, as Shaw's second battle followed closely on the heels of her first. "There was, indeed," she acknowledged, "barely time between in which to care for the wounded." Her second challenge involved an uproar over a dance scheduled to be held in the church building. The dance was sponsored by an organization called the Free Religious Group and was planned as part of the church's annual Christmas Fair. The East Dennis church had a policy forbidding dancing in the church building, and when Shaw attempted to enforce that policy at the insistence of the trustees, the determined dancers challenged her. Chaos broke out the night of the Christmas Fair until Shaw threatened to have the dancers arrested. She remained in the church hall that night to enforce the rule until she closed and locked the hall herself at midnight. Once again, church attendance records were broken the Sunday following the thwarted dance. The congregation that had gathered for excitement was not disappointed since Shaw read her resignation before she began her sermon. Believing it was her last chance "to tell the people and the place what I thought of them," she preached for an hour and half, reading the riot act to the congregation that failed to support her in enforcing their own policies. She later recalled:

> Under the arraignment my people writhed and squirmed. I ended:
> "What I am saying hurts you, but in your hearts you know you deserve every word of it. It is high time you saw yourselves as you are—a disgrace to the religion you profess and to the community you live in."[32]

And once again, Shaw's gamble paid off. Members of the congregation lined up for and against her, but she earned the respect of both her supporters and her adversaries. That night, at another well-attended church meeting, Captain Sears, her former adversary, appeared for the first time in several weeks. He asked to speak, but instead of continuing his attack on Shaw as she had expected, he commended her for the sermon she had

32. Ibid., 117.

delivered that morning (about which he—and the entire community—had heard). He agreed that it was time to cease the quarreling and back-biting that had divided the congregation for years and acknowledged that no minister before Shaw had "enough backbone to uphold the discipline of the church." He offered his support to Shaw: " 'I've come here to say I'm with the gal,' he ended. 'Put me down for my original subscription and ten dollars extra.' " "So we had the old man back again," Shaw recalled.

> He was a tower of strength, and he stood by me faithfully until he died. The trustees would not accept my resignation (indeed, they refused to consider it at all), and the congregation, when it had thought things over, apparently decided that there might be worse things in the pulpit than "the gal." It was even known to brag of what it called my "spunk," and perhaps it was this quality, rather than any other, which I most needed in that particular parish at that time.[33]

Indeed, Shaw recognized that her success in ministry resulted in large part from the strength and determination that had characterized her personality from her childhood when she worked side by side with her family to carve out an existence in the Michigan wilderness and from her young adulthood when she nearly worked herself to death trying to secure an education. In evaluating Shaw's ministry, biographer Ralph W. Spencer concluded that "she ran her churches with an authoritarian hand. She believed it was her church and she had the right to run it the way she felt it ought to be run." The drawback of this approach, of course, was that "she failed to permit any meaningful dialogue among the people, but chose the alternative pattern of ruling and running the church her way."[34] This authoritarian approach no doubt made the church a more palatable place for Shaw than it had been for Antoinette Brown Blackwell. Shaw obviously was not intimidated by outspoken parishioners or gossipy townspeople. She frequently risked her job and her reputation for her beliefs, but in what can best be described as the work of a divine presence of grace, the congregation always embraced her in the end.

Despite the peace that reigned after Shaw's battle with the Free Religious Group, she felt compelled to submit her resignation to the congregation two more times in her first three years at East Dennis to fight for

33. Ibid., 118–19.
34. Ralph W. Spencer, "Anna Howard Shaw," *Methodist History* 13 (1974–75): 43.

causes she "firmly believed in and eventually won."[35] The second battle involved an invitation Shaw extended to a local Unitarian minister to preach in the East Dennis church. Although Shaw had been welcomed into his pulpit, her congregation was reluctant to allow the liberal minister to preach in their church, and in response, she resigned. After much discussion generated by the tender of her resignation, the congregation agreed "that I could exchange pulpits not only with this minister, but with any other in good standing in his own church."[36] Her third resignation was prompted by the congregation's response to a sermon Shaw preached condemning a local saloon for corrupting the youth of East Dennis. In her characteristic way, Shaw preached against the saloon for three consecutive Sundays after having been advised to withhold her criticisms. Once again, she prevailed when her supporters rallied to her defense and rejected her resignation.

"That was my last big struggle," Shaw recalled. "During the remaining five years of my pastorate on Cape Cod the relations between my people and myself were wholly harmonious and beautiful."[37] By that time she had added the responsibility of serving as pastor for the Congregational Church at Dennis, two and a half miles away from East Dennis, a "temporary charge" that lasted for six and a half years. Her weeks were filled with pastoral responsibilities, sermon preparation, and an occasional lecture. Shaw described a typical Sunday to her friend Clara Osburn this way:

> It was a hard day yesterday. I preached to the children, then went to West Dennis to preach in the afternoon and forgot my sermon, so took a text and did the best I could. That was hard work, as I neither have the ability of the old Fathers, who never selected their text until they entered the pulpit: nor have I their faith to believe that the Lord will fill my mouth unless I have just filled my head with my subject. In the evening we had a Sunday School concert and I am always so anxious for fear the children will fail that I am about half sick. So you see my Sunday was a full and hard one.[38]

35. Shaw, *Story of a Pioneer*, 120.
36. Ibid.
37. Ibid., 121.
38. Ida Husted Harper, "Biography of Anna Howard Shaw," unpublished manuscript, 40, AHSP, SL, Fol. 357.

She offered an amusing glimpse into her personal feelings about the other responsibilities of ministry in this reflection on weddings and funerals:

> I prefer to attend weddings rather than funerals, though why is more than I can tell, for at the weddings I am helping to usher mortals into misery and at funerals I announce that they are out of it. It must be that I am wordly [*sic*], for I get a fee of ten dollars at my weddings and all my funerals have netted me nothing except it be a little or large amount of abuse. It is said that I do weddings beautifully and so long as I get the service read all right there is nothing to fear, as I do not have to make remarks of my own, lauding the bride and groom and all their relations. Now at a funeral it is different. The departed must be pictured as faultless and noble even if he never did a thing worth while and the greatest blessing he could bestow upon his family was to die and rid them of his care. Still they are supposed to be heart-broken mourners and the less there is to say about one the more is expected. So a minister, like a pilot, steers between the untrue and the family's feelings and sometimes it is hard work and if his conscience will not allow him to say anything good abuse follows. Especially is this true of those who do not believe in churches and ministers and religion and never pay a cent toward their support.[39]

In an interview in 1902, Shaw was asked about her pastoral ministry and described the wedding service she used:

> "While you held [your pastorate], I suppose you fulfilled every office? You christened, married, and buried as required among your people?"
>
> "Certainly; I performed every pastoral duty."
>
> "What marriage service did you use?"
>
> "I had one of my own arrangement. I never allowed a bride to promise to obey her husband. When the bridegroom would come to me to arrange for the wedding ceremony, I would say, 'Now, your wife will not want always to obey you if she has got sense of her own; and if she has not got sense, she is not fit to be married?' I used to ask them what they wished to promise each other, and generally they

---

39. Ibid., 40–41.

decided to vow to be faithful, kind, and loving to one another; that was all that was wanted, really."[40]

Both Shaw and the communities she served recognized her unique gifts for ministry. She was, she acknowledged, "considered the best minister to send for in hard cases."[41] Just as Brown Blackwell's difficulties in ministry appear, in retrospect, to be attributable to several factors that worked against her, Shaw's success can be attributed to several factors that worked in her favor, among them her personal style and inherent strength. Her ability to deal with conflict and to rise above defeat was proved repeatedly early in her life and then later in her pastoral ministry. Shaw's recollections of her ministry, note biographers Wil A. Linkugel and Martha Solomon,

> reveal much about her personality. While she admits the controversies were sometimes emotionally painful, she was sustained by her convictions. She handled the situations with remarkable forthrightness and assertiveness. She was quite comfortable with the role of leader and did not compromise with those who questioned her authority.

Those qualities, Linkugel and Solomon go on to state, "remained characteristic of her in later life." Her successes in the East Dennis pastorate "built Shaw's confidence in her abilities and in her rhetorical and leadership styles,"[42] confidence that, as will be seen, propelled her to national leadership in the woman suffrage movement.

Perhaps the most significant factor in Shaw's pastoral success was what appears to have been theological compatibility between pastor and people. Shaw never experienced the kind of theological angst that eventually proved devastating to Brown Blackwell's ministry. She believed in the church as the ultimate expression of Christian community, but she never had the strong denominational ties that characterized the religious lives of Brown Blackwell and Brown. Unlike the other two women, Shaw wrote little about the religious nature of her childhood and youth. She noted the

40. Mrs. Fenwick Miller, "Interviews with the American Suffrage Leaders: III.—The Rev. Dr. Anna Shaw," *Womanhood* (n.d.), 336, AHSP, SL, Fol. 361.

41. Harper, "Biography of Anna Howard Shaw," 41.

42. Wil A. Linkugel and Martha Solomon, *Anna Howard Shaw* (New York: Greenwood Press, 1991), 7.

strong Unitarian ties of her grandmother and mother in England and the price they paid "for being outside the fold of the Church of England." Her call to preach, which came when she was a teenager working in the woods, appeared to spring forth from no particular source. Even Shaw seemed baffled by it: "For some reason I wanted to preach—to talk to people, to tell them things. Just why, just what, I did not yet know."[43] She never knew—or at least never revealed—the reason.

Shaw's indeterminate church background might have served her well in the long run, for it made her less constrained by denominational rules. Her Methodist ties were the result of her encounter with H. C. Peck, the progressive presiding elder of the Methodist district in which she lived in Big Rapids. When denied ordination by the Methodist Episcopal Church, Shaw indicated no hesitation in moving her membership—and ordination quest—to the Methodist Protestant Church. Her East Dennis congregation had once been part of the Free Methodist Church but was independent by the time of Shaw's arrival. And the other Cape Cod church she served was a Congregational church. This ecumenical background demonstrates that Shaw, while never questioning the value of organized, institutional Christianity (as many of her suffrage sisters did), nevertheless did not feel great loyalty to any particular denomination. Her only preference appears to have been for congregations that were liberal in their ecclesiastical and social agendas.

While Shaw's congregation occasionally challenged her preaching, those challenges appear to be related to her style or to the issues she chose to address (such as the early congregational disputes) rather than to her theology. The residents of a seafaring community such as East Dennis were likely quite diverse in their theological views, but Shaw seemed able to preach a word that spoke to all of them. In her memories of her years on Cape Cod, Shaw recounted her visits with Relief Paine, a young invalid who became one of her closest friends. On her first visit with Paine, Shaw enjoyed regaling the young woman with stories of community life and her own experiences. At one point, Paine smiled at Shaw and said:

> "You are a queer minister. You have not offered to pray with me!"
> "I feel," I told her, "more like asking you to pray for me."
> Relief continued her analysis. "You have not told me that my

---

43. Shaw, *Story of a Pioneer*, 7, 44.

affliction was a visitation from God," she added; "that it was discipline and well for me I had it."

"I don't believe it was from God," I said. "I don't believe God had
anything to do with it. And I rejoice that you have not let it wreck
your life."

She pressed my hand. "Thank you for saying that," she mur-
mured. "If I thought God did it I could not love Him, and if I did not
love Him I could not live. Please come and see me *very* often—and
tell me stories!"[44]

This incident indicates something about Shaw's own theological perspective as well as something about one of the theological perspectives
represented among Shaw's parishioners. Most significantly, however, it
indicates that the two—Shaw's theology and the theology of her parishioners—were compatible at least most of the time. It is hard to imagine
an incident such as this occurring during Brown Blackwell's year in South
Butler, when her theological position was increasingly at odds with that
of her congregation, creating an untenable situation for both of them.
Shaw, on the other hand, exhibited a theological approach that was at least
tolerated and at best embraced by the people she served.

Shaw's theological and stylistic compatibility with her congregations
do not entirely account for her good experience on Cape Cod, however.
The ultimate factor contributing to her success was her ability to find
useful outlets for her abundant energy by means of commitments outside
her pastoral ministry. While engaged in the pastoral work of two congregations and preparations for three services each Sunday, Shaw entered
the doctoral program at Boston Medical School. "In her work among the
poor of Boston with the Home Missionary Society while she was in the
theological school," Harper wrote, "she had seen the great need of some
medical knowledge, of ministering to the body as well as the soul, and
she began to study medicine."[45] In a speech delivered in Birmingham,
Alabama, in 1915 while she was president of the National American
Woman Suffrage Association, Shaw recalled her decision to pursue a
medical degree. She had "attempted to help the homeless and the for-
saken and the betrayed women" by applying her knowledge of theology,
but, she said:

44. Ibid., 134.
45. Harper, "Biography of Anna Howard Shaw," 41.

In a little while I found that I had nothing to give that they wanted, and I also found out that, although I knew some things about theology, I knew very little about human beings; and I learned something there that I had not learned at any school. I learned to understand why the Master taught us to say: "Give us this day our daily bread" before He said: "Forgive us our sins"; for I learned that it is useless to talk virtue to a starving girl.[46]

Her brother James, a physician, encouraged her medical interest. Shaw wrote to a friend in July 1882:

What do you think my brother, Dr. James Shaw, is trying to do? He wants me to study medicine, even if I do not take a full course. I have often wished I knew something about it and then if my sex cut me loose from church work that would pay my expenses and keep me going, but I do not want to do anything that will interfere with my preaching. I would not be happy doing anything else.

She admitted that the medical course would serve "partly as an outlet for my surplus energy." By that time in her life she had become accustomed to hard work and seemed to thrive on the variety and extent of the demands placed on her. The trustees of the church granted her permission to spend several days each week at school in Boston. Harper reported, "She entered the School of Medicine of Boston University in 1882 and received her diploma in June, 1886. The reports of her final examination read: General Surgery 76; Materia Medica [*sic*] 90; Insanity and Nervous Diseases 91, etc., and during these years her parish work had not been neglected."[47]

Most of Shaw's excess energy, however, was devoted to nineteenth-century reforms. Like Brown Blackwell, Shaw began her work for reform years before she entered the pastorate. As a student at Albion College, she had lectured for the local temperance society in order to earn funds needed to remain in college:

My original fund of eighteen dollars was now supplemented by the proceeds of a series of lectures I gave on temperance. The temperance

46. Anna Howard Shaw, "A Speech by Dr. Anna Howard Shaw (President of the National American Woman Suffrage Association)," Birmingham, Ala., April 16, 1915 (New York: National Woman Suffrage Publishing, 1915), 3–4.
47. Harper, "Biography of Anna Howard Shaw," 41, 42.

women were not yet organized, but they had their speakers, and I was occasionally paid five dollars to hold forth for an hour or two in the little country school-houses of our region.[48]

It was not until she moved east to Boston, however, that she became enmeshed in the web of reformers and issues that dominated that part of the country. In Boston she encountered the preaching of two leading social reformers of the day: Phillips Brooks, the most eminent preacher in Boston, and James Freeman Clarke, a Unitarian minister, Transcendentalist, and avid abolitionist and supporter of woman's rights. She also was greatly influenced there by the lecturing of Mary Livermore, co-editor of the *Woman's Journal* and founding member of the American Woman Suffrage Association, and Frances Willard, prominent suffragist and president of the Woman's Christian Temperance Union, with whom Shaw became "closely associated in work and affection."[49]

It was also in Boston, which had long served as a center of woman's rights activism, that Shaw became acquainted and involved with the leadership of the woman suffrage movement. In an interview in 1902 she was asked when she had become interested in woman suffrage. " 'There never was a time in my memory when I was not interested,' " she responded. " 'I have always been speaking for Suffrage, and urging equal rights for women with men in every way.' "[50] Shaw had witnessed and experienced gender inequality throughout her life. As a child she witnessed the devastating effects on her family from the abuses and deprivations perpetrated by her father on her mother. As a young woman she experienced condemnation from her parents and siblings for her educational and pastoral pursuits. As a student she was denied the financial support and encouragement readily given to her male colleagues. As a newly trained and competent pastor she faced repeated rejection from the ecclesiastical communities in which she sought to assert her gifts and claim her God-given call to ministry. All of these experiences were attributable at their core to the gender inequalities that prevailed in and shaped American culture and institutions during the nineteenth century.

Anna Howard Shaw's path from parish ministry to suffrage work was also shaped by her personal confrontations with the deleterious effects of social injustice. Even after she obtained her medical degree and began her

48. Shaw, *Story of a Pioneer*, 72.
49. Ibid., 96.
50. Miller, "Interviews with the American Suffrage Leaders," 336.

medical work in the Boston slums, which she expected would satisfy her growing sense of helplessness in the face of human suffering, she continued to feel powerless against a social system that condemned many women to lives of poverty and disease:

> Here again, with my association with women of the streets, I realized the limitations of my work in the ministry and in medicine. As minister to soul and body one could do little for these women. For such as them, one's efforts must begin at the very foundation of the social structure. Laws for them must be made and enforced, and some of those laws could only be made and enforced by women.[51]

Shaw attributed her leadership in the suffrage movement to her acquaintance with Lucy Stone, by that time president of the Massachusetts Association, and Stone's husband, Henry Blackwell. Her work with Lucy Stone and Henry Blackwell, she recalled,

> developed in me a vital interest in the suffrage cause, which grew steadily from that time until it became the dominating influence in my life. I preached it in the pulpit, talked it to those I met outside of the church, lectured on it whenever I had an opportunity, and carried it into my medical work in the Boston slums when I was trying my prentice hand on helpless pauper patients.[52]

Stone and Blackwell recognized Shaw's potential as an eloquent advocate for their cause. "As early as August 1881," Ida Husted Harper, her biographer, wrote, "a letter from Lucy Stone asked: 'Can you give some woman suffrage lectures in September and October along on the Cape if all arrangements are made for you? We can pay five dollars a lecture and expenses.'"[53] In response to that request, Shaw added responsibilities as a lecturer for the Massachusetts Woman Suffrage Association to her already full life as pastor of two Cape Cod churches and student at Boston Medical School.

In contrast to Antoinette Brown Blackwell, Anna Howard Shaw seemed able to juggle her suffrage and parish work quite easily, but despite having a life that would strike most of us as overcommitted, she described

---

51. Shaw, *Story of a Pioneer*, 141–42.
52. Ibid., 141.
53. Harper, "Biography of Anna Howard Shaw," 42.

feeling that she was "getting into a rut" after four years in East Dennis. Her congregations, having already allowed her to enter the medical program in Boston, also allowed her to accept the responsibility of lecturing for suffrage. That permission, she said, "helped to keep me contented."[54] Rather than distracting her from her ministerial duties or fragmenting her life in a way that was detrimental to her well-being, as Brown Blackwell's woman's rights activity did for her, Shaw thrived on the threefold life of pastoral ministry, medicine, and reform work that she had established for herself by the early 1880s. Her activities outside the parish provided an outlet for her boundless energy and, as she and her parishioners no doubt recognized, made her a more effective pastor. For a while, Shaw managed to juggle all her professional responsibilities and feel that she was working toward her grand vision of justice and freedom for all people.

In 1885, after seven years of pastoral ministry, she eventually grew less satisfied with the routine of her life:

> There is a theory that every seven years each human being undergoes a complete physical reconstruction, with corresponding changes in his mental and spiritual make-up. Possibly it was due to this reconstruction that, at the end of seven years on Cape Cod, my soul sent forth a sudden call to arms. I was, it reminded me, taking life too easily; I was in danger of settling into an agreeable routine. The work of my two churches made little drain on my superabundant vitality, and not even the winning of a medical degree and the increasing demands of my activities on the lecture platform wholly eased my conscience. I was happy, for I loved my people and they seemed to love me. It would have been pleasant to go on almost indefinitely, living the life of a country minister and telling myself that what I could give to my flock made such a life worth while.

Shaw, however, felt deep in her heart the needs of the outside world, "and heard its prayer for workers." Her theological and medical degrees expanded her horizons, she said, and she sensed that her call was to serve a wider congregation than that represented by her Cape Cod churches or by the people whose medical needs she cared for in the Boston slums. She also heard the "rallying-cry" of the reformers who came to East Dennis to lecture. Those women "were fighting great battles," she realized, for

---

54. Shaw, *Story of a Pioneer*, 142.

suffrage, for temperance, and for social purity. "So many great avenues of life were opening up before me," she realized, "that my Cape Cod environment seemed almost a prison where I was held with tender force. I loved my people and they loved me—but the big outer world was calling, and I could not close my ears to its summons." Suffrage lecturing kept her contented and busy for a while, but eventually she could no longer resist that "summons" to the "big outer world." "So it was," Shaw wrote, "that, in 1885, I suddenly pulled myself up to a radical decision and sent my resignation to the trustees of the two churches whose pastor I had been since 1878."[55]

Shaw's resignation "caused a demonstration of regret which made it hard to keep to my resolution and leave these men and women whose friendship was among the dearest of my possessions." But her congregations accepted her decision and respected her new sense of call. They began offering all manner of tribute to what she had meant to them. One of the most amusing tributes

> came from a young girl in the parish, who broke into loud protests when she heard that I was going away. To comfort her I predicted that she would now have a man minister—doubtless a very nice man. But the young person continued to sniffle disconsolately.
>
> "I don't want a man," she wailed. "I don't like to see men in pulpits. They look so awkward." Her grief culminated in a final outburst. "They're all arms and legs!" she sobbed.

This incident remains amusing more than one hundred years later. But it is also profound in that it reveals how strong a role model for her parishioners Shaw had become during her time on Cape Cod. There would have been young members of her congregations who remembered no minister other than Shaw and for whom having a woman minister had become commonplace. Even many of the crusty old sailors who were among her flock and who surely had struggled to accept a woman in the pulpit expressed their affection for her. One of them, Captain Doane, who had grown to love Shaw, later admitted to her that he rarely went to church after she left. " 'When I heard you preach,' he explained, 'I gen'ally followed you through and I knowed where you was a-comin' out. But these young fellers that come from the theological school—why, Sister Shaw, the Lord Himself don't know where they're comin' out!' " He then

---

55. Ibid., 146, 142, 147.

referred to their earlier troubled relationship and how much had changed in the intervening years:

> "When you fust come to us," he said, "you had a lot of crooked places, an' we had a lot of crooked places; and we kind of run into each other, all of us. But before you left, Sister Shaw, why, all the crooked places was wore off and everything was as smooth as silk."
>
> "Yes," I agreed, "and that was the time to leave—when everything was running smoothly."[56]

A Congregation "thoroughly united and most congenial": Olympia Brown

Of these three nineteenth-century clergywomen, Olympia Brown had the most extensive ministry in parish settings. After spending several months with her family in Michigan while her brother recovered from a severe attack of rheumatism, and after studying elocution in Boston, Brown was ready to seek a church. In the spring of 1864, she contacted the Reverend A. A. Miner, head of the Universalist Association, the headquarters of which were located, conveniently, in Boston. In a less-than-enthusiastic response to Brown's inquiry, he warned her of the opposition to women ministers still prevalent in the denomination as well as his own ambivalence, saying, "It is no use opposing them. If they can't preach they won't preach. People don't do what they can't do."[57] Nevertheless he suggested that she pursue a pastorate that was vacant at the Universalist church in Weymouth Landing just south of Boston. Her reception by the trustees of the congregation proved to be the same as that of the church leaders she had encountered in Vermont: they reluctantly invited her to preach a trial sermon one Sunday, adding that she could stay if the congregation so desired. Her sermon must have impressed them, for the congregation voted overwhelmingly to hire her, and she remained their pastor for five years. After several months at Weymouth, the church arranged for a proper service of installation for Brown. The service, held on July 8, 1864, was led by several prominent Universalist ministers from the area.[58]

56. Ibid., 147–48, 150–51.

57. Olympia Brown, *An Autobiography*, ed. Gwendolen B. Willis, *Annual Journal of the Universalist Historical Society* 4 (1963): 33.

58. There is a copy of the church bulletin from Brown's installation at Weymouth in her papers. See OBP, SL, Fol. 10.

From Brown's own observations of the character of her congregation at Weymouth and her obvious compatibility with them, it is easy to see from the beginning that her ministry would not be troubled by the kind of theological and ideological problems that devastated Brown Blackwell's pastorate in South Butler. Those who embraced Universalist doctrine tended to be liberal in both their theological and social views, and the Weymouth congregation exemplified such Universalist views. "Looking back upon that time," Brown recalled,

> I think that the whole church must have been reformers since they were willing to accept a woman as pastor at a time when there was, perhaps, no woman pastor in the whole country and there are so few people who are willing to depart from old customs. The people of Weymouth were accustomed to going to Boston to hear [Wendell] Phillips and [William Lloyd] Garrison and other great speakers of that day and partook somewhat of the same spirit.[59]

She later recalled fondly the chairman of the board of trustees at Weymouth, Elias Richards, who "was so calm, so wise, so just, and his vision was so broad and his charity for his fellow men so far reaching, that he really seemed a model man." Richards was acquainted with some of the leading reformers of the day and invited them to lecture at Weymouth, a practice Brown encouraged as pastor. So it was that Brown, as pastor in a liberal tradition, a progressive community, and a congregation that "approved of every step of a forward nature," had a far more welcoming and comfortable situation in which to serve than Brown Blackwell and perhaps even Shaw. To add to her good experience at Weymouth, Brown met her future husband, John Willis, while serving there. Willis was a member of the board of trustees of the church and a well-respected and admired member of the community.

While Brown's congregation supported her ministry, as in the cases of Brown Blackwell and Shaw her fellow clergy did not. The assassination of Abraham Lincoln occurred about a year after Brown went to Weymouth. In an effort to acknowledge the shared grief of the nation, the ministers of the churches in Weymouth met to plan a memorial service for the slain president. The idea of a joint service, however, was abandoned as several ministers refused or hesitated to share in a service with Brown. "It

---

59. Olympia Brown, *Acquaintances, Old and New, Among Reformers* (Milwaukee, Wis.: Press of S. E. Tate Printing, 1911), 49.

presently became evident that they were all unwilling to unite in a service with a woman preacher," she recalled. "Therefore, we held our own service. I preached as good a memorial sermon as I could, and when the day was over all my church joined in approving my efforts."[60] Brown's experience with the Lincoln memorial service reveals the only tension in her relationships in Weymouth. On the one hand, she received great admiration and support from her congregation, which contributed significantly to her well-being and success as a pastor, especially a woman pastor. On the other hand, she lacked the support of colleagues in ministry. Obviously the former more than made up for the latter so that she was able to be content and serve effectively in Weymouth for five years.

In Weymouth Brown encountered neither the strident, destructive orthodoxy that Brown Blackwell encountered in her congregation (such an expression of orthodoxy being alien to the Universalist tradition) nor the divisive factions that Shaw discovered in East Dennis. She did, however, encounter some division prompted by the popular new religious ideology known as spiritualism. Her predecessor in the pastorate at Weymouth remained in the community as a proponent of spiritualism and held séances "which were attended by a number, who having been alienated from the church found an interest in these exhibitions of supposed spiritual power; some declaring that it would be impossible for them ever to attend church again after being so 'fed' at the spiritualist meetings." Brown assured those who questioned her on the subject that she was neither "illiberal or opposed to spiritualism" and was even open to the possibility of attending a séance. After that, the invitations to various séances in the community poured in, and she kept her word by attending some. But she remained unconvinced by the doctrines of spiritualism and concluded:

> I do not know what truth there may have been in the claims which were made, and these by persons whom I knew to be sincere and above intentional deception. But I can only say that I gained nothing of any kind from such experiences. On the contrary I found the whole subject a great stumbling block in my path, absorbing the interest and the time of my parishioners, and those who would have been such, and furnishing them nothing substantial in place of the work and thought which they cast aside.[61]

60. Brown, *Autobiography*, 35.
61. Ibid., 35, 37.

Brown's reaction to the newfound interest of some in her congregation demonstrates that at least a few her parishioners were more liberal than she. Despite that theological disparity between Brown and some of her flock, and despite the "stumbling block," as she called it, that spiritualism placed in her path, Brown continued to have a good relationship with her congregation and seemed quite content at Weymouth. While there she developed her homiletical and oratorical skills. She prepared and presented two sermons each week, eventually training herself to speak without a manuscript. "And from the time I left Weymouth until the present day," she wrote shortly before her death in 1926, "I have almost never used a manuscript."[62]

During her tenure at Weymouth, Brown made her first appearances on the suffrage platform. Susan B. Anthony, who had tried to coax Brown into helping with woman's rights work a few years earlier when Brown was serving the church in Marshfield, wrote to her again to invite her to assist with the reorganization of the postwar woman's movement. Brown agreed this time and traveled to New York City for the woman's rights convention where she was captivated by the oratory of Anthony, Elizabeth Cady Stanton, Henry Ward Beecher, Frederick Douglass, and other leading reformers of the day. At the convention, she joined several of those reformers in establishing the American Equal Rights Association, an organization committed to working for both woman's rights and rights for African Americans. With a leave of absence granted by her church, Brown joined Anthony and others on a six-week tour of New York state to campaign for equal rights at the end of 1866.

Six months after the New York tour, Brown once again interrupted her ministry in Weymouth with the permission of the church to spend several months campaigning in Kansas for an impartial suffrage amendment intended to enfranchise both women and African Americans. If the amendment passed, Kansas would become the first state in the nation to grant impartial suffrage. The success of the amendment would give an unprecedented boost to the movement for equal rights. Woman's rights organizers sought an eloquent, informed speaker to proclaim their cause across the Kansas frontier. Lucy Stone herself visited Brown at Weymouth to convince Brown that she had the ability and, with the grant of

---

62. Ibid., 37. Brown's papers include more than one hundred sermon manuscripts, some of which are more than forty pages in length, and sermon notes. It is remarkable that she was able to deliver those sermons extemporaneously after carefully writing them out by hand. See OBP, SL, Fols. 51–126.

an extended leave from the church, the freedom to spend four months campaigning in Kansas for the amendment.

Despite the hard work of Brown and many others, the Kansas amendment was defeated. Her work in Kansas, however, continued to receive accolades from leaders of the movement long after she had returned to Weymouth, making the defeat a bit easier to bear. Brown turned her disappointment into a renewed commitment to her parish work. While she was in Kansas, the congregation had done its part to affirm her ministry by refurbishing the church. The basement, previously rented out for a meat market, had been transformed into a reading room and lecture and social halls. The sanctuary also received new appointments, she recalled:

> A new pulpit had been built, and a new organ installed. I was afterward given, by Mr. George Baker, a beautiful work box made out of a part of the old pulpit. The people were in good spirits and ready for a campaign in behalf of Universalism. I shall never forget my pleasure when I knew how much they had done for the church in my absence.[63]

The support and affection Brown felt when she returned to Weymouth indicated once again her compatibility with the congregation. In her recollections of those years of her ministry, she gave every indication that the congregation believed in her work for suffrage and was prepared to "share" her with this important work for reform. There appeared to be no resistance to this second "ministry" to which Brown felt called. Once again, the ideological and theological compatibility between Brown and her people at Weymouth were great enough to allow her to commit significant time and energy to an ancillary field of service. In 1868, a year after the Kansas campaign and while she was still at Weymouth, Brown founded the New England Woman's Suffrage Association, the first association in the United States formed exclusively for the pursuit of woman suffrage. "The old Anti-slavery workers," Brown perceived, "in winning their victory felt that all other victories were comprised in that, and I saw that although they favored woman's suffrage they would do nothing for it unless we could make our reform a clear-cut, separate, and single question."[64]

63. Ibid., 38.
64. Ibid.

Brown accepted a call from the Universalist congregation at Bridgeport, Connecticut, and began her duties there on October 1, 1869. In the letter of call from Samuel Larkin, head of the trustees of the Bridgeport congregation, Brown was told of the opposition to her call "from only two of the male members of the society, one in oposition [*sic*] to a woman's preaching, the other didn't know how the female portion of the society would like it." "But for all that," Mr. Larkin assured her, "the larger portion by far are in favour of it."[65] Brown decided that Bridgeport offered her "a larger field of usefulness." The Weymouth congregation bade her farewell with thoughtful gifts and good resolutions concerning her work, and she "bade Weymouth goodbye with regret." In Bridgeport her challenges included church members who, though numerous, had lost interest in the church, let it deteriorate, and even had considered merging with another congregation. "I found the people unlike my Weymouth people," Brown remarked. "They had no such breadth of vision." Undaunted, she threw herself "into the work of interesting them, working in the Sunday School and preparing my sermons." Over her six years as pastor the congregation turned around and "took on a different aspect. In fact we succeeded in putting it on a good foundation and the Sunday School was very much improved. There was none in the city which the members attended with greater enthusiasm." P. T. Barnum, the famous showman, was a member of the congregation. "He was very friendly to me," she recalled, "and often made some complimentary remark as I came down from my pulpit."[66] A story from her ministry at Bridgeport claims that when Brown implored the congregation for more generosity in their giving, she would address Barnum personally, saying, "Mr. Barnum, I mean you." Apparently Barnum took no offense at her forwardness; according to the story, "Mr. Barnum never failed to oblige her."[67]

Life in Bridgeport grew increasingly complex for Olympia Brown. In addition to her work with the congregation, she became an indispensable part of the growing woman suffrage movement. In the spring of 1869 she assisted Susan B. Anthony in the organization of the National Woman Suffrage Association, which quickly gained a reputation for its radical tactics and ideology. The NWSA limited leadership positions to women, favored more liberal divorce laws, discouraged support for the Fourteenth and Fifteenth Amendments that prohibited woman suffrage, and worked

65. Samuel Larkin to Olympia Brown, June 1, 1869, OBP, SL, Fol. 130.
66. Brown, *Autobiography*, 38, 39.
67. Charlotte Coté, *Olympia Brown* (Racine, Wis.: Mother Courage Press, 1988), 106.

for a federal suffrage amendment rather than moving toward suffrage state by state. When, six months later, Lucy Stone and other suffrage leaders left the NWSA to form the American Woman Suffrage Association, meant to attract more conservative suffrage supporters, Brown committed herself to work for the new group as well. The two groups became increasingly alienated from each other, but Brown appears to have successfully supported both groups, distancing herself from the politicization and personal differences that characterized the woman's movement following the Civil War. Brown also added a new relationship to her already full life when she married John Henry Willis. Willis had followed her from Weymouth Landing to Bridgeport and became a persistent, supportive, and patient suitor as Brown managed to schedule visits with him in between her preaching, pastoral work, lecturing, and travel. The couple married in April 1873 at the home of family members in Rhode Island. While she was largely silent in her autobiographical materials about their relationship, her occasional references to Willis make it obvious that theirs was a strong and uniquely (for the time) egalitarian marriage. Brown admitted,

> My mother and many of my friends had advised me against marrying as they felt it would interfere with my preaching, but I thought that with a husband so entirely in sympathy with my work marriage could not interfere, but rather assist. And so it proved, for I could have married no better man. He shared in all my undertakings, and always stood for the right.[68]

Brown's fulfilling and seemingly contented life in Bridgeport began to unravel following the birth of her first child in 1874, when a small faction in the church that had always opposed the hiring of a woman minister became more vocal in its opposition to her. And while a majority of the members still supported her, some began to drift away due to the continuing dissension in the church. This experience proved to be one of the few incidents of blatant gender prejudice that Brown encountered in her several pastorates. All of her congregations expressed some doubt about the appropriateness of hiring a woman pastor, but all came to embrace Brown and respect her pastoral abilities. The small group of dissidents in Bridgeport worked hard to drum up support for their campaign against her by enlisting local ministers "to go among the people promulgating

---

68. Brown, *Autobiography*, 40.

this doctrine, 'what you need here is a good man.' "[69] Other factors worked against Brown as well, including the offense some members took at her references to political issues in the pulpit, disagreement with some of her liturgical practices, and a growing interest in spiritualism among members of the congregation.[70] When she left, Brown nonetheless still found much satisfaction in "an actual record of successful work for between six and seven years and an enlarged church and Sunday School."[71]

In 1876 Brown began a two-year hiatus from ministry during which she gave birth to her second child. But she sensed the call of the parish once again and sought a new congregation to serve. A Universalist church in Racine, Wisconsin, advertised for a pastor in January 1878, and the thought of renewing her Midwest ties appealed to Brown. When she contacted the clerk of the Racine (Universalist) Society, she received a rather discouraging reply describing the parish as "in a rundown and unfortunate condition." "A series of pastors," Brown was told, "easy-going, unpractical, some even spiritually unworthy, had left the church adrift, in debt, hopeless, and doubtful whether any pastor could again arouse them." Like Brown Blackwell and Shaw, Brown was undaunted by troubled congregations. And like her early female colleagues in ministry, she recognized the limitations imposed by her gender when seeking congregations to serve. Rather than begrudging the calls to larger, more prosperous congregations received by her male counterparts, Brown came to regard her ability to transform struggling churches as part of her unique gifts for ministry. In reflecting on her decision to accept the call to the Racine congregation, she stated:

> Those who may read this will think it strange that I could only find a field in run-down or comatose churches, but they must remember that the pulpits of all the prosperous churches were already occupied by men, and were looked forward to as the goal of all the young men coming into the ministry with whom I, at first the only woman preacher in the denomination, had to compete. All I could do was to take some place that had been abandoned by others and make something of it, and this I was only too glad to do.[72]

69. Ibid.
70. Coté, *Olympia Brown*, 112.
71. Brown, *Autobiography*, 40.
72. Ibid., 41.

Once again, Brown impressed a congregation with her preaching ability, and, after the second Sunday of her visit to Racine in February 1878, the church immediately called her to serve as pastor. Brown seemed uniquely suited to life in Racine. Her mother had by that time moved in with the family to help care for Brown's children, and her husband became publisher of the local newspaper and a respected member of the community. The contentment she felt in other areas of her life surely influenced the good work she was able to accomplish in the church. Brown found the church to be without conflict once a hardworking, responsible pastor was in place and the members to be "a very happy company of believers, bound together by our regard for the great principles of Universalism."[73] As a result of an intensive campaign marked by long days of pastoral visits, Brown managed to raise several thousand dollars to remodel the Church of the Good Shepherd.

Through the last quarter of the nineteenth century and throughout her ministry in Racine, Brown maintained ties to the growing suffrage movement. While her church was being renovated, she completed a lecture tour through the New England states, leaving her pulpit in the hands of her sister and another friend, both of whom she regarded as eloquent speakers. She also promoted suffrage through her own sermons[74] and by bringing to Racine national leaders of the suffrage movement such as Elizabeth Cady Stanton, Susan B. Anthony, Mary A. Livermore, and Theodore Tilton. When the suffrage movement divided after the Civil War into the National and American Suffrage Associations, both Susan B. Anthony and Lucy Stone, respective leaders of the two groups, vied for Brown's allegiance and efforts. Strident political and ideological debates characterized the movement through the 1870s. "I found it hard to keep from being entangled in these discussions," Brown admitted, "although I desired only to pursue my ministerial work, giving such time as I could spare from this to the work of women's enfranchisement."[75]

After several years of balancing pastoral and reform work along with

73. Ibid., 42.

74. Brown never hesitated to mix politics with religion, freely promoting social concerns such as temperance and woman's rights in her sermons. The references to these issues in her sermons are too numerous to mention, but one significant example is her sermon on the position of women and female education based on the New Testament story of Martha, who seeks knowledge at the feet of Jesus (OBP, SL, Fol. 83).

75. Brown, *Autobiography*, 62.

family responsibilities, Brown realized that "the demands of the movement for the enfranchisement of women were growing ever more pressing." She managed to serve her congregation while taking leaves for lecture tours and preparing petitions for Congress and state legislatures, insisting that her suffrage work had been "incidental to my preaching."[76] During her first six years in Racine, she assisted in the work of the Wisconsin State Woman's Suffrage Association and was named the association's president in 1884, a position she held for almost thirty years. But the defining moment in her move to full-time suffrage work occurred with the passage of the so-called School Suffrage Law by the Wisconsin Legislature in 1885. The law would allow women to vote in "any election pertaining to school matters." This "piecemeal" approach to achieving universal woman suffrage was working in other states. It required, however, an intentional effort to inform women of their new rights and to encourage them to participate in the electoral process, something foreign—and even frightening—to them. At this point in her life, Brown's call to suffrage work transcended her call to ministry, and she resigned her position at the Universalist Church in Racine in 1887 to assist with the state canvass of women voters.

Brown offered little reflection on her move from parish ministry to suffrage work. Her writings give "no clear explanation for this decision," notes Dana Greene, one of Brown's biographers. "There is no indication that she was frustrated with her work as a minister. Rather over the years she became more deeply involved in suffrage work and by 1887 she saw that there was much to be done in Wisconsin and no one ready to do it."[77] In Brown's words:

> As the years passed by it became more and more clear that I must give myself more to the suffrage work. There seemed to be no one else in Wisconsin fitted and willing to take upon herself the combined work of organizing, canvassing, speaking. . . . I brought the chief advocates of the suffrage cause to Racine for lectures and meetings but it was not possible for me to undertake lengthy trips about the state and still do justice to my parish and my family. The immediate occasion of my resignation therefore was the Suffrage Bill which passed the legislature of 1885 and was voted on and became a law in 1886. This law

76. Ibid., 43.
77. Dana Greene, ed., *Suffrage and Religious Principle* (Metuchen, N.J.: Scarecrow Press, 1983), 4.

provided that every woman having the proper voter's qualifications should have the right to vote "at any election pertaining to school matters."[78]

The decision to give up her church no doubt was a difficult one for Brown, but she realized that she would always serve as a preacher and pastor in some capacity. "I had held this post nine years," she recalled. "But I had no intention of giving up my ministry altogether. In fact, I preached a great deal after this resignation; four years in Mukwonago, Wisconsin; two in Columbus, and one in Neenah at different subsequent periods."[79] The congregation at first refused to accept her resignation, but Brown convinced them of the importance of the new work she felt called to do. While she never commented on the congregation's feelings toward her new "ministry," it is not difficult to imagine that while they regretted her departure, they understood her compelling call to suffrage work. The church—and the community—had become acquainted with many of the great reformers and ideologies of the day through the lecture series Brown organized. She had made her church "one of the most important social and educational influences" in the town of Racine. It was her duty, Brown declared, "as well as a pleasure, to bring to the town as many important speakers as I could command, and our church became known for its lecture courses and entertainments."[80] Brown had helped her congregation gain an appreciation for the urgency of woman suffrage, and they, in turn, must have recognized the importance of the work she was about to undertake.

Taking the World for Their Pastoral Charge:
From Preachers to Suffragists

In their own times and ways, Brown Blackwell, Brown, and Shaw eventually heeded the challenge once placed before Olympia Brown by Susan B. Anthony to "take the *World* for your *Pastoral Charge*."[81] While the particular circumstances surrounding their resignations from their respective congregations varied somewhat, historians Carl J. and Dorothy Schneider note that "the same thinking underlay the decision of each—

---

78. Brown, *Autobiography*, 62.
79. Ibid., 43.
80. Ibid.
81. Susan B. Anthony to Olympia Brown, March 12, 1868, OBP, SL, Fol. 129.

a recognition of the need for women's rights before women could serve the church to their full capacity."[82] They sensed calls to broader ministries and larger, more diverse congregations—ministries and congregations that comprised the essential work of woman suffrage. All three women were similarly inspired by a compelling vision of human equality that would replace the inequality they had witnessed and experienced in both sacred and secular realms. Their new calls were no less fervent than—nor entirely unrelated to—their previous calls; they would simply be fulfilled in a larger venue. Brown Blackwell, Brown, and Shaw eventually came to acknowledge the reality that they could hasten their wholistic vision of the kingdom of God—a kingdom characterized by gender and social equality—by promoting that vision in the political sphere rather than in the limited ecclesiastical spheres available to parish ministers. "Now in the latter half of the nineteenth century," the Schneiders state, "these feminist Christians shifted their energies away from religion toward political solutions for their situation."[83]

Antoinette Brown Blackwell

Antoinette Brown Blackwell is the only one of the three who might have admitted "giving up" ministry when she resigned from the South Butler Congregational Church and committed herself to traveling and lecturing for woman's rights. Her experience in parish ministry was the most short-lived and troubled of the three. But even she never intended to give up the ministry of preaching, to which she felt a primary allegiance. "The only reason for leaving Butler," she insisted in a letter to Horace Greeley, "is my *health* and the necessity for a few months leisure-time for rest, thought, and study; interspersed with lecturing."[84] She completed a series of lectures for the New York Antislavery Society at the end of 1854 and commenced a speaking tour on behalf of woman's rights early in 1855.

If a single factor loomed large in Brown Blackwell's move from parish ministry to reform work, it was undoubtedly her growing theological liberalism. Her writings and actions in the months following her resignation from the South Butler church reveal her struggle to balance her evolving

82. Carl J. and Dorothy Schneider, *In Their Own Right* (New York: Crossroad Publishing, 1997), 69.

83. Ibid.

84. Antoinette Brown Blackwell to Horace Greeley, September 6, 1854, as quoted in Cazden, *Antoinette Brown Blackwell*, 93.

theological convictions with her still-persistent call to ministry. Despite her rebellion against the constraints of Protestant orthodoxy that had, in large part, driven her from the pastorate, she continued to feel called to ministry and even to service to the church in some generalized form. She

> was never settled over another parish after resigning at South Butler. She preached when and where she could find a pulpit open to her, until as pastor emeritus of the little church at Elizabeth, N.J., she had a regularly monthly hearing. Yet it was as a *minister* that she thought of herself and wanted to be thought of, not as a reformer, nor a pioneer in other fields.[85]

Early in 1855, she pursued—at her own initiative this time—the possibility of preaching on Sundays in a rented hall, the idea once posed to her by Horace Greeley and Charles Dana. She admitted to Greeley that she could never again be "the *pastor of a Church*," but at the same time she also acknowledged that she "must be *a preacher for the people*."[86] She defined her religion at that time as "a free one" that interpreted truths as "revelation from Nature's God to the soul." Therefore, "one must be outside of all sectarian pressure to speak it freely. This can be better done in the city than the country—in NY than in any smaller place."[87] The kind of free religious exploration Brown Blackwell felt led to do was possible only in a context outside traditional ecclesiastical boundaries, so she arranged to rent a hall in New York City where she would, once each Sunday, "try to preach a *free gospel to the people*."[88]

Beginning in the spring of 1855, Brown Blackwell preached on Sundays in various halls in New York while continuing lecture tours on behalf of woman's rights. While preaching in New York, she encountered for the first time the devastating effects of urbanization on the poor. She joined other female reformers already at work to address the exigencies of poverty. Greeley solicited from her reports of her experiences among the poor and immigrant communities, imploring her to "expose the blackest evils in the severest language, as they deserve"[89] and asked her to write a

85. Gilson ms., 20.

86. Antoinette Brown Blackwell to Horace Greeley, January 8, 1855, as quoted in Cazden, *Antoinette Brown Blackwell*, 94.

87. Ibid.

88. Antoinette Brown Blackwell to Gerrit Smith, February 8, 1855, as quoted in Cazden, *Antoinette Brown Blackwell*, 95.

89. Antoinette Brown Blackwell to Samuel C. Blackwell, n.d., BFP, SL, Fol. 23.

series of articles on the topic for the *New York Tribune*. In the first article, titled "Shadows of Our Social System," she described the exigencies of poverty—starvation, insanity, illness, even death—as "shadows" in contrast to the benefits of economic and industrial progress:

> An opaqueness attaches to all finite powers, and throws a shade of imperfection over their best works. . . . Polished, enlightened, civilized, Christianized society has yet the black shadow, more or less dense; on its vine-trellised cottages, and its marble palaces, its temples of justice, and its halls of learning; on its costly churches built up as grand houses for God's people to fall asleep in, and on its church spires with their long fingers pointing far up toward heaven; on the cheek of the little maiden, and on the brow of the grave judge.[90]

In her assessment of the social situation, Brown Blackwell revealed her contempt for rigid, punitive theological understandings by relating a story of a young woman who believed that her devastating social lot was the result of having "committed sins enough before I was three years old to make it impossible for me ever to be forgiven." The young woman's guilt and despair had driven her to insanity and an asylum. Brown Blackwell encountered her there and tried to dissuade her from her paralyzing theological notion. "But on this point she was fixed," Brown Blackwell wrote. "From her babyhood she had been taught that a child of three years might commit sin enough to merit eternal punishment; and, in her present state, her own guilt magnified till it seemed too great to be forgiven."[91]

Another confirmation of the significance of the theological transformation that shaped Brown Blackwell's life following her parish ministry was her marriage to Samuel Blackwell. The brother of Henry Blackwell, who was soon to be the husband of Lucy Stone, Samuel had visited Antoinette in South Butler the previous year while traveling on business. The paths of Samuel and Antoinette crossed again in 1855 when they discovered that they had more in common than "the fact that his brother was in love with her closest friend. They were believers in woman's rights, abolition, temperance, but most important they were highly religious and, at the time they met, both losing their orthodoxy."[92] Antoinette Brown

---

90. Antoinette L. Brown, "Shadows of Our Social System," *New York Tribune*, May 3, 1855.
91. Ibid.
92. Elinor Rice Hays, *Those Extraordinary Blackwells* (New York: Harcourt, Brace & World, 1967), 121.

and Samuel Blackwell were married in the Brown family home on January 24, 1856. After the wedding, both spouses kept the promises they had made before they were married: Antoinette to continue her public speaking activity, and Sam to support her in doing so. Just a month after the wedding Brown Blackwell left her new home with Sam at the Blackwell family homestead in Cincinnati and went off on a lecture tour to Philadelphia and New Jersey.

Olympia Brown

Olympia Brown's move from preacher to suffragist revealed none of the theological or ecclesiastical angst exhibited by Brown Blackwell. Her call from parish ministry to a ministry of suffrage evolved over her more than twenty years of service to churches. The length of time she spent as a pastor makes her unique among this group of three clergywomen—indeed, it makes her unique among all clergywomen until late into the twentieth century. Her contentment and long tenure in parish ministry were due in large part to her commitment to and compatibility with the Univeralist tradition. The denomination itself was not always supportive of her, as evidenced by the mixed response of denominational leaders and fellow clergy to her ministry. But the Universalist tradition gave Brown a specific place in which to find her way as a woman pastor. It also provided her with liberal congregations with whom she shared similar theological, social, and political perspectives and that were, for the most part at least, progressive enough to welcome her ministry despite her gender. "Universalists and Unitarians," Carl and Dorothy Schneider remark, "tiny denominations, attracted a better-educated, more liberal membership than the Congregationalists and Methodists."[93] This close denominational affiliation, particularly with a liberal denomination, seemed critical to Brown's success in ministry. She also had at least a few women colleagues in the Universalist ministry with whom she shared the challenges and frustrations of being a clergywoman. The Reverend Phoebe Hanaford, whom Brown had encouraged to pursue ministry and for whose ordination Brown had preached in 1868, became a close friend and colleague with whom Brown shared a common commitment to the dual "callings" of the church and woman suffrage.

Despite her contentment in parish ministry, Brown finally gave in to

---

93. Schneider and Schneider, *In Their Own Right*, 69.

the compelling call to "take the *World* for [her] *Pastoral Charge*," as Susan B. Anthony had implored her nearly two decades earlier. Anthony had tried to entice Brown away from her pastoral commitments several times over the course of Brown's ministry. Brown appeased Anthony by speaking at state and national woman's rights gatherings and even joining extensive political tours while continuing to hold her pastoral positions. She resisted repeated invitations—and enticing salaries—to accept full-time suffrage positions, however, citing her commitment to and hard work to achieve her goal of ordination and pastoral service to the church.

When Brown finally did exchange her pastoral charge for suffrage work, she did so with a deep sense of the urgency of the need for woman's equality. Brown had witnessed the evolution of the woman's movement from its infancy when she, as a college student, carried a woman's rights petition door to door on the streets of Cleveland to its maturity as a vast, highly organized, fully funded national political movement. The closing decades of the nineteenth century were a critical time for the issue that had become the single objective of the decades-old woman's movement: full voting rights for women. States were beginning to consider particular or even universal suffrage laws pertaining to women. Wisconsin's passage of the School Suffrage Law represented for Brown the hard-won momentum of the movement. "I was determined to avail myself of it as it was the only suffrage law we had," she recalled. "Resigning my pastorate and securing a substitute for the fragment of a year (1887) which remained, I began to tour the state, instructing the women on the subject and urging them to vote at the next election."[94]

Brown found that, in much of the state, "people were pretty thoroughly waked up and in many places women voted and their votes were accepted." Her own city of Racine, however, was among the places where women's votes—including Brown's own—were rejected. Even though the suffrage law limited women's right to vote to "any election pertaining to school matters," Brown and the Wisconsin Woman Suffrage Association argued that, in Wisconsin, "*every* election 'pertained to school matters'" since school officials were elected at both spring and fall elections. Since "the candidates' names were on the same ballot with others and the law made no provision for women's using a separate ballot box . . . it seemed apparent that more was intended than would be

94. Brown, *Autobiography*, 63.

implied by a mere school suffrage law." Even "the members of the Senate committee who discussed the bill and referred it said that it was
intended to be, in effect, a full suffrage law." Not all the voting officials
agreed, however, and to prevent women from voting on issues and persons beyond school matters, they refused to allow them to vote at all. As
president of the Wisconsin Woman Suffrage Association, Brown initiated a lawsuit in November 1887 challenging those who prohibited
women from voting. "I was not in favor of bringing a suit," she later
recalled, "saying I preferred the law as it stood, in all its uncertainty, to
a decision against us. But others of the Executive Board of the Association did not agree with me and insisted that suit should be brought." A
judge of the Racine court ruled in her favor, but the state Supreme Court
overruled his verdict on appeal and interpreted the law as restricting
women's votes to school matters. "It was a great blow and caused discouragement to all the workers who had hoped to gain complete Suffrage under this law," Brown lamented. Not only that, but because the
law made no provision for separate ballot boxes, "it remained inopera-
tive for some fifteen years after its passage despite many efforts of the
women to avail themselves of it as a school law."[95] Not until 1901 were
separate ballot boxes provided for women in Wisconsin that enabled
them to vote on school issues and officers.

The furor and eventual court cases surrounding the School Suffrage
Law of Wisconsin surely confirmed Olympia Brown's decision to leave
parish ministry for suffrage work. By the late 1880s, there were enough
glimpses of progress toward woman suffrage to make her full-time efforts
worthwhile. Even her defeat by the Wisconsin Supreme Court ruling did
not discourage her; instead, she sublimated her anger by establishing *The
Wisconsin Citizen*, a state suffrage paper that was published continuously
from August 1887 until 1917. "Published once a month," Coté writes, "it
carried both state and national woman suffrage news, and it soon proved
to be an effective tool for educating women about working for the ballot."[96] *The Citizen*, as Wisconsin suffragists called it, became widely
respected within reform circles for the news and insights—often accompanied by sharp rhetoric—offered by Brown. It was one more manifestation of the sense of urgency that compelled Brown to make her move from
preacher to suffragist.

95. Ibid., 62, 63.
96. Coté, *Olympia Brown*, 128.

Anna Howard Shaw

Even Olympia Brown's sense of urgency in regard to the suffrage cause, however, was eclipsed by that demonstrated by Anna Howard Shaw. Shaw's difficult decision to leave her beloved congregations was motivated not by theological incompatibility with her people or specific frustration with her work but by an apprehension of the urgency of need for woman suffrage. Thirty years after leaving Cape Cod she recalled fondly the life and people she had known during her years as a pastor. "I am happy having known and loved the Cape as it was," she stated, "and in having gathered there a store of delightful memories. In later strenuous years it has rested me merely to think of the place, and long afterward I showed my continued love of it by building a home there, which I still possess." Immediately following her departure from Cape Cod, however, Shaw had little time for rest or reflection, "for now I was back in Boston, living my new life, and each crowded hour brought me more to do." Through her pastoral, medical, and political work she witnessed the increasingly devastating "shadows" of the social system that Brown Blackwell had described decades earlier. She also witnessed the growing concern for the welfare of women and children who were most vulnerable to the abusive effects of industrialization and urbanization. During the closing decades of the nineteenth century, the suffrage movement grew in strength and influence not only because of the increased efforts of suffragists but also in response to the rapidly changing sociopolitical climate of the United States. Thus, as an astute observer of the nature of life in urban America, Shaw noted the significance of the timing of her move from ministry to work for suffrage. "We were entering a deeply significant period," she recalled.

> For the first time women were going into industrial competition with men, and already men were intensely resenting their presence. Around me I saw women overworked and underpaid, doing men's work at half men's wages, not because their work was inferior, but because they were women. Again, too, I studied the obtrusive problems of the poor and of the women of the streets; and, looking at the whole social situation from every angle, I could find but one solution for women—the removal of the stigma of disfranchisement. As man's equal before the law, woman could demand her rights, asking favors from no one. With all my heart I joined in the crusade of the men and women who were fighting for her.

Despite the respect and appreciation Shaw had garnered as a pastor and despite her love for her people and her pastoral work, Shaw left parish ministry for suffrage work with a sense of peace, concluding, "My real work had begun."[97]

Being practical and having no one else to support her financially, Shaw realized that she could not survive without employment of some kind. "Of course, I had to earn my living," she realized; "but, though I had taken my medical degree only a few months before leaving Cape Cod, I had no intention of practising [*sic*] medicine. I had merely wished to add a certain amount of medical knowledge to my mental equipment." During the last two years of her pastorate, Shaw had been employed frequently as a lecturer for the Massachusetts Woman Suffrage Association under the presidency of Lucy Stone. The association was eager to have Shaw as a full-time lecturer and offered to pay her one hundred dollars a month to serve as a lecturer and organizer. With characteristic humility, Shaw accepted the position but refused the initial salary. "The amount seemed too large," she recalled, "and I told Mrs. Stone as much, after which I humbly fixed my salary at fifty dollars a month. At the end of a year of work I felt that I had 'made good'; then I asked for and received the one hundred dollars a month originally offered me."[98]

Shaw proved to be such a successful fund-raiser for the Massachusetts Association that she eventually requested a raise to one hundred and twenty-five dollars a month. She was assured that her work was worth that much, "but I was told that one hundred was the limit which could be paid, and I was reminded that this was a good salary for a woman." In response, Shaw left the Massachusetts Association and became an independent lecturer. During her first month as a freelancer, she earned three hundred dollars, proving to herself—and to others—her value as a lecturer. She eventually worked under the auspices of various lecture bureaus, earning herself a reputation as well as her first significant income. "I lectured night after night," she stated, "week after week, month after month, in 'Chautauquas' in the summer, all over the country in the winter, earning a large income and putting aside at that time the small surplus I still hold in preparation for the 'rainy day' every working-woman inwardly fears."[99]

As she traveled around the country and lectured on suffrage, Shaw described the sense of being part of a great cause that she regarded as

97. Shaw, *Story of a Pioneer*, 151, 152.
98. Ibid., 157.
99. Ibid., 158.

imbued by the very presence and purpose of God. That theological framework made her transition from parish ministry to a ministry of work for suffrage both logical and comfortable. Shaw never minced words about the difficulties she encountered as a professional lecturer or, later, as a national leader of the suffrage movement as they educated the nation on women's issues and campaigned for the ultimate freedom for women represented by the vote. She and her colleagues endured ridicule, prejudice, and hatred from outside the movement and squabbling, disunity, and petty jealousies among themselves. But she never expressed any regret for having chosen "the World" for her pastoral charge. Repeatedly in her speeches, sermons, and memoirs she revealed both her passion for the "cause" (often using a capital "C") of woman suffrage and her understanding of that cause as her life's ministry. When reflecting on her career in an address delivered before a student convocation at Temple University while she was head of the Woman's Committee of the Council of National Defense during World War I, Shaw eloquently concluded:

> I speak out of the fullness of a life's experience, forty years of which I have given to one great cause, for one purpose. The cause is called woman's enfranchisement, but it is much greater than that. If that were all, it would be narrow, selfish, and not part of a great whole. It is not that women may vote, but that the human in mankind may triumph. That civilization may conquer barbarism, may triumph over autocracy. That every child of God may have a fair chance to be and to become all that it is possible for it to attain. That democracy, which is not merely a form of government but the divine law of life emanating from the heart of the Infinite entering into the souls of men and transforming human character until some day it will respond in like spirit to the source from whence it springs. And when it does, we shall know that in Him there is neither male nor female, but all are alike one.[100]

While different factors contributed to the moves of Brown Blackwell, Brown, and Shaw from pastoral ministry to work for suffrage, all three women were adamant in reaffirming their original calls to ministry and their identity as preachers. They wanted to remain "preachers for the people," as Brown Blackwell described it, if not pastors of churches. They

---

100. Anna Howard Shaw, "Select Your Principle of Life," Address delivered at Temple University (Philadelphia, 1917), AHSP, SL, Fol. 470.

articulated a broader sense of call than that circumscribed by service to particular congregations, but it was a sense of call no less compelling or divine in nature than the calls that led them to their unprecedented ordinations. They continued to preach in pulpits and on platforms, occasionally to congregations gathered for worship but more often to gatherings of political and reform activists. In the process of their suffrage "ministries," they no doubt made converts of various sorts: converts to the gospel and to the gospel of female equality. Throughout the decades of their productive work for suffrage, they maintained and even promoted their clerical identities as the rare, precious, and hard-won gifts they were. Their writings and activities following their service to churches make it clear that these particular women did not "opt out of the clergy into other careers"[101] but moved into wider venues of ministry.

What is strikingly absent in the reasons for leaving parish ministry articulated by Brown Blackwell, Brown, and Shaw is any sense of gender discrimination directed at them by their churches. Any discrimination they might have felt was eclipsed by other issues such as theological incompatibility (Brown Blackwell) and the late-nineteenth-century momentum of the suffrage movement (Brown and Shaw). All three women expressed a sense of "going to" a new, larger call rather than "escaping from" something that had become intolerable. They worked hard to be faithful pastors, often battling against the odds of struggling churches, nonsupportive denominations, and mean-spirited clergy colleagues, and they offered gratitude for the grace demonstrated to them by the majority of their church members. By doing what they had been called to do—and doing it well and faithfully—they witnessed the changing of minds and hearts. With the achievement of ordination for women and their acceptance as pastors, Brown Blackwell, Brown, and Shaw felt they had already made their mark for equality in the church, freeing them to pursue their vision of gender equality in a larger venue. They continued to "break to them the bread of life," but that "life" now included the divine conviction that, as Shaw declared, "in Him there is neither male nor female, but all are alike one."

101. Schneider and Schneider, *In Their Own Right*, 92.

Chapter Four

"For the faith that was in them":

The Preachers as Suffragists

The thirty-third annual woman's rights convention opened on May 30, 1901, at the First Baptist Church of Minneapolis. The first national convention of the new century brought a change in the leadership of the National American Woman Suffrage Association. Carrie Chapman Catt, later regarded as the most successful and "easily the most admired suffragist of the twentieth century,"[1] occupied the president's chair for the first time following the long and much revered presidency of Susan B. Anthony. As had been the case from the first woman's rights gathering at Seneca Falls in 1848, the convention was thoroughly covered by the local press. The *Minneapolis Journal* reported on the opening ceremony:

> The formal opening of the suffrage convention yesterday afternoon was an impressive affair. Among the national officers seated on the platform were women who saw the first dawn of the suffrage movement, those who came into its fold midway of its life and those whose earnest endeavors are of more recent record. Among the first was the most honored member of the body, Miss Susan B. Anthony, and

---

1. William L. O'Neill, *Everyone Was Brave* (Chicago: Quadrangle Books, 1969), 123. After decades of work for suffrage in Iowa and five years of service as chairman of the NAWSA's organization committee, Catt was chosen by Anthony to succeed her as president. She served in that role for four years before resigning for personal reasons and being replaced by Anna Howard Shaw. She later led the New York state suffrage campaign to the passage of state suffrage for women in 1917 and reclaimed the presidency of the NAWSA in 1915 after Shaw's resignation, leading the national movement to victory in 1920.

among the latter is the president, Mrs. Carrie Chapman Catt. When the delegates rose and the Rev. Olympia Brown of Wisconsin stepped to the front of the platform and turned her face heavenward, saying, "In the name of liberty, Our Father, we thank thee," the impression even upon an unbeliever must have been that of entire consecration and one was reminded of when the early Christians met and consulted, fought and endured for the faith that was in them.[2]

Even an impartial observer such as this Minneapolis reporter recognized the depth of faith of many of the suffragists who led the woman's rights movement, seeing a parallel with the faith of early Christian martyrs. Theological language and religious commitment were neither incongruous with nor unique to the movement for woman's rights at any time throughout its history. Although a number of well-known leaders of the movement, including Lucretia Mott and Elizabeth Cady Stanton, publicly and vociferously critiqued the church, the clergy, biblical authority, and Protestant orthodoxy as impediments to the equality of women, many other leaders expressed their vision of female equality in theological terms and relied on biblical and theological arguments to defend woman's rights and to justify their own involvement in the movement. These religious suffragists bestowed "sacred significance" on "worldly arenas," as Robert Abzug described the work of earlier reformers in nineteenth-century America, creating "religious imaginations" that inspired their activities on behalf of political and social reform.[3]

Antoinette Brown Blackwell, Olympia Brown, and Anna Howard Shaw exemplified in their lives and work the compatibility of religious convictions and political equality for women, and as Evelyn Kirkley has suggested, they also revealed the various ways in which religion functioned in the movement for woman suffrage. The move these three women made from preaching to working as suffragists and the ways in which they justified that move as a broadened ministerial call demonstrate the role religion played as a motivating factor in their commitment to suffrage. Once

2. As recorded in Ida Husted Harper, ed., *History of Woman Suffrage*, vol. V (6 vols,; Rochester, N.Y.: National American Woman Suffrage Association, 1881–1922), 4–5. While the women in this study, and many of their colleagues in the suffrage movement, often attributed feminine qualities to God and made occasional references to God as Mother, they usually addressed God by the masculine term *Father* and used masculine pronouns in references to God. They also commonly used masculine language to refer to all of humanity. I have maintained their original language for purposes of this book.

3. Robert H. Abzug, *Cosmos Crumbling* (New York: Oxford University Press, 1994), viii.

they became suffrage orators, they relied on religious language, biblical imagery, and traditional moral (synonymous with Christian) values in arguing for women's right to vote. And they "made the vote a religious crusade, imbuing it with respectability and righteousness."[4] Moreover, their status as ordained ministers of major Protestant denominations lent a sense of *gravitas* to their involvement in the crusade for suffrage. Brown Blackwell, Brown, and Shaw were called upon regularly to pray and preach at suffrage and suffrage-related gatherings, and their ecclesiastical titles never went unmentioned in the official records of the movement.

Even though Brown Blackwell, Brown, and Shaw had diverse religious backgrounds and affiliated with different denominational groups during their ministerial and suffrage careers, the "religious imaginations," as Robert Abzug might have called them, that inspired and shaped their work for suffrage were remarkably similar. As might be expected given their progressive religious and social views, all three women shared a complex of theological views that could best be described as classic nineteenth-century liberal Protestantism. They believed in the Fatherhood of God, the brotherhood of man, and the freedom and equality of all people, terms that came to characterize nineteenth-century liberalism. They also subscribed to the notion of realized eschatology, the belief that the kingdom of God could become a reality on earth as the result of diligent work on the part of faithful reformers.

Understanding the religious imaginations that shaped the work of Brown Blackwell, Brown, and Shaw offers insight into their ability to transcend the traditional ideological barriers that separated the sacred and political realms. The conception of God shared by these three women was decidedly *unlike* the conception of God that was prevalent in American Protestantism during the early years of their lives. The traditional notion of God as an arbitrary, detached, and malicious Being who kept strict account of sinful transgressions and assigned helpless human beings to eternal bliss or punishment gave way by the mid-nineteenth century to the notion of a more merciful, nurturing God. And belief in the helplessness and dependency of human beings who were entirely at the mercy of that capricious God gave way to a belief in human agency and empowerment as a significant means to accomplishing the purposes of God on earth. These radical departures from long-held theological understandings, part of the "crumbling cosmos" described by Abzug, made it possible

4. Evelyn A. Kirkley, "'This work is God's cause': Religion in the Southern Woman Suffrage Movement, 1880–1920," *Church History* 59 (December 1990): 508.

for these three suffragists to engage in political and social reform that was fully undergirded by theological convictions.

A Country Transformed

By the time Olympia Brown and Anna Howard Shaw had moved to ministries of suffrage and Antoinette Brown Blackwell had returned to active participation in the movement during the last quarter of the nineteenth century,[5] the social and political landscape of the United States had been entirely transformed. The decades immediately following the Civil War brought unprecedented changes to all aspects of American life. The impact of industrialization, urbanization, immigration, intellectual innovation, and religious reconfiguration resulted in a nation that bore little resemblance to its antebellum ancestor. By the turn of the twentieth century, author Henry Adams commented on the country he no longer recognized:

> Certainly, when I return here after six months in Europe, my poor old senile brain whirls and whizzes for weeks. I do not any longer keep up a pretence of knowing where I am. My country in 1900 is something totally different from my own country of 1860. I am wholly a stranger in it. Neither I, nor anyone else, understands it.[6]

The transformation to which Adams referred had a significant impact on American Protestantism. During the first two centuries of its existence, the Protestant establishment in America had accommodated irresistible change even as it refused to relinquish a deeply rooted vision of Protestant America as the "redeemer nation" that would exemplify a moral order for all the world to emulate.[7] Despite philosophical, political, and ecclesiastical challenges, an unbowed coalition of Protestant forces had maintained their hold on American culture. American Protestantism had made peace with religious disestablishment and with the national spirit of indi-

---

5. Brown Blackwell had spent the 1860s raising her five daughters and the 1870s writing books and working for a variety of new women's organizations, including the Association for the Advancement of Women.

6. Henry Adams to Charles Milnes Gaskell, March 29, 1900, in *Letters of Henry Adams (1892–1918)*, ed. Worthington Chauncey Ford (Boston: Houghton Mifflin, 1938), 279.

7. See Ernest Lee Tuveson, *Redeemer Nation: The Idea of America's Millennial Role* (Chicago: University of Chicago Press, 1968).

vidualism, both of which, while fragmenting the Calvinist consensus of the nation's earliest centuries, actually bolstered Protestantism's hegemony through renewed religious enthusiasm and new expressions of faith. Reform organizations (including efforts for temperance, abolition, woman's rights, and moral reform) and benevolent societies (especially mission, Bible, and tract societies) represented a drive toward moral virtue rooted in religious piety. Such denominational and interdenominational groups swelled the ranks of Protestant churches. As historian Robert T. Handy concluded, "In many ways, the middle third of the nineteenth century was more of a 'Protestant Age' than was the colonial period with its established churches." Armed with the certainty of their convictions and guided by a vision of what America could be, Protestants "set out to evangelize and Christianize every aspect of American life."[8]

By the final third of the nineteenth century, however, the guardians of the Protestant tradition realized that their vision of a Protestant America was threatened by powerful and widespread forces. The populace was more diverse than ever before and proved to be less amenable to a particular interpretation of American life. "The culture they were trying to Christianize grew steadily less homogenous after the Civil War,"[9] Handy noted, evidenced by the persistent division between North and South, the growth of new religious traditions and practices, and the influx of non-Protestant immigrants. The "custodians of the empire . . . found that much of what they had considered to be distinctively Protestant was blurred in the American environment."[10]

As had occurred previously in American history, changes in the sociological configuration and economic fortunes of the nation created a perceived decline in its moral standards. The content of earlier moral declines had been articulated as a vague sense of social malaise often accompanied by a marked decrease in church attendance. The moral declension during the last quarter of the nineteenth century, however, was both more identifiable and more quantifiable than earlier declensions. The names and faces of those to whom the digression from Protestant moral standards was attributed, including immigrants, Roman Catholics, and factory workers, were recognizable; the numbers—how

---

8. Robert T. Handy, *The Protestant Quest for a Christian America, 1830–1930* (Philadelphia: Fortress Press, 1967), 10, 11.

9. Ibid., 12.

10. Martin E. Marty, *Protestantism in the United States: Righteous Empire*, 2d ed. (New York: Charles Scribner's Sons, 1986), 137.

many immigrants flocked to American cities, how many new Catholic parishes were established, how many arrests for intemperance occurred—were easily countable. According to social commentators of the era, the vague sense of moral dis-ease that pervaded post–Civil War America had a myriad of clearly identifiable root causes. In 1885 Josiah Strong, a Congregational minister and general secretary of the Evangelical Alliance for the United States, enumerated various "perils which threaten our future" and "the magnitude of the issues which hang on the present." His message was one of urgency, linking the preservation of America's destiny as "the chosen seat of enterprise for the world's conversion" to Christianity (in a particular Protestant expression, of course) to its success in mitigating the forces of modernity that challenged traditional assumptions.[11]

Protestantism's ethos began to fracture in the face of assaults on its moral assumptions—assumptions that seemed strangely out of step with the realities of modernity. Because, as historian Martin Marty has noted, the changes resulting from modernization "represented challenges to the world of meaning in which Protestantism was at home, they threatened Protestantism itself."[12] Church and religious leaders offered an oddly conflicted response to the challenges of the times. A "divided mind" emerged from within Protestant ranks concerning questions of ecclesiastical engagement with culture at the end of the nineteenth and beginning of the twentieth centuries.[13] The ultimate goal of maintaining a Christian America remained, but liberal and conservative religious voices disagreed as to the particular direction of that quest. The liberal approach to social reform eventuated in the social gospel, creating an alliance of liberal evangelicals who considered redemption of the social order to be as significant as or even more urgent than the redemption of individual lives. An equally fervent approach predicated social reform on the priority of personal salvation, giving rise to the massive revival campaigns of evangelists such as Dwight L. Moody as well as urban ministries such as the American branch of the Salvation Army. Both, according to Robert Handy, were

11. Josiah Strong, *Our Country: Its Possible Future and Its Present Crisis* (New York: Baker & Taylor, 1885; reprint, Cambridge, Mass.: Belknap Press of Harvard University Press, 1963), 6, 11.

12. Marty, *Protestantism in the United States*, 159.

13. See Ferenc Morton Szasz, *The Divided Mind of Protestant America, 1880–1930* (University: University of Alabama Press, 1982).

"powerful expressions of a similar fundamental motif. There were crucial differences in theology and social philosophy between social gospel and conservative Protestants, but both groups strove to make America Christian."[14]

Behind the various ministries and missions that emerged in response to the "perils," as Josiah Strong called them, of late-nineteenth-century America lay an enduring vision of what Protestant America was to look like, a vision that had permeated American history from its Puritan origins. While social reformers would have disagreed over the details of that vision, there would have been considerable agreement on qualities such as diligent work habits, temperance, Sabbath observance, family commitment, and sexual purity. There had been little "revisioning" of the historic "redeemer nation" vision of America that had shaped the previous two and a half centuries of American Protestantism. Those who perpetuated the Protestant worldview at the end of the nineteenth century did not fashion a new vision informed by changes to the social and cultural landscape of America. Instead, they looked backward to "preindustrial custom and religion . . . which predominated in the ethos in the first century of national life." They dusted off old "doctrines and ideals . . . antiques from village and rural America."[15] This reclamation of the values and rhetoric of the past in the face of unprecedented social change was, as Handy recognizes, nothing short of a "counter-reformation which was rooted in the conservative, evangelical, revivalistic Protestantism of the earlier nineteenth century, but showing a hardening and a narrowing of that tradition."[16]

The Functional Value of the Ballot

Oddly enough, many advocates of woman suffrage—considered a progressive if not radical idea—joined that "counter-reformation" by embracing the ideology and rhetoric of the movement to recapture an earlier moral vision of America. At the very time that the Protestant vision of America faced its most vehement challenges, the suffrage movement encountered challenges of its own. A continuing trend toward the radicalization of the movement in the last quarter of the nineteenth century,

14. Handy, *Protestant Quest*, 17.
15. Marty, *Protestantism in the United States*, 153.
16. Handy, *Protestant Quest*, 14.

as evidenced by the activities of some of its leaders,[17] and the organizational split of the national suffrage effort[18] reflected a troubled era that confronted the suffragists. As a result of the movement's perceived radicalization, "antisuffragists found it relatively simple to attach the stigma of 'home breakers,' 'religious crackpots,' and 'free thinkers' to suffrage advocates."[19] Increasingly, many who advocated woman suffrage realized that the rhetoric that had come to dominate the movement, with its emphasis on equality and rights, had fallen on deaf ears in many of the most influential corners of American society, most notably among legislators and church leaders who shaped public opinion. The idea that women deserved to vote solely on the basis of their human equality or their equality under a democratic constitution could be stated in "only so many ways," forcing suffragists "to seek other arguments which would keep the public's interest and advance their cause." In an effort to garner support and regain lost momentum at a critical time for the movement, suffragists were forced to attribute "functional values"[20] to the ballot, stating the practical reasons why voting women would be good for the country.

While extant materials from the century-long woman's movement reveal various arguments for woman's rights in general and woman suffrage in particular, certain arguments appear to have prevailed at specific times. Suffrage historians have defined the arguments and their periods of predominance in different ways. Aileen Kraditor was the first to identify two broad categories of arguments for woman suffrage and to suggest a time frame for the dominance of each. Kraditor distinguished between

17. Elizabeth Cady Stanton and Susan B. Anthony in particular came to be associated with radical views on marriage and religion. Stanton's publication of the first volume of the *Woman's Bible*, a feminist interpretation of Scripture, in 1895 confirmed the feelings of many who felt she had moved away from traditional religious beliefs.

18. The formal split of the American Equal Rights Association in 1869 into the National Woman Suffrage Association (NWSA) and the American Woman Suffrage Association (AWSA) denoted the ideological differences among suffragists by the second third of the nineteenth century. The NWSA, represented by its newspaper, the *Revolution*, took more radical stands on issues such as divorce, allowed only women to hold leadership roles, and worked for full federal suffrage for women. The AWSA welcomed men into all levels of the organization, had more conservative views on issues regarding marriage and family, and worked for state as well as federal suffrage laws.

19. Wil A. Linkugel, "The Woman Suffrage Argument of Anna Howard Shaw," *Quarterly Journal of Speech* 49 (April 1963): 170.

20. O'Neill, *Everyone Was Brave*, 49. Significant evidence of this rhetorical shift to the functional values of the ballot appears during the years of reorganization of the suffrage movement

two arguments used to justify women's enfranchisement: the "argument from justice" and the "argument from expediency." Early in the movement, Kraditor asserted, the primary arguments propounded by suffragists were based on a belief in human equality as a natural right. The founding principle of justice for all was new enough that it was assumed to have a wide-ranging rhetorical value for public debate. A common language of individual rights and corporate democratic principles shaped all dimensions of American rhetoric through the mid-nineteenth century. "The task of the pioneers of women's rights," according to Kraditor, "was to prove that this equality applied to women too."[21]

Later in the century, however, the theoretical principle of justice for all was challenged in light of new social and political realities. European immigrants, freed slaves, urban dwellers, and a large working class tested the sincerity of the language of equal rights that had dominated American political discourse since the Revolutionary era. In response, many suffragists moved away from their emphasis on equality and adopted instead a rhetoric in defense of woman suffrage that spoke to the problems and fears of the day. "At the time when the men of their group were taking cognizance of the ways in which men differed from each other," Kraditor noted, "new arguments for suffrage evolved, emphasizing the ways in which women differed from men. If the justice of the claim to political equality could no longer suffice, then the women's task was to show that expediency required it."[22]

While the arguments from expediency varied in terms of specific content, they revealed two dominant and related themes: the belief that women were morally superior to men and could—and should—exert that influence politically, and the belief that God had created women morally superior and intended for them to use their gifts in service to humanity. What is interesting is that this ideology was not new but was merely an extension of the earlier nineteenth-century ideology of True Womanhood.

---

following the Civil War. Speeches by the Reverends Gilbert Haven, Phoebe Hanaford, and Henry Ward Beecher at the 1869 gathering of the American Equal Rights Association reveal argumentation for woman suffrage based on the positive influence women's votes would have on the nation and even the world. See *History of Woman Suffrage*, II:388, 398–99.

21. Aileen S. Kraditor, *The Ideas of the Woman Suffrage Movement, 1890–1920* (Garden City, N.Y.: Doubleday, 1965), 43. The term "expediency" as used by Kraditor comes from a pamphlet written by suffragist Mary Putnam Jacobi, *"Common Sense" Applied to Woman Suffrage* (New York: G. P. Putnam's Sons, 1894).

22. Kraditor, *Ideas of the Woman Suffrage Movement*, 44.

The rhetoric of True Womanhood encouraged women's positive social influence through the private, domestic sphere as well as through networks of female organizations dedicated to specific social reforms. If women had the kind of beneficial influence on the domestic realm they were purported to have, would it not be to society's advantage to allow them to bring that influence to bear on the larger, public realm? Thus, still under the rubric of influence, suffragists at the close of the century called women to transform their social influence into blatant political influence by means of the ballot.

Suffragists predicated their belief in the functional value of the ballot on the assumption that women had divinely ordained and socially imperative responsibilities, a premise acceptable to the vast majority of Americans at the close of the nineteenth century who feared the moral disintegration of the nation. By addressing those national fears through the use of biblical imagery, theological language, and traditional understandings of gender characteristics, many suffragists discovered that they could locate themselves within mainstream American society. By doing so, they argued for their cause from a position of strength rather than a position of alienation. Earlier in the century, opposition to the ideology of woman's rights contributed to what was often perceived to be the radicalization of the woman's movement. Women with progressive views on gender roles found themselves marginalized by a society dedicated to the preservation of True Womanhood. In the era following the Civil War, however, the mitigating influences of massive cultural upheaval coalesced to create an atmosphere in which religious and moral arguments for women's participation in the political realm were both heard and affirmed.

Meeting the Challenge of the Antis

The rhetorical shift in the arguments used to support woman suffrage at the end of the nineteenth century was also prompted by the rise of a powerful antisuffrage movement. While there had been significant opposition to the idea of woman's rights from the inception of the movement, that opposition was composed of discrete voices with no consistent rhetoric and no central organization. By the end of the nineteenth century, however, the antis, as they came to be called, were efficiently organized and well financed. Several local chapters of the Association Opposed to the Extension of Suffrage to Women appeared around the turn of the century as state societies. A National Association was not founded until 1911, but by then the state societies had made considerable progress in their antisuffrage work. By the time the question of woman suffrage began appearing before state legislatures and Congress with regularity, the antisuffrage movement had become as formidable and legitimate a movement as the suffrage movement itself. It not only served to "isolate the women's rights movement; it also helped to define the boundaries within which the suffrage movement would operate."[23]

The specific arguments advanced by the antis were many and varied, but the most frequent line of argumentation invoked a biblical defense of separate gender spheres with apocalyptic warnings against any transgression of the divine order. "In contrast to pro-suffrage speakers, who were alleged to have depicted wedding rings as relics of barbarism," observes suffrage historian Thomas Jablonsky, "antis said that their organization stood for 'Home, Heaven, and Mother.'"[24] In an early antisuffrage monograph, Carlos White declared that "the Bible teaches the unity and inviolability of the family, and a distinction of sex as wide as that which exists in the United States." "The Innovators," as White called the suffragists, "are not fighting against man merely, but against God; and they must take the consequences."[25] Theologian Horace Bushnell, an early antisuffragist, constructed a cogent argument against woman suffrage based on his earlier work on natural theology. Bushnell considered the reforms for which women lobbied to be contrary to nature as God had established it. He accused suffragists of interfering with divine intention by trying "to make trumpets out of flutes, and sun-flowers out of violets." Women were "in a subject nature, and not merely in a subject condition— they are relatively frail and delicate, in a finer type of grace and color, a less coarse, stormy voice, and with a different unnerving quality which is distinctly feminine."[26]

Some of the most vehement opposition to woman suffrage came from women themselves. Catharine Beecher, author and sister of Henry Ward Beecher, contradicted arguments used by her brother and other suffragists by warning of the deleterious effects of woman suffrage on the sanctity

23. William H. Chafe, *Women and Equality: Changing Patterns in American Culture* (New York: Oxford University Press, 1977), 38.

24. Thomas Jablonsky, "Female Opposition: The Anti-Suffrage Campaign" in Jean H. Baker, ed., *Votes for Women: The Struggle for Suffrage Revisited* (New York: Oxford University Press, 2002), 123.

25. Carlos White, *Ecce Femina: An Attempt to Solve the Woman Question* (Boston: Lee & Shepard, 1870), 181.

26. Horace Bushnell, *Women's Suffrage: The Reform against Nature* (New York: Charles Scribner, 1870), 7.

of the home. She warned against "this *woman movement*" which, she claimed, was "uniting by cooperative influences, all the antagonisms that are warring on the family state." Inherent in the suffrage movement was an endorsement of such ideas as spiritualism, free love, and free divorce, all "the vicious indulgences consequent on unregulated civilization." Beecher defended what she believed were divinely intended gender distinctions and equated the separation of gender spheres with moral progress. "The more society has advanced in civilization and in Christian culture," she wrote, "the more perfectly have these *distinctive* divisions of responsibility for the two sexes been maintained."[27]

Because of their commitment to preserving the sanctity of the family and traditional Christian teachings and moral values, it is not surprising that antisuffragists found considerable support from Protestant churches and their leaders. Biblical interpretation had provided the ideological content for the doctrine of gender roles promulgated by the churches for centuries. Through the nineteenth century, evangelical Protestantism maintained a tenacious hold on the belief in woman's special nature amidst the calls for a greater public role for women in both church and society. Inherent in the Protestant notion of womanhood even at the end of the nineteenth century was the assumption of woman's unique moral nature, an assumption traditionalists felt was being assaulted by proponents of woman suffrage. As a result, the vast majority of Protestant churches and their clergy had been vociferous in their opposition to the woman's movement from its inception. While a few prominent clergymen, usually from liberal denominations and with ties to the abolition movement, openly supported the idea of woman's rights and, later, woman suffrage, most were either vehemently opposed or noticeably silent. Most of the extant sermons from the nineteenth century that address "the woman question" reiterate the value of domesticity and warn against any tampering with the "natural" order. Some denominations went so far as to issue statements against any kind of feminist activity.

As a result, ministerial opinion became even more important to the leaders of the woman suffrage movement in the final two decades of the struggle for the vote. In response to the negative publicity for suffrage generated by the antisuffrage movement, suffragists were eager to demonstrate that not all clergy had rejected their cause. After the turn of the century, the National American Woman Suffrage Association orga-

27. Catharine Beecher, *Woman Suffrage and Woman's Profession* (Hartford: Brown & Gross, 1871), 3, 5.

nized a Committee on Church Work to garner support for suffrage from churches and clergy. The committee countered the anti-Christian, anti-religious charges leveled at the suffragists by linking woman suffrage with Christian values. Mary E. Craigie, head of the committee, asked, "Would the extension of suffrage to women raise the standard of Christian citizenship? If so, should not our clergy and the church give their support to this reform movement?" Craigie criticized the clergy's timidity "to bear witness to truth against those whose good opinion we wish to keep." "There is needed today," she implored, "a courage of the pulpit as well as a courage of the Senate." She then presented the remarks of those who demonstrated such courage of the pulpit, encouraging other clergymen to "conscientiously admit that woman's influence has been for good in the home, in the church and in society, and cannot fail to be a power for good in the State, as well." Supporting "this great moral reform" of woman suffrage would "result in doubling the forces for righteousness throughout our land, and in raising the standard of Christian citizenship."[28]

The growing antisuffrage movement had placed the suffragists in a defensive posture by the end of the nineteenth century. The antis defined the content of the argumentation used in the rhetorical battle over woman suffrage. By appealing to the importance of preserving the standards and values of a Christian vision of America and by instilling fear over the transgression of divine intention if standards of gender distinctions and domestic traditions were violated, antisuffragists hoped both to inhibit support for suffrage and to preserve their traditional vision of America. What they did inadvertently, however, was give the suffrage movement a necessary boost as suffragists responded with their own religious defense of women's political equality. Suffragists reshaped their own rhetoric to make it more palatable to a broader constituency of Americans.

Antoinette Brown Blackwell: "The cause of woman suffrage was the cause of religion"

In 1916 as the struggle for woman suffrage came to a conclusion, Carrie Chapman Catt, then president of the National American Woman Suffrage Association, named Antoinette Brown Blackwell as one of the women who had "builded with others the foundation of political liberty

28. Mary E. Craigie, *Christian Citizenship* (New York: NAWSA, 1912), 1, 7–8, 14.

for American woman."[29] As one of the earliest and most persistent public voices for woman's rights in nineteenth- and then twentieth-century America, Brown Blackwell not only helped build the foundation that would yield political equality for women but also exhibited the evolution of the rhetoric used in defense of woman's rights over the course of the decades-long struggle for suffrage. She addressed the First National Woman's Rights Convention held in Worcester, Massachusetts, in 1850, and she lived to cast her ballot in the first national election open to women in 1920. Her speech and writings over those seventy years reflect not only her own changing philosophy and interests but also the changing emphases of the woman's movement.

Brown Blackwell's vocational path toward ministry coincided with the rise of a formal movement for woman's rights. Her completion of the graduate theological program at Oberlin College in 1850 occurred just two months before the First National Convention. Her struggle to obtain the education she desired and to serve the church as she felt called generated in her an interest in opening all doors—ecclesiastical, educational, social, political—to women. Thus she became a credible and valuable voice in the movement that was coalescing to secure wide-ranging rights for women. Two other qualities made her particularly attractive to the movement's leadership. One was her natural ability and training in public speaking, leading to frequent comments on her eloquence in the reports of woman's rights gatherings. The incipient woman's movement depended on articulate speakers to advance its agenda since rhetorical persuasion was the primary means of promoting social change in the mid-nineteenth century. The other quality that made her attractive to the movement's leadership was the obvious nature of her religious convictions. Just a week before her ordination in September 1853, Brown Blackwell preached to five thousand people gathered in Metropolitan Hall in New York City. The crowds had gathered for simultaneous meetings of woman's rights proponents and the Anti-Slavery Society. Brown Blackwell's preaching at a Sunday evening service "called out the denunciations of the religious press."[30] Later that week at the Woman's Rights Convention, Lucy Stone referred to the incident, defending Brown Blackwell's right to speak and noting her orthodoxy:

> It is said women could not be ministers of religion. Last Sunday, at Metropolitan Hall, Antoinette L. Brown conducted divine service,

29. Carrie Chapman Catt, "The Crisis," in Karlyn Kohrs Campbell, ed., *Man Cannot Speak for Her*, vol. 2, *Key Texts of the Early Feminists* (New York: Praeger, 1989), 494.

30. *History of Woman Suffrage*, I:546.

and was joined in it by the largest congregation assembled within the walls of any building in this city. . . . I tell you that some men in New York, knowing that they can hear the word of God from a woman, as well as from a man, have called her to be their pastor, and she is to be ordained this month. Some of you reporters said she was a Unitarian, but it is not so; she is among the most orthodox, and so is her church.[31]

Brown Blackwell confirmed Lucy Stone's testimony by demonstrating her orthodoxy in her early speeches on behalf of the incipient movement for woman's rights. Many years later, in reminiscences shared at the National American Woman Suffrage Convention of 1905, she remarked, "Ever since I made my first suffrage speech in 1848 I have believed that the cause of woman suffrage was the cause of religion and vice versa."[32] She gave her first national speech on woman's equality at the First National Woman's Rights Convention in 1850, and with that speech she appears to have established a theological defense of woman's rights. A brief reference to Brown Blackwell's speech in the minutes of the convention refers to "her logical argument on woman's position in the Bible, claiming her complete equality with man, the simultaneous creation of the sexes, and their moral responsibilities as individual and imperative."[33]

She reiterated her convictions two years later at the 1852 National Woman's Rights Convention in Syracuse,[34] arguing from a biblical rationale that God's intention in creation was the equality of man and woman. Even after the fall from grace, she stated, God's intention for gender equality remained. She believed that the pronouncement that man would rule over woman should be "properly translated as a prediction, not as God's command."[35] And the "submission enjoined upon the wife in the New Testament, is not the unrighteous rule predicted in the Old. It is a Christian submission due from man towards man, and from man towards woman." Numerous New Testament texts support such an interpretation, urging mutual submission among the disciples, apostles, and laborers in the church.[36] Even the pronouncement that man is the head of the woman,

---

31. Ibid., 554–55.
32. *History of Woman Suffrage*, V:133.
33. See *History of Woman Suffrage*, I:224.
34. See chapter 2 on Brown Blackwell's defense of women's right to preach.
35. Barbara S. Spies, "Antoinette Brown Blackwell" in Karlyn Kohrs Campbell, ed., *Women Public Speakers in the United States, 1800–1925* (Westport, Conn.: Greenwood Press, 1993), 64.
36. *History of Woman Suffrage*, I:535.

Brown Blackwell maintained, must be interpreted to "symbolize oneness, union. Christ so loved the Church He gave Himself for it, made it His own body, part and parcel of Himself. So ought men to love their wives."[37]

Even after her ill-fated attempt to address the World's Temperance Convention in New York in 1853—and perhaps because of it—Brown Blackwell held fast to her belief that ultimate justification for woman's equality depended not on secular arguments but on acceptance of the truth inherent in Scripture. At the October 1853 Fourth National Woman's Rights Convention held in Cleveland, she recounted her experience of being denied the chance to speak at the temperance gathering. She contended that she went to the convention—the *"World's"* temperance convention, she noted—"as an item of the world, to contend that the sons and daughters of the race, without distinction of sex, sect, class or color, should be recognized as belonging to the world, and I planted my feet upon the simple *rights of a delegate.*" When asked why she made her rights as a delegate an issue at that time, she answered:

> I have made it at all times and in all places, whenever and wherever Providence has given me the opportunity, and in whatever way it could be made to appear most prominent. Last spring, when woman claimed the supremacy—the right to hold all the offices in the Woman's State Temperance Society—I contended, from this platform, for the equality of man; the equal rights of all the members of this society. I have claimed everywhere the equality of humanity in Church and State; God helping me, I here pledge myself anew to Him, and to you all, to be true everywhere to the central principle— the soul of the Divine commandment, "Thou shalt love thy neighbor as thyself."[38]

Temperance, the cause she attempted to support by her appearance at the World's Convention, was a righteous cause. It was among the reforms that reflect the "heart and soul" of Christianity. Such reforms "seek to elevate mankind and better their condition, cling around our Christianity, and are a part of it."[39] Brown Blackwell argued that she went to the World's Convention

37. Ibid., 535.
38. Ibid., 507.
39. Ibid., 158. This account is a longer version of what is reported later in the first volume of *History of Woman Suffrage.*

only to claim in the name of Democracy and Christianity, that all be treated alike and impartially. The human soul is a holy thing; it is the temple of living joy or sorrow. It is freighted with vital realities. It can outlengthen Heaven itself, and it should be reverenced everywhere, and treated always as a holy thing. We only went there in the name of the world, in the name of humanity, to promote a good cause; and it is what I pledge myself now anew to do, at all times and under all circumstances, when the opportunity shall present itself to me. It was a good act, a Christian duty, to go there under those circumstances.[40]

At the early September 1853 woman's rights gathering and just days after she was "gagged" on the antislavery platform, as Horace Greeley's *New York Tribune* put it, Brown Blackwell turned her anger at her treatment by fellow abolitionists into eloquent rhetoric on behalf of woman's rights. She identified the fears inherent in those who opposed the movement for women's equality, including the fears of a transgression of natural laws, of religious declension, and of moral chaos:

Our cause is progressing triumphantly; and yet it is not without some to oppose it. . . . They suppose that a few mad-cap reformers are endeavoring to overthrow dame Nature, to invert society, to play the part of merciless innovators to imperil religion, to place all civil and religious freedom in jeopardy; that if our ends were accomplished all the public and private virtues would be melted as in a crucible and thrown on the ground, thence to cry aloud to heaven like the blood of righteous Abel.

The most objectionable dimension of the call for a greater sphere of activity for women, Brown Blackwell discerned, was the employment of women's intellect. "Intellectual women! Oh, they are monsters!" she mocked her detractors. "As soon allow wild beasts to roam at large as these to be let loose on society." She identified "the greatest wrong and injustice ever done to woman" as "that done to her intellectual nature." Using a biblical reference, she likened that intellectual injustice to "Goliath among the Philistines," an injustice that "overtops all the rest." "Such are the oppositions we meet," she concluded; "but they are all melting down like frost-work before the morning sun. The day is dawning when the

40. Ibid., 158.

intellect of woman shall be recognized as well as that of man, and when her rights shall meet an equal and cordial acknowledgement."[41]

Brown Blackwell was regarded as the resident theologian and biblical scholar at woman's rights gatherings throughout the 1850s. The chronicler of a state woman's rights meeting held in Saratoga Springs, New York, in August 1855 noted Brown Blackwell's presence at the convention and stated:

> Antoinette Brown was called on as usual to meet the Bible argument. A clergyman accused her of misapplying texts. He said Genesis iv. 7 did not allude to Cain and Abel, and that the language in Genesis iii. 16, as applied to Eve, did not mean the same thing. Miss Brown maintained her position that the texts were the same in letter and spirit; and that authority to all men over all women could be no more logically inferred from the one, than authority to all elder brothers over the younger could be from the other; and that there was no divine authority granted in either case.

Even though her participation in the woman's rights movement during the second half of the 1850s was limited due to the demands of marriage and motherhood, her ecclesiastical activities remained worthy of note by the movement's leaders. The *History of Woman Suffrage* noted her church work at the end of the 1850s: "In January, 1859, Antoinette L. Brown gave a series of Sunday sermons in Rochester, and in 1860 she preached in Hope Chapel, New York for six months."[42]

In May 1860, Brown Blackwell attended the National Woman's Rights Convention held at the Cooper Institute in New York City. One of the most heated debates of the convention focused on a series of proposed resolutions concerning marriage. Several leaders of the woman's movement, most notably Elizabeth Cady Stanton, supported the liberalization of divorce laws. Marriage, and its concomitant state of divorce, was one of the earliest issues addressed by woman's rights advocates in the nineteenth century. State laws pertaining to both marriage and divorce were long regarded as inequitable and oppressive toward women. Brown Blackwell became known as a staunch advocate of the institution of marriage and the maintenance of strict laws of divorce while arguing for equality and mutual responsibility between men and women within marriage. In establishing the foundation for her argument in favor of what she

41. Ibid., 553, 554.
42. Ibid., 624, 666.

called the "permanent and indissoluble" nature of marriage, she began with an appeal to the inviolable laws of God:

> I believe that the highest laws of life are those which we find written within our being; that the first moral laws which we are to obey are the laws which God's own finger has traced upon our own souls. Therefore, our first duty is to ourselves, and we may never, under any circumstances, yield this to any other. I say we are first responsible to ourselves, and to the God who has laid the obligation upon us, to make ourselves the grandest we may.

Brown Blackwell's understanding of marriage was based on her belief in the equality established by God in creation, an argument that would appear later in the century as one of the foundational arguments for woman suffrage employed by Olympia Brown and Anna Howard Shaw. In Brown Blackwell's words:

> I believe that God has so made man and woman, that it is not good for them to be alone, that they each need a co-worker. There is no work on God's footstool which man can do alone and do well, and there is no work which woman can do alone and do well. We need that the two should stand side by side everywhere. All over the world, we need this co-operation of the two classes—not because they are alike, but because they are unlike—in trying to make the whole world better.

Man and woman were created by God "to stand side by side, to stay up each other's hands, to take an interest in each other's welfare." In the same speech, she raised again the idea of woman's intellect that marked her argument in favor of woman's rights several years earlier and that would feature prominently in her later writings, contending:

> She [woman] need not absorb herself in her home, and God never intended that she should; and then, if she has lived according to the laws of physiology, and according to the laws of common-sense, she ought to be, at the age of fifty years, just where man is, just where our great men are, in the very prime of life! When her young children have gone out of her home, then let her enter in earnest upon the great work of life outside of home and its relations.[43]

43. Ibid., 724, 727, 728.

During the 1860s and1870s, Brown Blackwell found the expression of her own "great work of life" altered due to home and family obligations. She wrote more and traveled less, finding in writing an outlet for her intellectual curiosity while raising her children. In 1869 she gave birth both to her youngest daughter and to her first book. *Studies in General Science* represented a decade of study and reflection in the area of metaphysics generated by the popular theories promulgated by her contemporaries Charles Darwin and Herbert Spencer. Her intention in compiling several of her essays into *Studies* was to apply Darwinian principles to the apprehension of God as the "Author of the moral universe," the one in whom truths are "to be found at first hand, if one has power to discover or verify them for himself."[44] The ultimate confirmation of her religious application of Darwinism rested in her hope for social progress, manifested particularly in the equality of women.

A more direct application of the theories of "the accredited exponents of Evolution"[45] to issues of gender came with Brown Blackwell's publication of *The Sexes Throughout Nature* in 1875. For two years prior to its publication, she was engaged in a vigorous defense of female abilities in response to a published physiological study of the limitations of the female body. Dr. Edward Hammond Clarke, a physician and professor at Harvard Medical School, published a widely read and highly controversial work titled *Sex in Education, or a Fair Chance for Girls* in 1873.[46] Clarke particularly warned against intellectual exertion by women, claiming it would divert vital strength from the reproductive organs to the brain, leading to devastating conditions ranging from weakness to hysteria to infertility. Clarke's work represented a shift in the arena of argumentation concerning woman's rights from the theological and political realms to the scientific realm as well as the growing strength of the movement opposed to women's equality during the closing decades of the nineteenth century.

In a series of articles (some originally delivered as speeches) published in the *Woman's Journal* and in *The Sexes Throughout Nature*, Brown Blackwell defended the physical and intellectual abilities of women. She made

44. Antoinette Brown Blackwell, *Studies in General Science* (New York: G. P. Putnam's Sons, 1869), 15.

45. Antoinette Brown Blackwell, *The Sexes Throughout Nature* (New York: G. P. Putnam's Sons, 1875), 13.

46. Edward Hammond Clarke, *Sex in Education, or a Fair Chance for Girls* (Boston: James P. Osgood, 1873).

clear her intention to challenge Clarke's theory in her first article for the *Woman's Journal* on the subject "Sex and Work": "Dr. Clarke's recent book on 'Sex in Education,' seems to me to manifest a sufficient respect for women, to be courteous and kind in motives, the result of earnestness, observation, and humane thought; and yet to be so hopelessly one-sided that there is no choice left us except to hold up the subject afresh in certain other points of view."[47] In a subsequent article, Brown Blackwell noted, "The Dr. pronounces our national, rapidly growing method of Co-education in schools and colleges, 'a crime before God and humanity, that physiology protests against, and that experience weeps over.'"[48]

Even though a new scientific dimension had been added to the debate over women's rights and roles, the historic argument over woman's divinely intended nature endured. Her response to Clarke's theory, therefore, countered his arguments on theological as well as physiological grounds. She warned against any assumption that inequality marked God's creation of man and woman, asking:

> Who is prepared to show that they [men and women] are not started in life as equals, on an identical plane of evolution?
>
> It is hazardous to rely altogether upon *a priori* dogmatism, learned or unlearned, which forces one to set up the assumption that the Creator has been driven by partiality to model an unbalanced, unsymmetrical humanity; like an unshapely apple, one half large and desirable, but the other half small and unsavory.[49]

In an article published in May 1874 she asked:

> What unparalleled stupidity, then, could have induced the highest wisdom of the past Ages to debar the mother of the race from the noblest intellectual life? What blindness of vision it must have been, must still be, that can shut out her sympathies from the broadest general welfare! What narrow-mindedness, that can withhold her hand from any benevolent work, however comprehensive. She whom Nature especially enjoins to self-forgetfulness must be allowed to

47. Antoinette Brown Blackwell, "Sex and Work–No. 1," *Woman's Journal*, March 7, 1874, 73.

48. Antoinette Brown Blackwell, "Sex and Work–No. 3," *Woman's Journal*, March 21, 1874, 89.

49. Brown Blackwell, *Sexes Throughout Nature*, 179.

remember all other needs, those nearest at hand, those most remote and world-wide in their necessities. The natural mother of little children is also the natural mother of nations, and though it is already far on in the Nineteenth Century, she is resolute now in claiming her heritage.[50]

Brown Blackwell's portrayal of women as "the mother of the race" and "the natural mother of nations" demonstrated her appeal to the moral superiority of women, the strand of argumentation that gained prominence among woman suffrage advocates following the Civil War. In a paper read before the New England Women's Club, she reiterated that argument:

Since love and reverence for the home is ingrained in the feminine constitution, outside work is not likely seriously to impair its interests. Such an influence, if it should ever exist, must be superficial and temporary in its effects; for Nature is not at permanent warfare with herself. Nature, who incites both domestic instincts and wholesome outside activities, must be constrained to harmonize their influence, bringing out finally, from their combined results, a civilization much nobler than the world has known hitherto. No one love, however great, no one class of functions, however absorbing, can be enough for a character fashioned in the likeness of Mind Infinite and Universal in its sympathies.[51]

Women shared with men a concern for correcting the problems that plagued society. "The best women of to-day," she asserted, "seeing the evils, straightway begin to devise means to cure them. Their consciences are burdened by the crimes which strangers are committing; their hearts are broken by the public evils which laws are helpless to remedy." Both household and community responsibilities should be shared equally, Brown Blackwell believed. "Let them distribute life's duties honorably," she argued, "in honor preferring one another; mutual helpers when feasible, mutual sympathizers always."[52]

---

50. Antoinette Brown Blackwell, "Work in Relation to the Home–IV," *Woman's Journal*, May 23, 1874, 161.

51. Antoinette Brown Blackwell, "Work in Relation to the Home" (paper read before the New England Women's Club), *Woman's Journal*, May 2, 1874, 137.

52. Antoinette Brown Blackwell, "Work in Relation to the Home–II" (paper read before the New England Women's Club), *Woman's Journal*, May 9, 1874, 145.

Brown Blackwell argued that the call to women to exert moral influence over society was not antithetical to God's intention for creation but represented "a Divine impulse [that] has proved stronger than teaching." Referring to her scientific studies, she declared, "Nature has been getting more and more heterogeneous, like everything else." She anticipated a day when

> both men and women—not to an equal extent but, as added to housekeeping, in an equivalent degree—should be agriculturists, artisans, tradesmen, doctors, lawyers, preachers, teachers, scientists, artists, journalists, bookmakers, politicians, statesmen, sea-captains if they will and land captains also, if they can; heading volunteers in every department of thought and action.[53]

It was only "narrow-mindedness" that limited women or men to "any one class of topics or pursuits." Jesus himself exemplified the divine ideal of heterogeneous nature: "The divinest Man, in whom we delight to recognize the blending of masculine and feminine traits, with no near social ties, who had not where to lay his head, could yet find little children to be gathered into his arms, and in blessing them he was himself most blessed in return."[54] Women who resisted participation in a wider sphere of activity did so at their own peril. "Let every woman comprehend fully that inactivity is death," she warned. "The laws of Nature are not to be set aside for our benefit. Our Father worketh hitherto, and we must work."[55]

In 1905, her eightieth year, Brown Blackwell attended the National American Woman Suffrage Convention held in Portland, Oregon. It was at the Portland convention that she asserted her belief in the cause of woman suffrage as the cause of religion and vice versa. At the same gathering she spoke on the relationship of suffrage to education and, according to the stenographer of the convention, "showed the evolution in woman's work," an issue she had promoted through her previous three decades of speeches and writings. From her perspective of eight decades of life, most of them dedicated to the fervent struggle for woman's rights, Brown Blackwell was more convinced than ever that the time had come for woman's full political participation. "My grandmother taught me to

53. Ibid.

54. Brown Blackwell, "Work in Relation to the Home," 137.

55. Antoinette Brown Blackwell, "Sex and Work–No. 5," *Woman's Journal*, April 11, 1874, 113.

spin," she told those gathered at the convention, "but the men have relieved womankind from that task and as they have taken so many industrial burdens off of our hands it is our duty to relieve them of some of their burdens of State."[56]

Olympia Brown: "Breaking down all barriers"

The passage of the School Suffrage Law in Wisconsin and the possibilities it opened for general woman suffrage served as the catalyst for Olympia Brown's decision to resign from her Racine pastorate. Racine Circuit Court Judge John B. Winslow supported Brown's lawsuit challenging those who prohibited women from voting on issues beyond those related to school matters. His decision was overturned two months later by the Wisconsin Supreme Court. After the higher court's decision, Brown had the opportunity to address Wisconsin Supreme Court Justice Cassody. In her response, Brown revealed her conviction that the court's decision had more than secular, human consequences. The Supreme Court, she asserted, had been granted "the most sacred charge that can be entrusted to mortals; you hold in your hand the liberties and destinies of your fellow beings." She condemned the court for their carelessness in considering the issues at hand and for their lack of thorough investigation. Had the court demonstrated a more studied approach to the issues, the women of Wisconsin would have honored the decision "even though against our cause." And even more, had the justices had the "discernment and courage to decide the case in accordance with the letter, and manifest spirit of the law," all "believers in progress" would have rejoiced. "All courts would have looked to Wisconsin," she lamented, "as furnishing an illustrious example of judicial integrity. Your own conscience would have approved your conduct and the Divine Spirit would have blessed you with a new power to perceive the truth." As it was, Brown cautioned, the decision against her and the women of Wisconsin would echo throughout the history of the state: "I leave you to a posterity, that will class your decision with the Dred Scott decision and the tyrannies of the old world. I leave you to God who will overturn and overturn until his will be done and the right triumphs. I leave you to yourself, to answer to your own conscience for this crime against the women of the State."[57]

56. *History of Woman Suffrage*, V:138.
57. Olympia Brown, "Judge Cassody, of the Supreme Court of Wisconsin" (Racine, Wis., 1888).

Brown's statement before Judge Cassody revealed her conviction that the human injustices perpetrated against women had divine implications. God was ever watchful over the human machinations that shaped the lives of all people, including women. In her rhetoric supporting woman's rights, she repeatedly pointed to "the intimate connection between feminism and religious insight which is so obvious in her life and so essential in understanding the role of religion in social reform movements in nineteenth-century America."[58] For Brown, God was the source of the best of human efforts and visions. She believed that human equality was not humanly devised but divinely granted. God had created all human beings equally with certain unassailable and equal rights and regarded creation accordingly. In a sermon on Proverbs 3:33 titled "The Curse of the Lord" she asserted:

> God is God of justice. Wherever we note the working of the laws which govern the universe there we see the administration of absolute impartial justice. The omnipresent father considers not times or persons, he knows no difference between the darker and the lighter skin, the stronger and the weaker intellect, he endows all alike with inalienable rights, he gives to all the title deeds to liberty.[59]

The "first great principle" of American democracy, including the assertion that all are created free and entitled to life, liberty, and the pursuit of happiness *and* the "inherent right of suffrage," Brown declared in an address given to the National American Woman Suffrage Convention,

> is not rubbish left over from the philosophy of the eighteenth century, for it goes back, clear back, to the apostle Paul, when he announced that God created of "one blood all the nations of the earth"—back to the time when the great Master proclaimed that it was "neither at this mountain nor yet at Jerusalem that men should worship the Father," thus breaking down all barriers between clique and class and clan, and recognizing that all are one. This is no rubbish, but the eternal gospel, God's living truth.

---

58. Dana Greene, ed., *Suffrage and Religious Principle* (Metuchen, N.J.: Scarecrow Press, 1983), 1.

59. Olympia Brown, "The Curse of the Lord" (sermon, n.d.), OBP, SL, Fol. 118.

Olympia Brown was realistic about the opposition that advocates of woman suffrage faced despite the clear and cogent arguments she so carefully rooted in Christian and democratic principles. "We have against us the Congress of the United States, and the legislatures of the several States, and the courts, and the newspapers, and the ministers," she acknowledged. But in her characteristic and committed fashion, she declared, "But we have God Almighty on our side and we shall conquer."[60]

God revealed God's ultimate intention of justice for all through the teachings and practices of Christianity, Brown argued. She equated Christianity with democracy and declared—not unlike most American citizens of the nineteenth and early twentieth centuries—that America was a Christian nation with certain unique qualities as well as obligations. "We cannot estimate how much Christian teaching has had to do with the great movements in behalf of liberty," she stated in a speech delivered at the Suffrage School in Madison, Wisconsin, in 1914. "But it would be interesting had we time to trace the influence of religious conviction in leading to the demand for political equality."[61] A "Christian democracy" such as that of the United States "is the outgrowth of this Christian ideal of the worth of man and the duty of all men to work together, cooperating for the common good. A Christian government is simply a large society in which all unite, first of all for protection, then for improvement, then for the development of the Arts and the conveniences of our modern civilization." She compared the state to a club in which members unite, pay dues, and offer moral support for the club's well-being. The ballot serves as the means of that moral support. It "becomes the instrument whereby we make known our wishes with regard to this great society to which we belong and everyone is under an obligation to do the uttermost for the common good." She believed that the denial of the right to vote was contrary to the intentions of the founders of the Republic who were "men inspired by a great idea, that of the equality of the human race and the worth of the human being, and they aimed to found a great Christian Republic in which there should be 'neither Jew nor Greek, nor bond nor free, nor male nor female.' "[62]

---

60. Olympia Brown, "Where is the Mistake?" (address given before the National American Woman Suffrage Convention, February 21, 1890), *Woman's Tribune*, March 8, 1890, OBP, SL, Fol. 29.

61. Olympia Brown, "Preparation for the Progress of Women" (speech delivered at the Suffrage School in Madison, Wis., June 18–24, 1914), OBP, SL, Fol. 33.

62. Olympia Brown, "Address on Woman Suffrage" (n.d.; after 1909), OBP, SL, Fol. 49.

Brown believed that the hope of modern civilization, the common good of the country, and the liberty of women all depended on adherence to Christian principles. In a sermon repudiating the restrictions imposed on women due to limited educational opportunities, she predicted, "Christianity applied to our civilization would break down these barriers, do away with false and unjust prejudice and leave everyone free to follow the inspiration of her own genius, and the dictates of conscience." She saw progress occurring as "the words of Christ are beginning to be applied to the subject of women's education and duties and every year in the future will see a step taken in advance."[63] In a sermon encouraging the Universalist Church to support impartial suffrage, she declared, "Christianity speaks to the world of liberty and equality. It comes to break down the barriers which separate men from their kind. It comes to free the oppressed, to lift up the downtrodden and to strengthen the weak and dependent."[64] A prayer in the form of a poem attached to the same sermon manuscript closed with this declaration: " 'Save us from ourselves!' 'Give us to see.' That all have equal rights with Thee!"

Brown had always been convinced of the appropriateness of bringing religious ideology into secular worlds, even the political world. In college, many years before she became active in the suffrage movement, she wrote in an essay titled "Politics v. Piety," "We need a religious element in our politics, . . . religion and government, church and state, politics and piety must in some way or other be united." Even at that early stage of her thinking about woman's rights, Brown believed that the greatest hope for uniting politics and piety lay in the participation of women in the political process. In her college essay, she derided "the condition of our politics when men acknowledge that women can take no interest whatever in them, without becoming contaminated!" The best interest of the country rested in "the duty of the great and good to take a part in our political contests and though such a life be arduous and uncertain, though it involve toil and anxiety the good and the true must be willing to sacrifice themselves to some extent for their country." She identified women as the most obvious of "the good and the true." "Characterized by spiritual perception and intuition, it is they who are especially called to the work of renovating the political world," she argued; "it is theirs to redeem our government, from the blighting influence of corrupt minds."[65]

---

63. Olympia Brown, Sermon (untitled; n.d.), OBP, SL, Fol. 83.
64. Olympia Brown, Sermon (untitled; n.d.), OBP, SL, Fol. 86.
65. Olympia Brown, "Politics v. Piety" (essay, n.d.), OBP, SL, Fol. 40.

This early essay is only the first of Brown's many statements declaring her belief in the uniquely spiritual nature of women. Throughout her life, her belief in and appeal to what she regarded to be the religious proclivities of women formed an essential element of her defense of woman's rights and woman suffrage. "It is notorious, I think," she stated in a sermon delivered at the Church of Our Father in Washington, D.C., in 1885, "that women have taken especial interest in religion everywhere the world over, and in all ages." Women represented the majority of members of congregations across the country, and "the Sabbath-school and the prayer-meeting and the conference meeting would be impossibilities without woman's cooperation, woman's devotion, and woman's self-sacrifice." Even church treasuries and ministers' salaries would be impoverished without the support of women. "It is recognized all through the Bible," she argued, "—woman's peculiar fitness and adaptation to the great interests of the soul." When God created human beings, " 'male and female created he them'—not him. . . . And then, in the fullness of time, Jesus Christ came to the world and revealed himself peculiarly to women." Because of the Divine Spirit that so rested upon Mary, Christ came to the world "with a woman's tenderness in His nature, and woman's spiritual perception, with a woman's great sympathy for fallen, suffering, downtrodden humanity everywhere, and He revealed Himself first of all to woman."[66]

Brown echoed other suffragists in identifying the spiritual and moral superiority of women as a means to reversing the moral declension of a nation suffering the effects of political corruption, materialism, intemperance, and vice. In the face of overwhelming national problems at the turn of the twentieth century, Brown recognized "the necessity of an influence in the government which shall protect the home, which shall care for the children, which shall look to the establishment of righteousness and truth and justice in our communities." That influence, she concluded, "must come from the women. It is only by their influence and their voices that we can hope to secure a true Republic and save our nation from premature destruction." Given the ballot, women would use their influence "in favor of the great philanthropies, in favor of those things that tend to building up purity and truth in our communities. Woman Suffrage is the only possible salvation for this country."[67] Woman's mater-

---

66. Olympia Brown, "Women and Skepticism" (sermon delivered at the Church of Our Father, Washington, D.C., January 25, 1885), OBP, SL, Fol. 28.

67. Brown, "Address on Woman Suffrage."

nal nature was just the "remedy" for the proliferation of crime and moral degeneration that afflicted the nation: "As in the sick room it is the mother's tender touch that soothes the child's pain and calls back the glow of health, so in this sin-sick world, it must be the loving sympathy of mothers that shall win back the erring and restore them to mental health and moral beauty."[68]

Brown associated Christian principles not only with democracy and freedom but also with the exaltation of women. "It is the glory of Christianity that it has recognized and enthroned womanhood," she stated.[69]

> [Christianity] broke down the old barriers and admitted women to the public assemblies, recognized their right to speak as they were moved and to bear their testimony in the great congregation, and from that day to this Christianity and the Christian Church have been upheld, inspired, sustained and honored by the work of women and a very large proportion of the membership is composed of women.[70]

In several of her statements connecting woman's rights to Christian principles, Brown pointed to Christ's unique relationship with and high regard for women during his earthly life. "He first revealed himself as the promised messiah to a woman," she reminded her listeners in a sermon.[71] Jesus "wrought his first miracle at the command of a woman, and as a recognition of the supremacy of motherhood; he revealed the great truths that he came to bring to women, and he sent women forth to proclaim the risen Lord."[72] Women "were last at the cross and first at the sepulchre, and when he rose from the dead he revealed himself first of all to a woman and bade her go and proclaim the risen Lord."[73] She stated in her sermon on "Women and Skepticism":

> Today, as of old, He speaks to sorrowing, downtrodden and oppressed woman, and now, as then, He says: "Woman, why weepest

68. Olympia Brown, "Crime and the Remedy" (address before the Parliament of Religions, Art Institute, Chicago, September 22, 1893), OBP, SL, Fol. 29.

69. Ibid.

70. Olympia Brown, "Why the Church Should Demand the Ballot for Women" (n.d.), OBP, SL, Fol. 49.

71. Olympia Brown, Portions of sermons, OBP, SL, Fol. 125.

72. Brown, "Crime and the Remedy."

73. Brown, "Why the Church Should Demand the Ballot for Women."

thou? Go tell my disciples that I am risen from the dead." Christ is risen: He rises today, let us shake off the grave clothes that have hung about our race through the ages of the past; let us rise out of that lethargy, and put on new life that is with Christ in God; and, brothers and sisters, let us walk forth together in the light and liberty of the children of God.[74]

Because of its regard for women, "a church or any other organization for Christian work without women would be an anomalous affair. Women from the very first have been the very life of the Church." Thus, she argued, the church should demand the ballot for women. The church represented "a great power for righteousness in the administration of our public affairs. Society today needs the votes of the church women in settling the great moral problems of our time." If the church were to "maintain the dignity and self-respect that belong to such an organization, if it would do its grandest work, [it] must secure the ballot for its women."[75]

Brown countered the argument that freedom for women would lead to skepticism and immorality and infidelity in marriage. On the contrary, she averred, using in support of her contention the fact that liberty, according to history, had made men more noble and responsible in their conduct. "Now if liberty does all this for men," she asked, "if it makes them true and brave and strong, self-reliant and earnest, why should it not have the same effect upon women?" That effect would be even greater when liberty was applied to the already religious and virtuous nature of woman. She pointed to examples of American women such as Abigail Adams and Lucretia Mott whose Christian character had influenced many lives while helping to shape the nation's history. Denying the participation of such godly women in the political arena meant disregarding "a reserve force in our community that shall rise up and infuse into our political and social life an element of faith, of charity, of purity, and of hope." Because they have been "by nature and by the peculiarities of their circumstances and experiences fitted for religious impression," women offer the unique ability to bring the Divine into everyday experience. There come to women

revelations of truth and duty which no man in all this world ever can experience. . . . She looks above things that are seen and passing, recognizing the things that are unseen and everlasting. God speaks to

74. Brown, "Women and Skepticism."
75. Brown, "Why the Church Should Demand the Ballot for Women."

her soul and she feels the Divine presence. . . . Let us have [women] in the councils of the State and in the places of influence, and let them translate the songs of the angels into human laws and incarnate them in human institutions, that there may be a high and pure moral standard placed before all the people; that we may rise out of our materialism and our sensualism to live for the highest aims, to aspire to realize here on the earth that kingdom which is peace and righteousness and joy in the Holy Ghost.[76]

As Christ had sent women to proclaim the risen Lord, "so today he commands women to go abroad publishing the Gospel of a world's salvation, not only by words but by life and by deeds."[77]

No matter how inclined toward good woman's nature was, however, women could "do nothing for God or humanity with your hands tied. The first thing is to free yourself from this bondage in order to help some good cause."[78] Inhibiting women's inclination toward good work meant interfering with divine intention: "And shall men, churches or governments dare longer to prohibit women from obeying the command and fulfilling the Divine decree? All reforms wait for woman's freedom." Once women were free, she predicted, they would

> not go about getting up strawberry festivals, and oyster suppers, and crazy quilt lotteries, but we shall vote appropriations. At present, women are utterly powerless with regard to the great evils which they are asked to overcome, and the first service we can render to the church or to the anti-church—the first service that we can render to humanity or to God, is to get ourselves into a position of independence.[79]

Anna Howard Shaw: "The Heavenly Vision"

Three years after leaving her Cape Cod churches, Anna Howard Shaw preached what would be her most popular and oft-delivered suffrage sermon, "The Heavenly Vision." In that sermon Shaw revealed her strong theological and political convictions, convictions that comfortably coexisted

76. Ibid.
77. Brown, "Crime and the Remedy."
78. Brown, "Where is the Mistake?"
79. Brown, "Crime and the Remedy."

within her vision of God's intention for creation. Appealing to biblical and historical examples, she painted a convincing portrait of the evil and vice that had marked the centuries of humankind while men ruled the world and the influence of women was ignored:

> Patiently, prone upon the earth, Sphinx-like, sat woman limited by sin, limited by social custom, limited by false theories, limited by narrow bigotry and by still narrower creeds, listening to the tramp of the weary millions as they passed on through the centuries, patiently listening, toiling and waiting, humbly bearing the pain and weariness which seemed to fall to her lot.

After centuries of this patient waiting upon the earth, the woman of the nineteenth century "lifted her eyes above the earth to heaven and away from the jarring strifes which surrounded her." There she encountered a vision so full of wonder and light "that her soul burst its prison-house of bondage as she beheld the vision of the grandeur and dignity of womanhood." That vision was not one of her own wishful imagination but a liberating gift from God:

> The truth stood before her, and she knew it was not the purpose of the Divine that she should crouch beneath the bonds of selfishness and custom, that she should yield blindly to prejudice and ignorance. She learned that she was created not from the side of man, but rather created *by* the side of man. The world had suffered that she had not kept her divinely-appointed place. Then she remembered the words of prophecy, that salvation was to come to the race not through the man but through the descendant of the woman.

The women of the nineteenth century, Shaw believed, were those to whom the "heavenly vision" of a divine, moral life had been granted. Through the ages, God had revealed in visions great truths for the improvement of humanity. Now, in the "sunset hour of the Nineteenth Century," God revealed similar truth through women, "diverse and varied," who had "come together here and now with one harmonious purpose—that of lifting humanity, both men and women, into a higher, purer, truer life." Like the apostle Paul and even Jesus before them, women were obligated to obey the call of God and, "rising above all selfishness," gather up their "varied gifts and accomplishments to consecrate them to God and humanity." Then, "influenced by lofty motives, with her own womanly nature in her, stimulated by the wail of humanity and the glory of God, woman may go forth and enter into any field of usefulness which God and the world opens up before her."[80]

In this sermon and in her other suffrage presentations, Shaw wove together her beliefs in God's divine intention for women as morally superior beings, the inextricable relationship between democratic principles and human equality, and the timeliness of women's influence upon the political realm. While it might be true that "Dr. Shaw said little about religious issues in her suffrage speeches,"[81] her entire ideological argumentation for woman suffrage was cast in a theological framework. To disregard that framework is to disregard the essential nature of who she was, what she believed, and why she spoke and acted as she did. She avoided using suffrage rhetoric for proselytizing or for preaching religious doctrine, but she unabashedly built her arguments on widely held theological beliefs.

In one of her standard lectures, "God's Women," Shaw presented a theological defense of woman suffrage that began with the assertion of gender equality from the time of creation. "We have proved by the Bible," she stated, "that when God created man in the beginning in his own image, He created man, male and female man, and called their name Adam, and to this male and female man, who He called Adam, He gave all things." With characteristic humor, she went on to explain her understanding of God's intention in this two-in-one creation:

> The race has believed all this time that Adam was Mr. Adam, and not Mrs. Adam at all. Eve was not Mrs. Adam because she was the wife of Mr. Adam. She was no more Mrs. Adam because she was the wife of Mr. Adam than Adam was Mr. Adam because he was the husband of Mrs. Adam; not a bit. They were each Adam, and neither of them alone was Adam. They were Adam together. You can never have a male Adam or a female Adam. You must have a male and female Adam, and you have manhood and womanhood—humanity.[82]

She reiterated in many speeches and in many ways her belief in God's intention that man and woman were created equally to work side by side.

80. Anna Howard Shaw, "The Heavenly Vision," *Woman's Tribune*, March 27, 1888, 3.

81. Linkugel, "The Woman Suffrage Argument of Anna Howard Shaw," 172.

82. Anna Howard Shaw, "God's Women," in *National Council of Women in the United States*, ed. Rachel Foster Avery (Philadelphia: J. B. Lippincott, 1891), 243–44.

She referred to the assumption in western countries that "the voice of the people is the voice of God, . . . that the laws of our land were the crystallized voice of the Deity."

Those who made that correct claim, however, often forgot "that in the compass of the people's voice there is a soprano as well as a bass, and that if the voice of the people is the voice of God, we will never know what His voice is until the bass and soprano unite in harmonious sound, the resultant of which will be the voice of God."[83] God had declared from the beginning that man and woman were to dwell together. "Now," she stated quite simply in a 1915 suffrage speech, "all that is meant by the woman-suffrage movement lies in that first divine utterance to man: 'It is not good for man to stand alone'—either in the home, or the state, or even in the Garden of Eden."[84] The equality God introduced at creation was the most persuasive argument for woman suffrage. "There are no new arguments," she believed, "there never have been any for woman's suffrage; there never has been a new argument for it since the day when God created man in His own image, male and female, and gave them dominion over the world. That is the only argument there ever has been or ever will be in favor of woman's suffrage."[85]

In order to bolster the biblical argument for equality, she recounted events from Old Testament history in which God had raised up women to assure the success of the nation of Israel. First among those divinely appointed women was Deborah, judge over Israel. No one who was not recognized by the people of Israel to have been chosen by God could have assumed such a position. Nor can anyone assume, she went on, "that God did not know what He was doing when he chose Deborah to be a judge in Israel." Shaw refuted an argument posed in a speech by a bishop who preceded her on the platform during a suffrage tour. The bishop delineated the things women may and may not be permitted to do. As Shaw quoted his speech, the bishop inferred that Deborah and any other woman of leadership was not God's woman. "If then she was not God's woman," she asked, "whose woman was she? And if God is not able to recognize His own, what will become of us at the last? We believe that this

83. Anna Howard Shaw, "The Fate of Republics," AHSP, SL, Fol. 423.

84. Anna Howard Shaw, "A Speech by Doctor Anna Howard Shaw," Birmingham, Ala., April 16, 1915 (New York: National Woman Suffrage Publishing, 1915), 3–4.

85. Anna Howard Shaw, "Woman Suffrage as an Educator" (address delivered before the Equal Franchise Society at the Garden Theatre, January 13, 1910 [New York: The Equal Franchise Society, n.d.]).

judge in Israel was divinely ordained for the work, because otherwise she could not have done her work so well." Other women of the Bible— Miriam, Ruth, Rachel, the Marys—demonstrated similar selfless leadership in response to the call of God. These were "God's women," and if

> God chose a woman to act in these cases, when the world needed a clear brain, a tender, affectionate, loving, motherly heart, a firm and determined will, and chose the woman to do it, and if when the people needed a leader to guide them out of bondage to freedom He chose a woman to be among the leading instruments of that great undertaking, who shall dare to say, be he layman or priest, that such a woman is not God's woman?[86]

With this list of specifically feminine qualities, Shaw demonstrated her belief in woman's unique, God-given nature. Like Antoinette Brown Blackwell and Olympia Brown, Shaw believed that women were endowed with particular gifts that manifested themselves in certain characteristics such as pure hearts, maternal natures, and religious affections. And also like Brown Blackwell and Brown, Shaw believed that women were not to ignore or hoard those divine qualities but to use them for the moral uplift of humankind:

> The mother-heart of woman, the mother-heart that reaches out to the race and finds a wrong and rights it, finds a broken heart and heals it, finds a bruised life ready to be broken and sustains it—a woman instinct with mother-love, which is the expression of the Divine love; a woman who, finding any wrong, any weakness, any pain, any sorrow, anywhere in the world, reaches out her hand to right the wrong, to heal the pain, to comfort the suffering—such a woman is God's woman.[87]

Shaw's full-time work for suffrage grew out of her increasing exposure to the desperate nature of many women's lives, so it is not surprising that the inherent goodness and the existential needs of women served as the philosophical foundation for her suffrage rhetoric. "Every suffragist I have ever met has been a lover of home," she declared in her autobiography, "and only the conviction that she is fighting for her home, her children, for

86. Shaw, "God's Women," 245, 246.
87. Ibid., 249.

other women, or for all of these, has sustained her in her public work."[88] The differences among women were obliterated as they united to follow the heavenly vision of improving humanity: "Diverse and varied as are our races, diverse and varied as are our theories, diverse as are our religious beliefs, yet we come together here and now with one harmonious purpose—that of lifting humanity, both men and women, into a higher, purer, truer life."[89]

The ultimate application of woman's unique gifts and superior moral nature, however, would occur, Shaw argued, when she used her nature for the moral improvement of the United States. In an address on behalf of the Ohio Woman's Christian Temperance Union, Shaw noted that the "battles" of her day were more serious than the battles of previous eras in the history of the United States. "Theirs were the first material struggles of a new century; our problems are ethical and spiritual; and it takes clearer brains, purer hearts and more determined purpose to solve them than it did to solve the simpler problems of the last century." From that assertion she argued that "because we need these clearer brains and these purer hearts, and these higher convictions of justice and duty, that it is the right, and ought to be the purpose, of all the women of this country to demand every bit of power which will enable them to do for their children the very best and noblest service which can be done by free women in a free country."[90] First, however, women had to be convinced of their usefulness. They needed to discover "self-respect, belief in themselves, and a high opinion of the service for which God put women into the world and which women have so loyally rendered since the beginning of time." Once women acknowledged "the dignity of women's work and women's service," their faithfulness "in these great responsibilities, the obligations to the home, to society, to the church and to the country, which women have borne in the past, we will realize that they have been but the preparation for the new responsibilities which may come to women during all the period of their lives."[91]

In her most famous lecture, "The Fate of Republics," Shaw described

---

88. Anna Howard Shaw with Elizabeth Jordan, *The Story of a Pioneer* (New York: Harper & Brothers Publishers, 1915), 269.

89. Shaw, "The Heavenly Vision."

90. Anna Howard Shaw, "Influence Versus Power" (excerpts from an address), Ohio WCTU leaflet, AHSP, SL, Fol. 421.

91. Anna Howard Shaw, "Address at a Meeting of the Women's Section, Maryland Council of Defense" (Academy of Music, Baltimore, Md., January 4, 1918), 5.

the fate of nations that excluded women and their gifts from participation in government: those republics "have always become weak and have ultimately come to their death through the decay of the moral and spiritual side of their life." She defended the proposition that the moral character of the nation would be improved when women were allowed to participate fully in the political process by answering her own question, "Wherein does the nature of women differ from that of men in such a way that if they voted they would be able to affect the government?" "It is universally admitted that women are more moral than men," she declared unequivocally. Women were more temperate, more peace-loving, and more law-abiding than men. "The great moral factor of the world is its womanhood."[92]

Besides exhibiting moral superiority, women also exhibited greater religious affections than men. "Women are also more religious than men," Shaw declared in language similar to that of Olympia Brown; "nearly three-fourths of the church members are women, and nine-tenths of the spiritual and philanthropic work of the world is done by them." Women are "the teachers of the young, we are the mothers of the race. If you want the noblest men you must have the noblest mothers."[93] Woman's moral influence had already been demonstrated, transforming professional and industrial worlds. At a congressional hearing on behalf of woman suffrage in 1900, she dismissed the fear of the degradation of women's morality should they become engaged in public activity. The statistics show, she remarked, "that in those occupations in which women are able to earn a livelihood in an honorable and respectable manner they have raised the standard of morality rather than lowered it."[94] After hearing testimonies at the 1906 National American Woman Suffrage Association (NAWSA) convention by elected officials who attributed their success to the influence of good women, President Shaw commented, "Now if a good woman can develop the best in an individual man, may not all the good women together develop the best in a whole State?"[95] Recalling the history of the nation in her "Fate of Republics" speech, she noted that the United States had more than its share of "parents" to guide its settlement, "but they have all been fathers—pilgrim fathers, Plymouth

92. Shaw, "The Fate of Republics."
93. Anna Howard Shaw, Speech before the NAWSA Convention (1892), *History of Woman Suffrage*, II:200.
94. Anna Howard Shaw, Congressional hearing, *History of Woman Suffrage*, IV:380.
95. *History of Woman Suffrage*, IV:154.

fathers, forefathers, revolutionary fathers, city fathers, and church fathers, fathers of every description." But, she continued, "we have never had a mother. In this lies the weakness of all republics. They have been fathered to death. The great need of our country today is a little mothering to undo the evils of too much fathering."[96]

Shaw dismissed objections to this potential infusion of morality and religion into politics and repudiated fears for the obliteration of lines separating church and state. "[God] has no place for the politics of any country in which there is no room for the Decalogue or the golden rule," she declared boldly. "What we need more than the settlement of any of the problems which are at present agitating the political mind is an infusion of the golden rule into politics, and of the Decalogue into the laws of the land." But such a display of religious fervor had to be more than superficial. "This cannot be accomplished either by putting the name of [the] Deity into the Constitution, or by the union of church and state, but by bringing to bear upon the government the influence of that class of people who are the spiritual strength of the church."[97]

Like Antoinette Brown Blackwell, Olympia Brown and other suffrage preachers, Shaw had high hopes for the moral influence of women. Women held the potential to transform American society if not the world. When women awakened to the "heavenly vision" divinely set before them, they would come to the service of humanity "each bearing her torch of living truth, casting over the world the light of the vision that dawned upon her own soul." The content of that light would serve to "transform this world, bringing humanity into harmonious relations with itself and infusing justice into citizenship, honesty into business, purity into social relations, and the spirit of the golden rule over all life."[98] Women would work to reconfigure the economic structure of society, giving people rather than charity "an opportunity to develop and make themselves capable of earning the bread." Instead of spending their time and energy in "fool charities," voting women would see to it that "there will not be so much need of charity and philanthropy."[99]

Shaw took the occasion of a Sunday suffrage gathering to note the appropriateness of considering a very political issue on the Sabbath, stating:

96. Shaw, "The Fate of Republics."
97. Ibid.
98. Shaw, "The Heavenly Vision."
99. Anna Howard Shaw, "The Fundamental Principle of a Republic," as recorded in Wil A. Linkugel and Martha Solomon, *Anna Howard Shaw* (New York: Greenwood Press, 1991), 157.

I know of no better sermon for Sunday afternoon than for men and women to discuss the fundamental principles of the government under which they live. No man is fitted to become a citizen of the Kingdom of Heaven who is not a good citizen on this earth. No man who thinks this earth and its problems unworthy of consideration understands the moving of the Divine Spirit, and anyone who thinks that woman suffrage is not a proper subject for discussion on Sunday afternoon, does not comprehend the profound, sublime and divine principles of democracy.

Having established the appropriateness of a Sunday discussion of woman suffrage, Shaw made one of her boldest statements associating democratic values with divine principles:

Democracy is not merely a form of government; it is a great spiritual force emanating from the heart of the Infinite, permeating the universe and transforming the lives of men until the day comes when it shall take possession of them, and shall govern their lives. Then will men be fitted to lift their faces to the Source from whence the spirit of democracy flows, and answer back in the spirit, in their recognition of that fundamental principle of democracy, "One is our father, even God, and we are members one of another." And as soon as the spirit of democracy takes possession of us, we shall not quibble as to whether it is male or female, bond or free, Jew or Greek; we shall recognize only that every child has an equal right with every other human child of God, in the things that belong to God. Liberty, justice, freedom, belong alike to God's human children.[100]

Inherent in all of Shaw's suffrage rhetoric is a vision of social progress for America. She was often derided as a "dreamer" for that vision, a description she proudly accepted. "We are told that to assume that women will help purify political life and develop a more ideal government but proves us to be dreamers of dreams," she told suffragists at the 1905 NAWSA convention.

Yes, we are in a goodly company of dreamers, of Confucius, of Buddha, of Jesus, of the English Commons fighting for the Magna Carta,

100. Shaw, "A Speech by Doctor Anna Howard Shaw."

of the Pilgrims, of the American Revolutionists, of the Anti-slavery men and women. The seers and leaders of all times have been dreamers. Every step of progress the world has made is the crystallization of a dream into reality.[101]

The dawn of political equality for women was one manifestation of the realization of her dream of social progress. It was a logical component of her philosophical progressivism. History, particularly Christian history, revealed "how prejudice and ignorance, how bigotry and the creeds and narrow views of men have stayed the progress of truth," but the growth of truth, Shaw believed, "like the growth of a flower, is progressive."[102] Shaw was, indeed, an exponent of the social gospel theology that dominated liberal religious thought in America at the turn of the twentieth century.[103] She believed the kingdom of God could be realized on earth through the upward, progressive improvement of society. Her rhetoric reflected her theology of divine immanence and her conviction that God worked through human lives and human history to bring about a new kingdom on earth that more closely reflected divine intention. She encouraged clergywomen to

> teach that the Kingdom of Heaven is set up here and now; let her show by example that service is the sum of human excellence; let her declare that love is the fulfillment of the perfect law, that it alone is the dynamic force in human lives which is to redeem the world from its greed, its injustice and its barbarism; let love be the keynote of all her thinking and acting, for out of it alone can come the great social, moral and religious harmony which shall usher in "the new Heaven and the new Earth wherein dwelleth righteousness."[104]

She not only equated the enfranchisement of women with movement toward a more enlightened political climate but regarded woman suffrage as a sign of the dawn of God's kingdom through the spirit of American democracy. "The idealists dream and the dream is told," she proclaimed to her fellow suffragists, "and the practical men listen and ponder and

101. *History of Woman Suffrage*, IV:126.
102. Shaw, "The Heavenly Vision."
103. For more on Shaw's social gospel theology, see Ralph W. Spencer, "Anna Howard Shaw," *Methodist History* 13 (1974–75): 48–50.
104. Anna Howard Shaw, "Women in the Ministry" (1879).

bring back the truth and apply it to human life, and progress and growth and higher human ideals come into being and so the world moves ever on."[105] The only hope for progress rested with those, particularly women, who were willing to move beyond dreams to action: "The life which God intends us to live is not one long dream of truth and its power," she cautioned. "He calls us to lift ourselves upon our feet, and, in the dignity of a truer, nobler womanhood than we have heretofore known, to stand face to face with truth and open up a way for it to enter into our souls, and there to bloom into the eternal flower of constant purpose and of a new life."[106] Those who chose to follow the vision of truth God had instilled in them through the work of reform were brought "into the knowledge that all progress is one. That a reform no more than an individual can live to itself. That truth, all truth, is the atmosphere of the Infinite Mind, and is in its source and aim one with God."[107]

Shaw summarized her theological and political convictions in this statement from a speech delivered at a student convocation held at Temple University in 1917, two years before the end of her life:

> I speak out of the fullness of a life's experience, forty years of which I have given to one great cause, for one purpose. The cause is called woman's enfranchisement, but it is much greater than that. If that were all, it would be narrow, selfish, and not part of a great whole. It is not that woman may vote, but that the human in mankind may triumph. That civilization may conquer barbarism, may triumph over autocracy. That every child of God may have a fair chance to be and to become all that it is possible for it to attain.[108]

The "heavenly vision," of which Shaw dreamed and for which she preached and worked so earnestly, would become reality

> when every man and woman into whose soul the light of truth has burned goes forth in the name and in the spirit of his Master to give this truth to the world that the world by it may be lifted out of its bigotry and sin, out of its false life into the fullness of a truer and broader living. . . . Then when this light shall have rested upon us all, and we

105. *History of Woman Suffrage*, IV:126.
106. Shaw, "The Heavenly Vision."
107. Anna Howard Shaw, "Select Your Principle of Life," AHSP, SL, Fol. 470.
108. Ibid.

are filled with his spirit we shall be ready to give ourselves to the world, and then will the world receive us in the name of Him through whom we come, whose name is love—God.[109]

The "orthodox of the orthodox"

In her autobiography, Shaw recounted an incident from the many days she spent on the suffrage circuit with Susan B. Anthony. The two women were lecturing in "an especially pious town," a fact that did not go unnoticed by the speakers. "Just before I went on the platform," Shaw recalled, "Miss Anthony remarked, peacefully, 'These people have always claimed that I am irreligious. They will not accept the fact that I am a Quaker— or, rather, they seem to think a Quaker is an infidel. I am glad you are a Methodist, for now they cannot claim that we are not orthodox.'" Anthony went on to introduce Shaw not only as a Methodist minister but as the "orthodox of the orthodox."[110] The incident Shaw recalled revealed the tenor of the suffrage movement during the decades leading up to the passage of the Nineteenth Amendment. As both suffragists and antisuffragists sought to make inroads in public sentiment and political action, the stakes became higher and the rhetoric and tactics more strident. The value of "orthodox" women, as Shaw was described by Anthony and as Antoinette Brown Blackwell was described by Lucy Stone decades earlier, to the suffrage cause increased as the movement gained strength and encountered equally vehement opposition from antisuffragists.

Antoinette Brown Blackwell, Olympia Brown, and Anna Howard Shaw represented a cadre of women and men, clergy and laity, who tempered the perceived radicalism of the suffrage movement in its final decades by infusing it with a religious dimension. Their theological and biblical language, their appeals to traditional moral values, and their very identities as people of faith and religious leaders made them more acceptable and more persuasive as suffrage advocates than many of their secular fellow reformers. They appealed to the expedient potential of women's political power in a nation threatened by diminishing moral standards and portrayed the cause of woman suffrage in terms of a divine quest for the moral salvation of America. In doing so, they reverted to the early-nineteenth-century ideology of True Womanhood, linking the idea of the True

109. Shaw, "The Heavenly Vision."
110. Shaw, *Story of a Pioneer*, 192.

Woman with woman suffrage. They created thereby an effective vehicle for broad suffrage support from two formerly antithetical images, making the idea of woman suffrage palatable for traditional women. This linkage also revealed the powerful dimension of social class that pervaded the suffrage movement during its final few decades. These suffrage preachers appealed to the sense of *noblesse oblige* that mobilized women at the close of the nineteenth century to organize clubs and associations devoted to benevolence and reform. Through the words and ideology of these clergywomen-cum-suffragists who represented traditional values, woman suffrage was transformed from a self-serving right demanded by radical, nonorthodox women to a female obligation necessary to preserve the religious and moral integrity of America.

Much of the success of Brown Blackwell, Brown, and Shaw as suffrage orators came as the result of their rhetorical appeals to their listeners. In a study of the suffrage press, Martha M. Solomon asserted, "Because all human cooperation entails communication, that process of transformation into a social movement will have rhetorical interaction at its core."[111] The woman suffrage movement and the tradition of transformative social movements in which it stood reveal the validity of that assertion. The language these women preachers used to promote the goal of woman suffrage was far from arbitrary. The particular rhetorical strategies and the precise words these preachers used to assert their views differed at times, but beneath their words existed a common understanding of the intention of their speech. That intention was to promote a particular worldview they shared, inherent in which was the fear of a waning Protestant ethos and the loss of the traditional moral attributes that accompanied it. The rhetorical worlds Brown Blackwell, Brown, and Shaw created through their sermons, speeches, and essays enabled them to become some of the most popular apologists for the suffrage cause. In their embrace of religious sentiment in defense of woman's rights, they made an idea that once was deemed radical and untenable acceptable to the moderate majority of American citizens. They represented the public voices of the later, moderate woman suffrage movement, voices that appropriated ideas and language of the larger culture and adapted them to craft a rhetoric in support of woman suffrage.

The rhetoric used by suffrage preachers identified the values and fears of white, middle-class American society in the decades of transition

111. Martha M. Solomon, ed., *A Voice of Their Own: The Woman Suffrage Press, 1840–1910* (Tuscaloosa: University of Alabama Press, 1991), 3.

preceding and following the turn of the twentieth century. They advocated a challenge to social and political tradition in the specific form of women's enfranchisement but did so in what has been referred to as the "value language"[112] of the prevailing culture. The most obvious way in which Brown Blackwell, Brown, and Shaw employed the value language of their culture was in their continual reassertions of the divinely assigned gender attributes. God had created women with a particular nature and with particular affinities, including a superior moral nature. This belief represented a departure from earlier Christian assertions of women's susceptibility to sin and evil and from nineteenth-century philosophical notions that men and women were equal in every respect. Womanhood was "the great moral factor of the world," as Shaw put it. God had created women more susceptible to religious sentiment than men and better suited for molding moral character. The proof of this divine intention was obvious in the influence women had asserted for good from biblical days onward.

From this foundational belief in woman's moral nature, these preachers moved to the requisite application of that nature to the social sphere. Women's understanding of politics and issues pertaining to a wider sphere of existence would enhance their positive influence on sons and husbands who were engaged in that wider sphere. The ballot in women's hands would enable them to enact public legislation that would give them greater control over the moral character of their homes and families. Moving beyond the domestic sphere of influence, however, voting women would create of the nation something akin to a morally responsible family, simply on a much larger scale. The social vision they portrayed was one of mutuality and complementariness with women and men working together to bring their best gender attributes to bear on the complexities of life in American society. You cannot "build up homes without men," Shaw contended. In the same way, you cannot "build up the state without women." God intentionally "placed man and woman together in the world in families and in society," Brown stated. Man's "observation and reason" were completed by woman's "perception and ready inference," enabling them to address "the great needs of the world." Such argumentation placed the defense of suffrage in an entirely different philosophical framework, a framework devoid of the strident and offensive idea of rights that bore the taint of selfishness and radicalism.

---

112. Herbert W. Simons, "Requirements, Problems, and Strategies: A Theory of Persuasion for Social Movements," *Quarterly Journal of Speech* 56 (February 1970): 7.

Unfortunately, in their zeal to gain support for woman suffrage, Brown Blackwell, Brown, and Shaw, like many of their colleagues in the movement, sometimes succumbed to what could be interpreted as racist and xenophobic rhetoric in their defense of woman suffrage. Such argumentation was not unheard of in the closing decades of the nineteenth century. An incipient racism began to appear in suffrage rhetoric shortly after the passage of the Fourteenth and Fifteenth Amendments, which granted African American men the right to vote but, for the first time in American political history, specifically denied all women the same right. The rhetoric concerning race used by suffragists had a "yes, but" quality about it. They declared their support for African American suffrage but qualified it by stating their belief in the priority of woman suffrage.

This dark side of the rhetoric of suffragists extended beyond race to nationality. Shaw warned against the overwhelming of "America's womanhood" by "external forces" that were characterized by ignorance and, often, criminal proclivities. She feared for the stability of a nation that insisted on enfranchising "ignorance and vice" while disenfranchising "intelligence and virtue." Brown invoked similar arguments in her rhetoric questioning immigration policies. Like Shaw, she attributed negative, stereotypical qualities of ignorance and immorality to foreigners who had come to America from the Old World. Immigrants were blamed for promoting intemperance and the growth of the alcohol industry. Foreigners who had come from European countries were accused of bringing with them habits acceptable to their cultures but abhorrent to the moral sensibilities of Americans.

The racist and xenophobic language that haunts some of the suffrage rhetoric of Brown Blackwell, Brown, and Shaw is particularly perplexing in light of their commitment to abolition and human rights. Antoinette Brown Blackwell, like many early women speakers, gained much of her public speaking experience and her reputation as an orator on the antislavery platform. Her first journalistic efforts after leaving the church in South Butler exposed the horrors of life among the lower classes of New York City. Olympia Brown worked and preached against the Civil War and the evils of slavery while serving as a pastor. Anna Howard Shaw obtained a medical degree and left parish ministry in large part because of the sufferings of impoverished women that she witnessed on the streets of Boston. In the larger framework of their lives and work, the dark side of their suffrage rhetoric points to the employment of particular ideology for the sake of expediency. They sought to restore a lost manner of life and to construct a vision of an ideal, monolithic world in response to the social dislocation that pervaded nineteenth-century America. Through their words, they induced hope in the restoration of a world their listeners believed had once existed but that appeared lost forever. In contrast to the depravity of society they saw when they looked around them, these preacher-suffragists were idealists who shared a vision of what life in America could be when influenced by women and men who advocated particular religious and moral values and cultural norms.

That vision, while certainly romantic, had a deeply religious character. Women's enfranchisement was cast in a larger theological framework that included a presumption of divine authority and of divine initiative in human affairs. Such a theological context for the defense of suffrage was essential in light of the fact that most of the rhetoric opposing suffrage came from religious communities and from religious leaders who invoked biblical and theological arguments to circumscribe the appropriate sphere of female activity. Brown Blackwell, Brown, and Shaw countered that religious perspective with a mixture of their own theological constructs, biblical hermeneutics, and patriotic visions. They believed woman suffrage was part of a larger understanding of God's intention for America. Their speech revealed a lingering vision of the kingdom of God in America that had defined the American mythos since the Puritan settlement.

In pursuing that vision, they collapsed the barriers between church and state and between private and public spheres. They found ways to fulfill their vocational calls by redefining sacred space and by bridging the ecclesiastical and secular worlds. They saw nothing incongruous in preaching from suffrage platforms or promoting suffrage in the pulpit. Much of their popularity as speakers and their success in winning converts to the cause of woman suffrage resulted from their ecclesiastical identities. They were trusted leaders who spoke in familiar language. They truly believed women brought honesty, purity, and other similar virtues to public life, and they truly believed the condition of American society required the restoration of such virtues. Inherent in their suffrage rhetoric is a rejection of the way things were and a fervent—albeit sometimes naïve—hope for the way things could be. They believed in the progressive nature of human history and in America as the conduit of progress toward the revelation of God's kingdom in all its fullness. All three women would gladly have accepted the accusation once made against Shaw of being "dreamers of dreams." They shared a dream, a "heavenly vision" of moral progress that would be hastened by woman suffrage, one important step toward the realization of the eternal truth of God.

Chapter Five

They "have trodden many thorny paths":

Three Lives of Reform

In a letter of tribute written in 1893 recalling the life and work of Olympia Brown, Lucretia Effinger, Brown's roommate at Antioch College, reflected on her dear friend's purpose as a young woman. Olympia Brown, Effinger stated, sought "to take hold some where of the world's work and win for women some larger recognition than had yet been accorded them." Since those early days of her life, Effinger concluded, Brown's "feet have trodden many thorny paths and she has ever stood in the front of the battle for equal rights and opportunities for women."[1]

Effinger's words are an appropriate description not only of Brown but also of her preacher-suffragist sisters Antoinette Brown Blackwell and Anna Howard Shaw in their quests to fulfill their calls to serve God and humanity. They faced skeptical families, scornful professors, uncooperative colleagues, and hostile critics. But faith, persistence, and the support of individuals and congregations who affirmed their gifts and visions enabled them, in Effinger's words, to "win for women some larger recognition than had yet been accorded them." After they had achieved their personal goals of ordination to pastoral ministries, no goal was more urgent and no accomplishment more gratifying for Brown Blackwell, Brown, and Shaw than political equality for women, which, they believed, would lead to equality for women in all arenas of American society, including the church. The hope of woman's rights inspired them at the ends of their lives as obviously as it had shaped the beginnings of their

---

1. Letter from Lucretia Effinger, 1893, OBP, SL, Fol.1.

lives, making the road to women's enfranchisement the final thorny path they traveled.

The Passage of the Nineteenth Amendment

The woman suffrage movement's "Armageddon,"[2] as it has been called, occurred in Nashville, Tennessee, in August 1920, when, after considerable debate and vacillation, the Tennessee state house passed the woman suffrage amendment to the United States Constitution by two votes. The years leading up to that momentous vote were riddled with problems. The first decade and a half of the twentieth century was in the suffrage movement known as the "doldrums"[3] among suffrage historians. Although individual states continued to pass legislation authorizing woman suffrage, suffragists had a difficult time getting their issue on the national agenda. Theodore Roosevelt, the 1912 presidential candidate of the newly formed Progressive Party, included woman suffrage in his campaign platform, but the issue was not on the agenda of the Democratic Party and its nominee, Woodrow Wilson, the winner of the election.

At the same time, the National Association Opposed to Woman Suffrage, founded in 1911, was growing in strength while the National American Woman Suffrage Association faced organizational disagreements that hampered its unity and effectiveness. Anna Howard Shaw stepped down as president of the NAWSA in 1915 with the group's appreciation for her oratorical skill in shaping the movement but disappointment with her organizational ability. Her successor, Carrie Chapman Catt, introduced what she called her Winning Plan, which focused all efforts on the passage of a federal amendment. Catt, along with other suffrage leaders, believed that the panoply of efforts that characterized the Progressive Era, the era of early-twentieth-century social and political reforms (including work for peace, temperance, and urban reform), had fragmented the efforts of suffragists. Many suffragists—Brown Blackwell, Brown, and Shaw included—regarded wide-ranging reform work as the means to broader support for suffrage. Catt believed the opposite, however, maintaining that suffrage was the means to the realization of other reform

---

2. Anastatia Sims, "Armageddon in Tennessee: The Final Battle Over the Nineteenth Amendment," in Marjorie Spruill Wheeler, ed., *One Woman, One Vote: Rediscovering the Woman Suffrage Movement* (Troutdale, Oreg.: NewSage Press, 1995), 333.

3. Eleanor Flexner, *Century of Struggle* (New York: Atheneum, 1974), 262.

objectives.[4] In order to fulfill her Winning Plan, Catt fashioned her version of a modern phenomenon, the single-issue political pressure group. She refused to allow any other cause to divert the focus of the NAWSA's agenda, saying, "As a matter of fact we do not care a ginger snap about anything but that Federal Amendment."[5]

Whether as the result of the concerted efforts of Catt and her fellow suffragists or a changing political climate, the passage of a federal woman suffrage amendment, known by then as the Susan B. Anthony Amendment, appeared imminent by the beginning of the 1920s. New York state had adopted a suffrage amendment in 1917, and with such a large and influential state joining the growing list of states that approved woman suffrage, "the suffrage bandwagon seemed to be gaining momentum," according to suffrage historian Anastatia Sims.[6] President Woodrow Wilson eventually yielded to pressure from suffragists and endorsed a federal suffrage amendment in 1918. The amendment was approved by the House of Representatives in 1918 but failed to achieve the two-thirds vote required for approval by the Senate. After much lobbying by the NAWSA and the National Woman's Party,[7] Senate approval joined another overwhelming House vote in May 1919. The woman suffrage amendment was ratified officially by Congress on June 4, 1919.

The celebrations of the suffragists were short-lived, however, since they realized that their next task, gaining ratification of the amendment by three-fourths (thirty-six) of the states, would not be easy. By June of 1920, twelve months after Congress's approval of the amendment, ratification by thirty-five states had occurred. After weeks of disappointing news from state legislatures, including defeat by Delaware, deadlocks in Vermont and Connecticut, and growing opposition in North Carolina, the only hope for final ratification rested with the state of Tennessee.

4. Robert Booth Fowler, "Carrie Chapman Catt, Strategist," in Wheeler, *One Woman, One Vote*, 298.

5. C. C. Catt to Ethel M. Smith (August 3, 1917) as recorded in ibid.

6. Sims, "Armageddon in Tennessee," 333.

7. The National Woman's Party, originally known as the Congressional Union, began in 1913 as a committee of the NAWSA, led by Alice Paul and other radical suffragists who eventually rejected the passive tactics of the NAWSA and broke away to form an independent organization. It became known for its militancy, including a willingness to break the law and resist governmental authority and engage in hunger strikes and violent protest. Paul spent time early in the 1900s working with radical suffragists in England and Scotland. She was jailed in England and force-fed as a result of a hunger strike in which she participated. She brought some of the radical tactics of the British "suffragettes" with her on her return to the United States in 1910.

Tennessee's Governor Albert H. Roberts, at the urging of President Wilson, called for a special session of the state legislature to be held August 9, 1920, to consider the suffrage amendment. Supporters and opponents of the amendment descended on Nashville for a long, hot summer of debate and lobbying. Carrie Chapman Catt was summoned to Nashville by local suffragists. She arrived with an overnight bag but stayed for two months.[8]

When the bill reached the Tennessee House floor on August 18 after several postponements by the opposition, it appeared that the suffragists were still two votes short. Yet another motion to table the amendment was made, but it failed on the tying vote of Representative Banks Turner, forcing a vote on the amendment. The suffragists had not counted Turner's support in their tally of legislators, but he was persuaded by his friend Governor Roberts and the Democratic Party to ensure Tennessee did not become the state held responsible for the amendment's defeat. Even with Turner's support for the amendment, the suffragists remained one vote short. Harry Burn, a representative from rural East Tennessee, twenty-four and the youngest member of the House, had previously sided with the antisuffragists in their motions to table the amendment, and he represented a conservative district opposed to the suffrage amendment, so suffragists were not hopeful of his support. What they did not know, however, was that Burn carried in his coat pocket a letter from his mother, a staunch suffragist, urging his vote for woman suffrage:

> Hurrah! And vote for suffrage and don't keep them in doubt. I notice some of the speeches against. They were very bitter. I have been watching to see how you stood, but have noticed nothing yet. Don't forget to be a good boy and help Mrs. Catt put "Rat" in Ratification.[9]

Burn was "a good boy" and voted "aye" when his name was called. A few minutes later, Banks Turner also voted in favor of the amendment, which was approved forty-nine to forty-seven, making woman suffrage a federal law. The antisuffrage forces refused to accept defeat and maneuvered to have the decision reversed. Through their supporters in the legislature, they worked for days to pass a motion to reconsider the vote. When those efforts failed, they tried to prevent the governor from signing the ratification certificate and the secretary of state from issuing the

8. Flexner, *Century of Struggle*, 322.
9. Ibid., 323.

certificate. The ratification process continued, however, and the procla-mation certifying Tennessee's adoption of the Nineteenth Amendment was signed early on August 26, 1920, enfranchising twenty-six million women of voting age.[10]

Faithful to the End: The Last Years

Olympia Brown

On September 12, 1920, three weeks after the ratification of the Nine-teenth Amendment, Olympia Brown, 85, preached her last sermon, as the guest minister at the Universalist congregation she had served for several years in Racine, Wisconsin. She titled her sermon "The Opening Doors" (from her text, Psalm 24:7: "Lift up your heads, O ye gates; and be ye lift up, ye everlasting doors") and used it as an occasion to celebrate homilet-ically the hope she had for the full political participation of women in the United States. She spoke of the decades that had passed since she resigned as the church's pastor in 1887 and of the many things that had transpired in those years spanning portions of two centuries. "But the grandest thing," she proclaimed with certainty, "has been the lifting up of the gates and the opening of the doors to the woman of America, giving liberty to twenty-seven million women, thus opening to them a new and larger life and a higher ideal."

The relationship between democracy, divine intention, and liberty that had long characterized Brown's suffrage rhetoric was evident in her final public statement as she declared, "The foundation of democracy is the realization that every human being is a child of God, entitled to the oppor-tunities of life, worthy of respect, and requiring an atmosphere of justice and liberty for his development." The granting of full suffrage rights to women, Brown believed, would contribute to the fulfillment of the noblest aspirations inherent in every human being as a creation of God: "The greatness of men, the grand capabilities of women attest the worth of the human being fashioned in the image of God." She related an experience that confirmed and even surpassed her hope for woman suffrage:

> When the other day I saw crowds of women of all conditions com-ing into the polling booth all filled with great enthusiasm, forgetting old prejudices, old associations and former interest, only seeking to

10. Ibid., 324.

know how to serve the state, ready to leave their usual amusements and associations and give themselves to new subjects of study, not to serve any particular party, but only to learn how to help the world I said, they are grander than I thought. They have "meat to eat that the world knows not of," there is a Divine Life in them which this new experience is revealing.[11]

By the time Olympia Brown cast her ballot for the first time in a national election, one of the few "old pioneers,"[12] as she once referred to herself and her contemporaries, of the woman's rights movement to live to do so, she was firmly ensconced in more radical political ideology than had characterized her earlier life. Although she never lost faith in women's ability to effect the moral transformation of America nor in her belief in God's intention of equality for women in all spheres of life, she did lose faith in the means by which woman suffrage would be realized. The disputes among suffragists and what she—and many others—perceived to be weak leadership within the NAWSA (including the leadership of Anna Howard Shaw) through the first decade of the twentieth century resulted in what Brown recalled as "a period of indifference":

> People no longer came to meetings from curiosity; ridicule had lost its force; the stale old jokes no longer amused; no one even came to scoff. And yet women kept on courageously working in all possible ways, but apparently without success. Suffrage was defeated unaccountably. No state had adopted woman suffrage since 1894. . . . The ten years preceding 1910 I have called the Great Desert of woman suffrage. Of course women were working everywhere; the annual conventions of the National American Association were held, resolutions were passed, literature was circulated and petitions were signed, but apparently without result.[13]

In an effort to counteract that "period of indifference," Brown joined the Congressional Union, later renamed the National Woman's Party

---

11. Olympia Brown, "The Opening Doors" (sermon preached in the Universalist Church, Racine, Wis., September 12, 1920), OBP, SL, Fol. 36.

12. Olympia Brown, *Acquaintances, Old and New, Among Reformers* (Milwaukee, Wis.: Press of S. E. Tate Printing, 1911), 92.

13. Olympia Brown, "Reminiscences of a Pioneer," *Suffragist* (September 1920), OBP, SL, Fol. 36.

(NWP), in 1913, believing that the time had come for more militant tactics in pursuit of woman suffrage. "To her it seemed a re-birth of the old radicalism of Susan B. Anthony and Elizabeth Cady Stanton," her daughter, Gwendolen B. Willis, observed.[14] The National Woman's Party was vocal and active in its opposition to the reelection of President Wilson in 1916. Its members and many less-radical suffragists held him responsible for the repeated failure of a suffrage amendment. While a fervent advocate of other manifestations of justice and human rights, Wilson first opposed woman suffrage and then supported it grudgingly and only by means of state authorization rather than federal legislation. Despite opposition from suffragists, Wilson was reelected in 1916, a result of his efforts toward world peace. Two months after his election, however, suffragists organized the first in a series of protest marches in Washington, D.C. Olympia Brown, having celebrated her eighty-second birthday just days earlier, joined the protesters on January 10, 1917, bundled up against the wintry Washington weather, to march back and forth in front of the White House. The protesters carried signs bearing Wilson's own words. Brown carried a sign that read, "We cannot any longer delay justice in the United States," no doubt fully aware of the irony those words evoked in the minds of the women seeking the vote.[15]

Wilson continued to oppose the suffrage amendment, and the protests also continued, growing in size and causing embarrassment for Wilson's presidency. Rather than changing his stand on woman suffrage, however, Wilson had a number of the women arrested and put in jail. The brutal treatment some of the jailed women received, especially those who were held at a workhouse in Virginia, garnered much publicity and sympathy from the general public, and the numbers of protesters increased rather than diminished after the incident. More than a thousand protesters, including Olympia Brown, showed up on March 4, 1917, in a cold rain for a demonstration organized by the NWP. Gilson Gardner, a Boston reporter, described the scene:

> To see a thousand women—young women, middle-aged and old women—and there were women in the line who had passed their three-score and ten—marching in a rain that almost froze as it fell;

14. Olympia Brown, *An Autobiography*, ed. Gwendolen B. Willis, *Annual Journal of the Universalist Historical Society* 4 (1963): 74.
15. Charlotte Coté, *Olympia Brown* (Racine, Wis.: Mother Courage Press, 1988), 157.

to see them standing and marching and holding their heavy banners, momentarily growing heavier—holding them against a wind that was half gale—hour after hour, until their gloves were wet, their clothes soaked through; . . . to see these women keep their lines and go through their program fully, losing only those who fainted or fell from exhaustion, was a sight to impress even the dulled and jaded senses of one who has seen much.[16]

The leaders of the NAWSA, particularly President Carrie Chapman Catt and Honorary President Anna Howard Shaw, condemned the NWP and its protest marches, fearing that any publicity earned by militant women would work against the suffrage cause in the long run. Olympia Brown disagreed, citing the courageous and even illegal activities of Susan B. Anthony in earlier years of the movement. Anthony had gone to the polls and voted in 1872, for which she was arrested and jailed. She had marched for woman's rights at the national Centennial Celebration in Philadelphia in 1876. In an article for the *Suffragist*, Brown wrote:

> We ask, not what Miss Anthony did, but what she would do were she here today. Still it is interesting to know her opinion, and it is reassuring to find that in most things she was entirely in accord with the spirit and purpose of the present workers. If some of our methods were unheard of in her day, we may be sure that she would approve them now, were she here, and the criticisms which we meet in our time are mild when compared with those which Miss Anthony endured.[17]

Because of her activities in Washington and her association with the NWP, Brown found herself ostracized from the Wisconsin State Suffrage Association when she returned home to Wisconsin in the spring of 1917. A year later, when she offered to campaign for suffrage in Wisconsin, her offer was declined by the president of the Wisconsin association due to what was described as Brown's apparent disagreement with the "methods and aims" of the Wisconsin women.[18]

16. As recorded in Inez Haynes Irwin, *The Story of the Woman's Party* (New York: Harcourt, Brace and Company, 1921), 204.

17. Olympia Brown, "Miss Anthony and the Suffrage Movement," *Suffragist*, March 31, 1917.

18. Coté, *Olympia Brown*, 161.

In addition to her efforts toward woman suffrage in the years just prior to the passage of the Nineteenth Amendment, Olympia Brown joined many suffragists, both moderate and radical, who worked for peace after the United States was drawn into World War I and international turmoil. She regarded increased militarism as the greatest problem facing both her country and the world. Three weeks after the passage of the Nineteenth Amendment, she wrote of her hopes for the nation now that women were empowered to vote. Women had achieved a "great victory," she acknowledged, but many things remained to be done for them, including "justice in wages, in law, and in public opinion." And yet, she went on,

> urgent as these subjects are, it seems to me that we should first consider the great danger that threatens our country at the present time. The danger is militarism, the same which we fought against Germany to destroy. I could wish that the whole womanhood of America would join and with one voice denounce the whole military system, compulsory service, military training, and the expenditure of millions of the people's money for munitions of war. Surely the united voice of all the women would be heard. Militarism would be swept away and our country consecrated to "peace on earth, goodwill to men." Such an accomplishment would be worthy of the great struggles and sacrifices that have been made to give women the ballot.[19]

When she preached her last sermon, "The Opening Doors," in celebration of the victory American women had achieved in obtaining the vote, Brown continued her lifelong tradition of mingling politics with religion in the pulpit. Her commitment to Universalist principles and liberal theology remained as strong as ever:

> We have hoped to make the world safe for democracy; to establish a league of peace; but the very first necessity in reform work is the recognition of Divine capabilities in man. The foundation of democracy is the realization that every human being is a child of God, entitled to the opportunities of life, worthy of respect, and requiring an atmosphere of justice and liberty for his development.

19. Brown, "Reminiscences of a Pioneer."

But the world could never be made safe for democracy by fighting, she believed. Only "by showing the power of Justice done to each humble individual shall we be able to create a firm basis for the state. We can establish a league of peace only by teaching the nations the great lesson of the Fatherhood of God and the Brotherhood of Man."[20]

Olympia Brown continued to work for peace as fervently as she had worked for woman suffrage until her death in 1926 at age ninety-one. In the years preceding her death, she joined the Women's International League for Peace and Freedom, the League of Nations, the American Civil Liberties Union, and the League of Women Voters, the organization that succeeded the NAWSA following the passage of the Nineteenth Amendment. Over the course of seventy years, she had left her feminist mark on both church and society. Her distinction as the second woman ordained to the ministry—and the first ordained by action of a regional body of a connectional denomination—gave her unique respect in many circles and access to ecclesiastical and public forums closed to other suffragists. As a Midwestern suffrage leader who held office in national associations, she helped bridge the distance between the eastern leadership of the movement and those who labored in other parts of the country.

Most significantly, however, Brown brought the idea of woman suffrage into the resistant realm of the church and brought the church into the debate on suffrage by proclaiming a vision of morality that exalted the role of women in the establishment of a society based on justice and virtue. As Dana Greene, her biographer, notes,

> The writings and speeches of Olympia Brown offer a unique understanding of what it meant to be a religious person in late nineteenth- and early twentieth-century America. For Brown it meant to be actively dedicated to the advance of the goal toward which all history moved, the realization of "democratic Christianity." The way Brown chose to live her religion was in single-minded dedication to one objective, the enfranchisement of women. For her this was no puny goal, but one of enormous magnitude and meaning.

All of her commitments—her pursuit of the rights of women, her pastoral ministry, her work against militarism and for peace—"spoke of her loyalty to truth." That loyalty sustained her journey over the many "thorny paths" she trod and left the witness of a life that, as Greene suggests,

20. Brown, "The Opening Doors."

"manifests the fruitfulness of religious insight in providing the goals and ideals for reform in American history."[21]

Upon her death, the tributes to Olympia Brown poured in from friends and acquaintances. The *Baltimore Sun*, the newspaper of the city in which she lived with her daughter for the closing years of her life, praised her for carrying throughout her life "the dauntless courage and the mental freshness of the frontier environment whence she came."[22] In the eulogy for Brown, her friend and fellow suffragist Frances R. Greene suggested that the finest tribute admirers of Olympia Brown could offer her would be for every woman to vote in the next election.[23] Other tributes to her life came many years later. A memorial tablet to Brown was hung in the Memorial Universalist Church in Washington, D.C., in 1930 by her children. It notes her designation as the first woman to receive ordination and bears her favorite quotation: "He who works in harmony with justice is immortal." The Racine, Wisconsin, church she served was renamed the Olympia Brown Church, and an elementary school in Racine was named for her in the 1970s. In 1963, the hundredth anniversary of Brown's ordination was celebrated with the establishment of a scholarship in her honor by the New York State American University Women and by the dedication of a memorial plaque at St. Lawrence Theological School in Canton, New York, her alma mater. The plaque at St. Lawrence appropriately sums up her full and faithful life: "Preacher of Universalism, Pioneer and Champion of Women's Citizenship Rights, Forerunner of the New Era."

Antoinette Brown Blackwell

Along with Olympia Brown, Antoinette Brown Blackwell was among the "old pioneers" of the woman's rights movement who lived to cast ballots on November 2, 1920, in the first national election open to women. At the time, she lived with her youngest daughter, Agnes Blackwell Jones, in Montclair, New Jersey, because a fire had damaged the Blackwell family home in Elizabeth. Brown Blackwell, ninety-five years old at the time, had registered to vote by mail. The election between Republican Warren G. Harding and Democrat James M. Cox generated much debate between Agnes, who supported the Democratic Party, and Antoinette, who

---

21. Dana Greene, ed., *Suffrage and Religious Principle* (Metuchen, N.J.: Scarecrow Press, 1983), 1, 13.

22. Brown, *Autobiography*, 76.

23. Coté, *Olympia Brown*, 175.

favored the Republican Party. Nevertheless, Brown Blackwell refused to reveal her choice of candidate until it was time to register her vote, saying only, "Yes, my dear, I will vote as I think best when the time comes."[24] In a biography of her mother, Agnes recorded this newspaper account of her mother's participation in that historic Election Day:

> They drove over to Elizabeth by automobile, picking up a camp stool at a neighbor's so that Mrs. Blackwell might rest if the line of voters was long, but when she appeared, about noon, the line made way for her. The signing of her own name was quite an occasion, as she could not see, and the officials were most kind. The daughter and a clerk went into the booth with her and when the clerk asked for instructions she said in a voice which could be heard by all, "I wish to vote the Republican ticket, all things considered at the present time. It seems to me the wisest plan." Her decision was greeted with applause by the waiting lines of voters.[25]

Age and physical limitations rendered Antoinette Brown Blackwell less active in the final years of the suffrage movement than were Olympia Brown or Anna Howard Shaw. She continued to be productive in many ways, however, and was frequently honored at suffrage gatherings for her many contributions to the equality of women in church and society. She published three books in the first fifteen years of the twentieth century. In 1902, she turned her hand to poetry with the publication of *Sea Drift*, a series of poems reflecting her ongoing efforts to demonstrate the unity of the spiritual, physical, and moral realms. *The Making of the Universe*, her version of natural theology, in which she argued for evidence of God, the Creator, through the natural world and human-made creations, appeared in 1914. It was followed by her final book, *The Social Side of Mind and Action*, in 1915. By then Europe was at war, lending urgency to Brown Blackwell's call for morality and mutual assistance among human communities. "The old authoritative foundations of moral and religious guidance and assurance," she wrote in the introduction, "—foundations that for so long seemed more stable than the earth itself,—have either crumbled to powder, or broken into fragments."[26]

24. Agnes Blackwell Jones, "Postscript," November 20, 1926, BFP, SL, Fol 11.
25. Ibid.
26. Antoinette Brown Blackwell, *The Social Side of Mind and Action* (New York: Neale Publishing, 1915), 9.

As long as she was able, the "preacher for the people" also pursued her call to preach. Although she found no permanent position as a parish minister after joining the American Unitarian Association in 1878, she continued to preach in Unitarian and other churches. In 1903, she finally got her wish of a pastorate when she learned of a newly organized Unitarian Society near her home in Elizabeth, New Jersey, and was invited to conduct its Sunday services. The congregation "for a time held its meetings in a hired hall, then later occupied the public library for its hour or two on Sundays," she recalled. But "a radical church in a conservative neighborhood could hardly be expected to build itself up satisfactorily under such conditions. It was decided to erect a small church building in what was then almost the western limit of the town."[27] Brown Blackwell donated a portion of her property in Elizabeth for construction of a church building, which was completed in 1908. "Without her courage and patient assistance the church would probably never have been built," noted Sarah Gilson, the editor of her autobiography.[28]

A permanent minister was hired for the established church, but Brown Blackwell was granted the title "Minister Emeritus" and preached at the church once a month until 1915, when she curtailed her preaching responsibilities due to failing health. Sarah Gilson, who often heard Brown Blackwell preach, commented, "In old age her preaching was of two kinds—sometimes metaphysical, when it was beyond the grasp of her hearers. . . . The other sermons were made up of plain, sustaining spiritual advice." Her work in establishing and serving All Souls Church, as it was named, gave Brown Blackwell a great sense of accomplishment in the later years of her life. In her autobiographical reflections recorded in 1909, she commented hopefully on the church's success: "The region is fast building up, the outlook for the church is a fairly good one. The congregation is now steadily growing and its various religious and social meetings are filling a real need in the community. The people are extremely harmonious and all interested in the improvement of their environment."[29]

The Unitarian pastorate was one of two confirmations of her lifelong call to preach that came to her late in life, the other being an invitation from Henry Churchill King, president of Oberlin College, to attend the

27. Memoirs told by Brown Blackwell in 1909 to Mrs. Claude U. (Sarah) Gilson, 220, BFP, SL, Fols. 3–14.
28. Ibid.
29. Ibid., 20, 220.

Oberlin commencement in June 1908 to receive an honorary doctor of divinity degree. Although the official recognition of her work in theology came fifty-five years late, Brown Blackwell graciously accepted the invitation and the degree. Sarah Gilson commented:

> She was never resentful [of her treatment by Oberlin]. When in June 1908 Oberlin asked her to come to the 75th anniversary [of Oberlin College] and receive the degree of D.D., she spent no time in reflecting how little Oberlin had done to speed her on her way into the ministry. Not a word did she say about the change in the views of Oberlin, nor that the recognition came late. She simply smiled and devoted her attention to obtaining the proper kind of doctor's gown.[30]

"So times change," Brown Blackwell remarked philosophically in noting the belated recognition.[31]

On November 5, 1921, Antoinette Brown Blackwell died at Agnes's home. "It is a beautiful experience to see one live to be 96½ without losing any lovely traits of character," Agnes wrote of her mother. "Always straightforward and true and with an optimism and understanding of man and his ways as related to the Creator and his eternal life. She inspired all who came within her influence."[32] In the tributes to her life before and after her death, Brown Blackwell was remembered for her vast and varied contributions to the political, educational, and intellectual achievements of women. "Yet it was as a *minister* that she thought of herself," Sarah Gilson observed, "and wanted to be thought of, not as a reformer, nor a pioneer in other fields. She neither had the close fellowship nor the support of many of the leaders in her chosen denomination. Yet she went on to become the beloved and venerated leader of all women in any denomination who entered the ministry."[33]

Anna Howard Shaw

Unlike Antoinette Brown Blackwell and Olympia Brown, Anna Howard Shaw did not live to cast her ballot in 1920. She died in July 1919, just one

---

30. Ibid., 17.
31. Antoinette Brown Blackwell, "Life Work," 7, ms., n.d., BFP, SL, Fol. 1.
32. Jones, "Postscript."
33. Gilson ms., 20.

year prior to the passage of the Nineteenth Amendment. Although she did not see the culmination of her work for the "great Cause," as she often called it, she sensed its nearness and surely knew the role she had played in its realization. She worked tirelessly for woman suffrage as president of the NAWSA from 1904 to 1915 through the critical and difficult years known as the "doldrums" of the movement, often amidst criticism of her leadership. She had accepted the presidency in 1904 reluctantly, realizing the challenges ahead of her, and only under the "command" of Susan B. Anthony, for whom she had the utmost respect and with whom she had a deep friendship. Anthony was eighty-four and quite frail at the time. "It was no time for me to rebel against her wishes," Shaw recalled, "but I yielded with the heaviest heart I have ever carried, and after my election to the presidency at the national convention in Washington I left the stage, went into a dark corner of the wings, and for the first time since my girlhood 'cried myself sick.' "[34]

Shaw's years of leadership of the NAWSA proved to be as challenging as she had anticipated, given the fragmentation of the suffrage movement over tactics (evidenced by the founding of the National Woman's Party) and the increasing efforts of antisuffragists to counter the tally of states approving woman suffrage. Nevertheless, the things she remembered most vividly from those years were not the challenges but the opportunities her position afforded her. She traveled across the United States, working in states in which constitutional amendments mandating woman suffrage were pending, and around the world as a representative to international suffrage gatherings. At a convention in Vienna in 1913, she recalled receiving the "ovation of my life" and making an amusing "conversion" of one of her auditors:

> I was immensely surprised and deeply touched by the unexpected tribute [of a standing ovation]; but any undue elation I might have experienced was checked by the memory of the skeptical snort with which one of my auditors had received me. He was very German, and very, very frank. After one pained look at me he rose to leave the hall.
>
> "*That* old woman!" he exclaimed. "She cannot make herself heard."
>
> He was half-way down the aisle when the opening words of my address caught up with him and stopped him. Whatever their

34. Anna Howard Shaw with Elizabeth Jordan, *The Story of a Pioneer* (New York: Harper & Brothers Publishers, 1915), 286.

meaning may have been, it was at least carried to the far ends of that great hall, for the old fellow had piqued me a bit and I had given my voice its fullest volume. He crowded into an already over-occupied pew and stared at me with goggling eyes.

"*Mein Gott!*" he gasped. "*Mein Gott*, she could be heard *anywhere.*"[35]

She left Vienna with memories of her oratorical triumph as well as a basket of tiny fir trees that she planted on the grounds of her home in Pennsylvania.

Shortly before she resigned in 1915 after more than a decade as president of the NAWSA, Anna Howard Shaw recalled "with gratitude and elation" the progress of work for woman suffrage:

> Our membership has grown from 17,000 women to more than 200,000, and the number of auxiliary societies has increased in proportion. . . . From an original yearly expenditure of $14,000 or $15,000 in our campaign work, we now expend from $40,000 to $50,000. . . . In 1906 full suffrage prevailed in four states; we now have it in twelve. Our movement has advanced from its academic stage until it has become a vital political factor; no reform in the country is more heralded by the press or receives more attention from the public.[36]

At the same time, she was honest about the "troubles" and "differences" among members of the NAWSA during her tenure:

> At every annual convention since the one at Washington in 1910 there has been an effort to depose me from the presidency. There have been some splendid fighters among my opponents—fine and high-minded women who sincerely believe that at sixty-eight I am getting too old for my big job. Possibly I am. Certainly I shall resign it with alacrity when the majority of women in the organization wish me to do so.[37]

The time came in 1915 when the women of the NAWSA and Shaw herself felt it was time for her to resign. She delivered her farewell address to

35. Ibid., 333.
36. Ibid., 335–36.
37. Ibid., 336.

the NAWSA in December 1915. In that address, she reiterated the "heavenly vision" that inspired her lifelong work for reform:

> We might well despair if we viewed life for a day. It is only when viewed as a whole that the real reformer is able with unfaltering faith to follow her vision to its goal. The reformer who believes that there is a power reaching through all the ages and that this power is a constant presence working with unfailing purpose toward a single goal, must believe that we shall ultimately know the meaning and purpose of life. It is that we may lay hold of this faith anew, that we may draw from its infinite supply the spirit that we all need to keep us steadily on the march, as well as to take counsel one with the other, that we have gathered from all parts of our country in our Annual Convention.[38]

Shaw's lifetime of reform had passed quickly. "I sometimes feel that it has indeed been hundreds of years since my work began," she remarked in her autobiography, published in 1915, "and then again it seems so brief a time that, by listening for a moment, I fancy I can hear the echo of my childish voice preaching to the trees in the Michigan woods."[39] Her accomplishments from preacher to the trees to international representative for woman's rights were praised by Carrie Chapman Catt, Shaw's successor as president of the NAWSA: "Where in all the world's history has any movement among men produced so invincible an advocate as our own Dr. Anna Howard Shaw? Those whom she has led to the light are Legion."[40]

A year after completing her work as president of the NAWSA, Shaw again accepted a position of leadership in service to her country. Spending the winter of 1916–17 in Florida, she was summoned to Washington by the secretary of war, Newton D. Baker. The Council of National Defense sought to involve women in the war effort during World War I by creating a Woman's Committee, and Secretary Baker asked Shaw to serve as its chairwoman. The Woman's Committee was to prepare women for American involvement in the war and coordinate existing organizations

38. Anna Howard Shaw, "An Address," December 1915 (New York: National Woman Suffrage Publishing, 1915), 1–2.

39. Shaw, *Story of a Pioneer*, 337.

40. Carrie Chapman Catt, "The Crisis," in Karlyn Kohrs Campbell, ed., *Man Cannot Speak for Her*, vol. 2 (New York: Praeger, 1989), 494.

for the provision of food, clothing, shelter, and other needs as wartime warranted. For the next two years, Shaw delivered addresses from the Atlantic to the Pacific, organized state societies, and attended countless board meetings and conferences. She gave advice on everything from how to dry fruits and vegetables (there was a shortage of containers for canning) to how to maintain morale in the face of devastating losses. Whatever the subject or manner of her work for the Council of National Defense, however, Shaw's ultimate message was the equality of women and the benefits of their enfranchisement. In an address in 1917, she connected suffrage and women's work for freedom:

> It is because we love our country so much and because we are so anxious to give ourselves entirely to the great service of winning the war, that we want the freedom of American women now. We suffragists would be thrice traitors if at this time of the great struggle of the world for democracy we should fail to ask for the fundamental principles here which America is trying to help bring to other countries.[41]

By early 1918 the progress of state suffrage laws (especially in New York) and the federal suffrage amendment (including President Wilson's endorsement and the House approval) made Shaw more hopeful about the dawning political possibilities for women. In a lecture to the Women's Section of the Maryland Council of Defense in January 1918, she commented on the "responsibilities" that would soon be incumbent upon American women:

> The preparation that the women of this country need first of all is self-respect, belief in themselves, and a high opinion of the service for which God put women into the world and which women have so loyally rendered since the beginning of time. If we can get hold of the idea of the dignity of women's work and women's service, then we may recognize that women who have been faithful in these great responsibilities, the obligations to the home, to society, to the church and to the country, which women have borne in the past, we will realize that they have been but the preparation for the new responsibilities which may come to women during all the period of their lives.[42]

41. *History of Woman Suffrage*, V:758.
42. Anna Howard Shaw, "Address at a Meeting of the Women's Section, Maryland Council of Defense" (Academy of Music, Baltimore, Md., January 4, 1918), 5.

When the Woman's Committee was dissolved in February 1919, many commendations were offered to Shaw and her colleagues. "It would be difficult to overestimate the importance of the function the committee has served in being both a vast bureau for the dissemination of information, and itself a wellspring of inspiration and zeal," stated President Woodrow Wilson. Secretary of War Baker, who had originally requested Shaw's service, commented that she and her committee "wrought a work the like of which has never been seen before and her reward was to see its success."[43] More formal recognition of Shaw's great service to the country came in May 1919 when she was awarded the Distinguished Service Medal, becoming the first living American woman to receive that honor. The award ceremony was yet another opportunity to connect the patriotic contributions of women in the war effort to their need for enfranchisement, and in her remarks Shaw noted:

> I realize that in conferring upon me the Distinguished Service Medal, the President and the Secretary of War are not expressing their appreciation of what I as an individual have done but of the collective service of the women of the country. . . . and while I appreciate the honor and am prouder to wear this decoration than to receive any other recognition save my political freedom, which is the first desire of a loyal American, I nevertheless look upon this as the beginning of the recognition by the country of the service and loyalty of women, and above all that the part women are called upon to take in times of war is recognized as equally necessary in times of peace. This departure on the part of the national government through the President and Secretary of War gives the greater promise of the time near at hand when every citizen of the United States will be esteemed a government asset because of his or her loyalty and service rather than because of sex.[44]

Shaw treasured the medal for the remaining months of her life, and it was pinned to her lapel later that year when she was buried.

The more involved Anna Howard Shaw became with the Council of National Defense during the war, the more she felt drawn to the cause of peace. As her work with the Woman's Committee wound down, she

43. As quoted in Wil A. Linkugel and Martha Solomon, *Anna Howard Shaw* (New York: Greenwood Press, 1991), 89–90.
44. *History of Woman Suffrage*, V:758.

accepted a position on the executive committee of the League to Enforce Peace, a peace advocacy group started in New York state before the war. During the war, note Shaw biographers Wil Linkugel and Martha Solomon, "Shaw often argued that women were innately pacifists because of their clear realization of the costs of war. Her speeches after the beginning of World War I had consistently included passages that emotionally depicted the psychological costs of war for women, when they saw their husbands and sons sacrificed to the cause."[45]

The league both during and after the war encouraged the United States government to support the founding of an international organization to promote world peace, and when President Wilson's proposal for a League of Nations was included in the Treaty of Versailles, the group worked for congressional approval of both the treaty and the League of Nations. In May 1919, Shaw was invited by the League to Enforce Peace to join former United States President William Howard Taft and Abbott Lawrence Lowell, president of Harvard University, on a national speaking tour to promote Wilson's peace plan. The original plan that she speak once a day was amended in response to popular demand, and Shaw was soon delivering four or five speeches a day, sometimes in different cities. After one especially exhausting day in Indianapolis when she had eight engagements, Shaw was stricken with pneumonia and hospitalized for two weeks. She returned to her home outside Philadelphia but never recovered from the illness and died there on July 2, 1919. A few days before her death, she revised a transcript of one of her speeches on the tour at the request of the league. The speech, titled "What the War Meant to Women," included her final eloquent words on her beloved causes of woman's rights and peace:

> We women, the mothers of the race, have given everything, have suffered everything, have sacrificed everything, and we come to you now and say, "The time has come when we will no longer sit quietly by and bear and rear sons to die at the will of a few men. We will not endure it. We demand either that you shall do something to prevent war or that we shall be permitted to try to do something ourselves.[46]

Anna Howard Shaw's impact on the nation was evident in the tributes

---

45. Linkugel and Solomon, *Anna Howard Shaw*, 91.
46. Anna Howard Shaw, "What the War Meant to Women" (League to Enforce Peace, 1919), 18.

paid her after her death. "It is literally true that a nation mourned the death of Anna Howard Shaw," reported the writers of the *History of Woman Suffrage*. Newspapers across the country eulogized her, noting "friend and foe alike yielded to the unsurpassed charm of her personality and the rare qualities of her mind and heart."[47] Former President Taft, with whom she was traveling when she became ill, remarked on "the very great privilege of listening to her persuasive eloquence and her genial wit and humor, which she always used to enforce her arguments. She thought nothing of the sacrifice she had to make and was only intent upon the consummation of our purpose. She was a remarkable woman." Even President Woodrow Wilson, long her adversary, praised her many contributions to American life:

> It was not my privilege to know Dr. Shaw until the later years of her life but I had the advantage then of seeing her in many lights. I saw her acting with such vigor and intelligence in the service of the Government, and, through the Government, of mankind, as to win my warmest admiration. I had already had occasion to see the extraordinary quality of her clear and effective mind and to know how powerful and persuasive an advocate she was. When the war came I saw her in action and she won my sincere admiration and homage.[48]

More tangible tributes to Shaw's life have come in the years since her death. Buildings, academic chairs, and lectureships on college and university campuses have been named for her. The SS *Anna Howard Shaw* was launched during World War II by the New England Building Company in Portland, Maine. In October 1988 a life-sized sculpture of Shaw was placed in a park next to the community library in Grand Rapids, Michigan, her childhood home. On December 12, 1926, the Methodist Protestant Church in Tarrytown, New York, where Shaw had been ordained forty-six years earlier, dedicated a memorial window in her honor. The Reverend Caroline Bartlett Crane delivered the memorial address, recounting the life of the woman who was, Crane declared, "always in spirit a preacher." The window in the iconoclastic church would serve as an appropriate witness to the life and spirit of Anna Howard Shaw, Crane stated:

47. *History of Woman Suffrage*, V:757.
48. Ibid., 760.

So future generations—especially future generations of women—will turn, not to the place where Anne Hutchinson stood at the bar of excommunication, or where defenseless women accused of witchcraft were burned to death; they will turn, instead, to a spot like this where, near half a century ago, a young woman with the love of God in her heart, and a truly celestial fire of eloquence on her tongue, was given by the spiritual forefathers of the men and women now present her free charter to go forth and preach the gospel of good tidings to all men.[49]

One suspects that Shaw would have been grateful to have "died with her boots on." She often joked that work was her favorite form of recreation. She worked tirelessly during her seventy-two years, manifesting a life lived in appreciation for God's divine goodness and in service to the establishment of God's justice on earth. In reflecting on her life for a student convocation at Temple University in 1917 during her tenure with the Woman's Committee of the Council of National Defense, Shaw did not deny the struggles inherent in any human life, especially her own. But the spirit of optimism and the grand, divine vision that shaped her life and work dominated the advice she offered to those just beginning their careers:

There are two things in life which make its struggle, its pain, its losses, its joys and its victories worth while. They are, first, to be so possessed by a fundamental principle of right that it becomes consuming fire. The other is to have a heart filled with a great love for humanity.

Possessed by these two passions, no struggle can become too severe, no waiting too wearisome, no life useless. In the midst of a multitude or alone with God, at home or abroad, with friends or with enemies, life is worthwhile.[50]

Endings and Beginnings of the Struggle for Woman's Rights

There was little noticeable change in American life immediately after women first exercised their right to vote. Neither the great hopes of the

---

49. Caroline Bartlett Crane, "Dr. Anna Howard Shaw" in *Methodist Recorder*, January 1, 1927, AHSP, SL, Fol. 361.

50. Anna Howard Shaw, Address delivered at Temple University (Philadelphia, 1917), AHSP, SL, Fol. 470.

suffragists nor the great fears of the antisuffragists came to pass. The nation was not magically transformed into a place of goodness and moral virtue; nor did great numbers of women divorce their husbands and abandon their families to pursue masculine professions or personal dreams. It quickly became evident that women would be no more able than men to stem the tide of social change (or social decay, as many regarded it) that engulfed the nation in the 1920s. The constitutional amendment legislating Prohibition was enacted in 1919 without the votes of women (albeit with several decades of female efforts toward temperance reform). The women's voting bloc, much touted by voices on both sides of the suffrage issue, turned out to be more a rhetorical strategy than a political reality as women proved to be as diverse in their political allegiances as men. As historian Nancy F. Cott has noted, there was considerable disunity among suffragists prior to 1920, and that did not vanish as a result of legislative victory: In "matters great and small . . . there were strategic, ideological, class-based and race-based differences among groups of women that were acted out in the public arena before as well as after 1920."[51]

The question of how and to what extent women effected social and political change after 1920 remains much debated. The long struggle for equality that ended with the enfranchisement of women, however, appears in historical retrospect to have been a significant turning point in their achievement of many other freedoms and accomplishments. Some of those freedoms—such as shortened skirts and bobbed hair—were trivial, while others—new educational and professional opportunities—were essential for the continued progress of women. But trivial or monumental, the freedoms for women that followed their enfranchisement were symbolic of a far greater psychological freedom engendered by their political equality.

Even the churches responded to the emergence of the New Woman in the 1920s and 1930s. In the years immediately following passage of the Nineteenth Amendment, some of the mainline Protestant churches most opposed to women's ordination in the nineteenth century, such as the Presbyterian and Methodist Episcopal Churches, at least began discussing the question of women's ordination and opened some church offices to women.[52] Several denominations opened schools or programs

51. Nancy F. Cott, "Across the Great Divide: Women in Politics Before and After 1920," in Wheeler, *One Woman, One Vote,* 355–56.

52. The Presbyterian Church in the U.S.A., for instance, voted to ordain women to its two lay offices of deacon and elder in 1922 and 1931, respectively.

for women in the first quarter of the twentieth century to train them as missionaries or Christian educators. By the 1930s, women began to make their mark in theological education, evidenced by the appointment of Georgia Harkness as professor of applied theology at Garrett Biblical Institute in Illinois. Dr. Harkness was the first woman to teach in a theological seminary in a discipline other than Christian education. In 1919 the Association of Women Preachers was founded as an organization of American clergywomen. The association's journal, *Woman's Pulpit*, continues to be published today.

Despite these gains, progress for women in the churches was neither rapid nor steady. Theological disputes within denominations, the preoccupation of the nation with the realities of the Depression and World War II, and continued debate over women's rights and roles hampered women's movement into church leadership. Historians Carl and Dorothy Schneider state that "in the first sixty years of the twentieth century, little happened for clergywomen."[53] Their numbers were extremely small at midcentury. Even traditions that had earlier been open to women's ordination or at least preaching, including the Congregational and Universalist traditions of Antoinette Brown Blackwell and Olympia Brown, became more resistant to women's ministries as a result of the increasing professionalization of the clergy and institutionalization of the churches.[54] It was not until the second half of the century that most denominations ordained women to full clerical status and not until the last quarter of the century that women have been ordained in significant numbers and accepted in congregational and other ministries of the church.[55]

The 150th anniversary of the ordination of Antoinette Brown Blackwell occurred on September 15, 2003. Women of the United States can rejoice in the political, ecclesiastical, social, and professional gains they have achieved in that century and a half. At the same time, there is the painful realization of gender inequities that persist in all corners of American society. But the greater and more heartening realization is that, because of the faithful persistence of women like Antoinette Brown Black-

53. Carl J. and Dorothy Schneider, *In Their Own Right* (New York: Crossroad Publishing, 1997), 126.

54. Ibid., 127.

55. Further information on the history of women's ordination can be found in Mark Chaves, *Ordaining Women* (Cambridge, Mass.: Harvard University Press, 1997); Rosemary Skinner Keller and Rosemary Radford Ruether, eds., *In Our Own Voices: Four Centuries of American Women's Religious Writing* (San Francisco: HarperSanFrancisco, 1995); and Schneider and Schneider, *In Their Own Right*.

well, Olympia Brown, and Anna Howard Shaw, the doors of progress have been opened, never to be shuttered again. Elinor Rice Hays, biographer of the Blackwell family, summarized well the contributions of brave women reformers of the nineteenth century in these words about Antoinette Brown Blackwell:

> The work she and her friends and colleagues had done had immeasurably extended the horizons of women. The elevation of politics, the international understanding, the ennobling of human life which they believed would come from women's freer participation in the world's work may seem today the bitterest of ironies. But they erred in expecting too much, not in achieving too little. No woman in our society will ever again be so limited in possibility as the women who lived before these early rebels fought their battle.[56]

56. Elinor Rice Hays, *Those Extraordinary Blackwells* (New York: Harcourt, Brace & World, 1967), 308.

Index